Borderland Circuitry

IMMIGRATION SURVEILLANCE IN THE UNITED STATES AND BEYOND

Ana Muñiz

UNIVERSITY OF CALIFORNIA PRESS

University of California Press
Oakland, California

Library of Congress Cataloging-in-Publication Data

Names: Muñiz, Ana, 1984– author.
Title: Borderland circuitry : immigration surveillance in the United
    States and beyond / Ana Muñiz.
Description: Oakland, California : University of California Press,
    [2022] | Includes bibliographical references and index.
Identifiers: LCCN 2021061570 (print) | LCCN 2021061571 (ebook) |
    ISBN 9780520379480 (cloth) | ISBN 9780520379497 (paperback) |
    ISBN 9780520976764 (epub)
Subjects: LCSH: Immigration enforcement—United States—21st
    century. | Immigration enforcement—21st century. | Data mining in
    law enforcement. | Data centers—United States. | Mexican-American
    Border Region. | BISAC: SOCIAL SCIENCE / Criminology | SOCIAL
    SCIENCE / Human Geography
Classification: LCC JV6483 .M85 2022 (print) | LCC JV6483 (ebook) |
    DDC 363.28/50973—dc23/eng/20220124
LC record available at https://lccn.loc.gov/2021061570
LC ebook record available at https://lccn.loc.gov/2021061571

Manufactured in the United States of America

31 30 29 28 27 26 25 24 23 22
10 9 8 7 6 5 4 3 2 1

For the borderlands, old and new.

Contents

Illustrations

TABLES

1 The Land Gets Tangled in Walls and Circuitry

STEEL BLOOMING IN THE BORDERLANDS

In 1987 Gloria Anzaldúa wrote of the US-Mexico border, "This is my home / this thin edge of / barbwire."[1] Indeed, when I was young, the border in much of Arizona's Sonoran Desert where I grew up consisted of a spiked metal string limply tied between rotting wooden posts. In a few places, it still is. For the most part, however, the barrier along the nearly two-thousand-mile scar has become increasingly formidable.[2] Over the years, hunks of metal have been hauled in. Motion sensors have been implanted in the ground. Cholla cactus drop fat yellow fruit under infrared, watchtowers, choppers, drones, and semiautomatics.[3] And now, as construction proceeds on a reinforced border wall, the barrier is set for another, more expansive iteration.

Surrounding the brutality is a beauty of shattering clarity. Land so beautiful, it calls people from all directions. There are people who arrive on Sonoran land through Arizona's northern border, from Iowa, Wisconsin, and Ohio. Sometimes these northern border crossers buy houses on this land. Sometimes the people from the northern border pay the people who live in the southern borderlands to tend to the ocotillo, aloe vera, and ancient creosote bushes in their front yards. Here, the two groups of people who move across the desert—one authorized, the other unauthorized—meet.

I used to sit in the cab of a white Chevy truck, the old kind with the gear shift on the steering wheel, watching my father dig his hands under the root ball, trying to extract a plant intact. Over sixty miles away from the nearest international boundary, Border Patrol would interrupt groups of laborers at work, walking down the line of hunched backs to ask, "Where are you from?" It strikes me many years later that it is the same question police officers on the streets of Los Angeles ask youth of color they stop for questioning as a coded gang interrogation. *Where are you from?* Are you a transgressor of one border or another? Are you entitled to mobility? African American studies scholar Hazel Carby writes that this question—*Where are you from?*—is not primarily about geographic origin as much as it is an interrogation of racial belonging.[4] You cannot look this way, cannot talk this way, and be one of us.

The materiality of the border, then, is both formidable and deceiving. The centrality of The Wall to public discourse in recent years and its uncontroversial materiality has obscured a more expansive and ubiquitous borderland made up of surveillance circuits, which has grown and become a routine way to detect supposed transgressors of myriad borders. As the physical wall has become more formidable, so has the digital surveillance infrastructure. This digital surveillance borderland is mighty, but its materiality is less clear than that of The Wall; it is often only evident to racialized and criminalized subjects, making its range and reach largely imperceptible for those exempted from its grasp.

This book addresses this gap by deconstructing the technological circuitry of immigration, domestic, and international law enforcement, studying how it targets immigrants deemed "criminal"—a category that applies to progressively broader groups of migrants—and exploring the precarization effects the borderland circuitry has on people subjected to it. In my approach, I follow the lead of criminologists Nancy Wonders and Lynn Jones, who urge scholars to conceptualize border*ing* as a process, as something that continually requires doing and undoing, rather than as solely a physical place or static thing.[5]

Here I trace new surveillance trends—many of which have been explored by surveillance scholars in the context of local police and federal intelligence agencies—in the less-examined immigration system. I contribute a novel empirical mapping of surveillance circuits and border building at, within, and beyond US borders. While my inquiry is geographically far-reaching, I use the US-Mexico border as an anchoring point, to which I return again and again. I examine empirical changes in the form and consequence of borders in tandem with my own experiences as a person who is from, and continues to be deeply shaped by, the borderlands.

CODED BORDERS

The invisible circuitry of the borderlands loomed large in the background of the most recent hardening of The Wall. In the hopes of further limiting mobility for some people in the borderlands, in 2017 the US government began to search for contractors to construct a border wall from San Diego, California, to Brownsville, Texas. In the call for proposals to build a prototype, the US government defined *wall* as "an 18–30ft. tall barrier designed to prevent illegal entry and drug[.]"[6] The definition ends with the word *drug* and without punctuation. It is curious that the definition is unfinished, though perhaps appropriate, as the construction of both the border and its people is an ongoing political project.

The buildup of the border barrier has happened before. In 1945, the Immigration and Naturalization Service (INS) removed wire fencing from a Japanese internment camp and reinstalled it along six miles of the California-Mexico border.[7] More fencing appeared in the San Diego sector in 1990, followed by new stretches in 1994 in Naco, El Paso, and San Diego.[8] In the case of Naco, the barrier consisted of landing strips the military had left unused in the deserts of the first Gulf War—symbolism for which a novelist would kill.[9] The Army Corps of Engineers installed more barriers in Tucson, McAllen, and Laredo in 1997.[10] The border received an infusion of surveillance technology, towers, drones, sensors, and night vision cameras with the 2005 Secure Border Initiative, and the 2006 Secure Fence Act promised 850 miles of double-layered fencing.[11] In some places, World War II–style Normandy fencing has been installed. Right now, much of the border fencing looks like bars on a jail cell.[12]

As the 2017 solicitations for border wall construction rolled out, the federal government released another call, to less fanfare, for contractors to develop a "continuous monitoring and alert system to track 500,000 identities per month" and amass information on "criminal aliens," including "FBI numbers; State Identification Numbers; real time jail booking data; credit history; insurance claims; phone number account information; wireless phone accounts; wire transfer data; driver's license information; Vehicle Registration Information; property information; pay day loan information; public court records; incarceration data; employment address data; Individual Taxpayer Identification Number (ITIN) data; and employer records."[13] My borderland home is made not only of concrete and steel, but of code as well, and it goes well beyond the demarcated international boundary.

Thus, the imposing and immediate physicality of The Wall is not its only imposition. Rather, The Wall is significant because of the diffusion of its function and its violence—sensual, symbolic, and, as I show throughout this book, technological—through time, space, and myriad institutions. While the spectacular physicality of the border wall dominates the landscape, more practically relevant to daily mass enforcement may be the construction of interoperable digital infrastructure to classify and surveil immigrants and other groups at the border as well as far away from the border.

Immigration enforcement agencies are building mass surveillance systems. Drawing from the work of surveillance scholars David Lyon, John Gilliom, Torin Monahan, Simone Browne, and Saher Selod, I define *surveillance* as the monitoring of people based on racialization and the gathering and analysis of their information in order to make decisions about them, sort them into categories, control them, and reify borders.[14] Surveillance is an old practice and an inherently racialized one; slaves in the United States were subjected to an extensive surveillance apparatus that included written identification manifests and lantern laws.[15] The practice of surveillance is thus rooted in paradigms of racial control and continues to be deployed to disproportionately target racially subjugated groups.[16] The specific practices and technologies of surveillance change over time and space but most often sustain the racial ordering established by European colonization and transatlantic slavery.[17] The slave ship, the plantation, the encomienda, the Spanish mission, and the reservation birthed surveillance in the Americas.

Late twenty-first-century technological developments have enabled a set of "new surveillance" practices in which surveilling agents deploy advanced technology in order to extract or create information.[18] This book asks how the development and deployment of new surveillance infrastructure since the 1980s has shaped US law enforcement practices and discourses. I answer this question by focusing on a multifaceted development that I call *borderland circuitry*. I argue that US law enforcement agencies deploy surveillance and information-sharing programs along particular geographic circuits and as a result construct punitive digital borderland spaces that enable detention, deportation, brutality, and precarity against an expanding group of criminalized immigrants.

BORDERLAND CIRCUITRY AND ITS SUBJECTS

Consider two presences on the US-Mexico border. One is a barrier whose purpose is largely one of iconography, a way to loudly communicate a dividing line that differentiates two political jurisdictions from one another. It is made to be seen and feared. The other is a network of surveillance technology that is largely invisible, by design unseen, omnipresent, almost mystical. The physical barrier is immovable and no more than inches or at most, feet, thick. The network of surveillance technology, on the other hand, flows far and wide in all directions, linking up to an extensive network of data repositories accessed by diverse law enforcement organizations.

Seminal immigration surveillance scholar Anil Kalhan has argued that as a result of digital surveillance technology, the function of the border—to screen individuals, prevent entry, or authorize entry—has been decoupled from the territorial boundary.[19] Automated and interoperable technology hase made immigration status immediately accessible in multiple domains such that in a sense, the border is now "everywhere."[20] As theorized by Étienne Balibar, the border is no longer a singular place but rather a diffuse legal construct that migrants encounter in the form of checkpoints and screenings in multiple locations.[21]

The Border Patrol has been explicit about this change, describing the purpose of its land, air, and sea forces as doing border control work within and outside of US territory, stating: "The border is not merely a physical frontier. Effectively securing it requires attention to processes that begin outside U.S. borders, occur at the border and continue to all interior regions of the U.S."[22] Similarly, during a 2011 lecture at Brooklyn Law School, Alan Bersin, the commissioner of US Customs and Border Protection (CBP) under President Barack Obama, characterized the outward surge of the border as central to homeland security: "The earlier that we can identify, intercept, and neutralize threats to the homeland, the safer our people will be.

The further away geographically from the physical line that we can achieve these ends, the safer our country will be."[23]

The movement of the border outward beyond US territory is empirically apparent, for example, in an information-sharing program I review in chapter 7 that enables US immigration authorities to share criminal history information on deported people with the government of their home countries, one of which is Guatemala. Research demonstrates that Guatemalan police have attempted to incarcerate and even assault people who return from the United States with criminal records and gang allegations against them.[24] When US immigration authorities share information and cooperate with foreign partners to incapacitate migrants in their home countries such that they are prevented from migrating back to the United States, then US immigration authorities have pushed the function of American borders into another country. Through information sharing, the border stretches out to impede people before they reach the physical border, even before they leave their home countries.[25]

Similarly, when migrants do cross into US territory, federal and local law enforcement continue to subject them to border-like surveillance and control deep in the country's interior via interconnected databases and information-sharing programs. For example, legal scholar Ayelet Shachar notes that unauthorized immigrants can be subjected to expedited removal within one hundred miles of the border fourteen days after they have physically crossed, effectively treating immigrants within US borders as if they had been stopped at the border. Shachar explains, "The border has been detached from its traditional location at the perimeter of the country's edges—it has now 'moved' 100 miles into the interior."[26]

While it is true, to some degree, that bordering and surveillance are omnipresent, in practice, certain people and places are surveilled more than others. Thus, I find widespread claims that the border is everywhere and that surveillance and state violence "is aimed at all of us" difficult to truly grasp and make real.[27] Rather, as border studies scholar Mark B. Salter argues, "the border is not everywhere for every-one" in the same way.[28] Therefore I set out to uncover and concretely map some of these new borderlands, to identify the state agents who are central to their construction, illuminate the most frequent targets of new surveillance and policing, and identify the specific mechanisms that have enabled the slow expansion of enforcement.[29] To accomplish this I draw from a trove of never before seen documents accessed through years of lawsuits against law enforcement organizations, supplemented by interviews and ethnographic observations.[30] *Borderland circuitry* refers to the particular geographic patterns or circuits along which authorities deploy surveillance and information-sharing programs and as a result enable enforcement against an expanding group of criminalized immigrants.[31] Specifically, I explicate three components.

First I deconstruct the technological circuitry of immigration enforcement—the guts of the data systems themselves—which allows me to map information exchange, a form of digital border construction between local law enforcement agencies primarily in the Western and Southwestern United States; federal law enforcement agencies in the United States; and law enforcement agencies in Mexico, Central America, and the Caribbean. Borderland circuitry thus describes cross-jurisdictional surveillance crystallizing along particular routes as a result of information-sharing partnerships. In the process, border control functions are externalized beyond US territory and internalized into the country's interior.[32]

My second task is to examine how authorities use borderland circuitry to target people—both US citizens and noncitizens—who have criminal records or are otherwise deemed to be dangerous, particularly alleged gang members, and exclude them from full membership in the polity. The border is a moving target, and so are categorical boundaries. Throughout American history, territory and substantive citizenship have not cleanly aligned. Instead, legal scholar Kunal Parker argues, "Designation as foreign is not a function of coming from the territorial outside. It is a *political strategy*."[33] Groups of people are *made* foreign in order to do something to them that could otherwise not be done: detain, punish, control, or forcibly move.

It has long been so. Before the Fugitive Slave Law of 1850 enabled the creation of a federal bureaucracy to oversee forced movement, immigration control occurred at the local level with states and towns instituting their own exclusion and deportation laws targeting unwanted entrants, most often free Black people and the poor.[34] After the abolition of slavery, legislators openly debated whether African Americans were citizens or mere "inhabitants," an illustration of how people born geographically within the US can be rendered foreign by virtue of their race.[35] Slave states punished Black people who allegedly broke laws with state-level deportation, frequently after the completion of a prison sentence, a model that resembles the current practice of deporting "criminal aliens" after the completion of criminal punishment.

Where the US government has not been able to physically expel subjugated groups from national territory, it has instituted spatial restrictions by building internal borders. The US government legally constructed Indigenous people as foreigners within US territory, thus enabling the forced removal of Native Americans from their land and confinement to reservations.[36] Connections survive in official nomenclature; Native Americans were "removed" to reservations, and *removal* is still the term used when deporting immigrants to other countries.[37]

As such, models of social control initially deployed against noncitizens become models to be used against groups of targeted citizens who are rendered foreign.[38] The forced internment of people of Japanese descent in the 1940s exemplifies both how noncitizens are subjected to extreme treatment as well as how citizens may be transformed into foreigners in order to be detained.[39] Similarly, during the Great Depression of the 1930s, approximately one million people of Mexican descent living in the United States were deported to Mexico, including a large proportion of American citizens.[40] When, as a child, I used to watch Border Patrol agents interrogate laborers in Tucson, they harassed US citizen, undocumented, and lawful permanent resident workers alike. Their Latino ethnicity marked them with a foreignness that no birthright or naturalized citizenship could counteract.

In this book I illustrate that it is through racialized classifications, specifically by being classified as an alleged criminal alien or gang member, that people are currently rendered foreign and violable, and understanding the relatively new technology that facilitates these old processes is critical. Through a deconstruction of data systems, I demonstrate that the pool of "criminal" or "dangerous" immigrants is expanding, not because immigrants are committing more crimes or joining gangs in greater numbers, but because policies enable the application of criminalizing categories to progressively broader groups of immigrants. Borderland circuitry thus both targets purportedly dangerous immigrants as well as US citizens and in a circular manner, actively constructs them as such.

Importantly, the information on which authorities rely in order to label people dangerous or criminal is questionable. For example, gang labeling practices, detailed in chapters 3 and 4, are based on subjective assessments by frontline officers. Those officers then enter their racialized, often unjustifiable, sometimes fabricated, gang labels into data systems, where the information is transformed into hard data. Unreliable information becomes authoritative fact by virtue of its presence in a database.[41]

Negative categorizations are important because they allow law enforcement agencies to do something with a given individual that they otherwise could not. Criminologists Travis Linnemann and Bill McClanahan contend that "the continuum of police power starts with classification [. . .] making classification the initial and therefore an essential police power."[42] The initial categorization of a person as a criminal alien or alleged gang member triggers and justifies—legally, morally, and politically—subsequent actions, including extended detention, prioritized deportation, horrific brutality, and information sharing with other law enforcement organizations.

Moreover, classification is a racially coded police power. Historian Nikhil Pal Singh argues that as categories of illegality and criminality become "part of the logic of an administrative apparatus," they "do the work of racial sorting without explicitly maintaining the forms of racial codification that had been central to its origination."[43] The explicitly racist origins of the terms *criminal* and *illegal* are lost to widespread amnesia, but their racist function continues, arguably more effectively.

My third, and last, task is to consider the implications for people subjected to borderland circuitry. Shachar argues that US immigration authorities' constant reshaping of the nation's territorial and membership boundaries is a key method for restricting both geographical and substantive access to the country. Immigration authorities can select whom to exclude, whom to render foreign, by shifting these boundaries in response to perceived threats.[44] The practice of rearranging borders and substantive access creates precarity. Anzaldúa's *fronterizas* (people from the borderlands) are caught in between two cultures, forced to try to bridge them both, and often belonging to neither.[45] "This is my home / this thin edge of / barbwire" can be read as a solemn refrain.[46]

Criminal aliens and alleged gang members face heightened vulnerability to surveillance, detention, and state violence in the United States, and if they are deported, they carry the stigmatized identity back to their country of origin, potentially resulting in exclusion from labor markets, social rejection, and amplified susceptibility to victimization and state violence. As borderland circuitry makes surveillance and control more widespread while inhibiting movement and settlement, more and more people may find themselves as permanent fronterizas: neither here nor there, precluded from accessing basic needs from any one nation-state. Thus borderland circuitry speaks to three dynamics: geographies of surveillance, expanding criminalization, and the spread of precarity.

We will not and cannot, in the tangle of digital circuitry, lose sight of The Wall gleaming in the desert. Along with the proliferation of digital borderlands, there remains "something unique about the state border," something undeniable about the physical space, particularly of the US-Mexico border.[47] We will return there because the combination of these two racialized phenomena—the spectacle of The Wall and the far-reaching, insidious nature of surveillance technology—is complementary.

As I ride across my own borderland, I wonder if it is under so much sunlight that borderland people are, to those in power, the most cloaked in darkness, the most unknowable, untamable, and threatening. Borderlands have often been portrayed as lawless spaces where rebels, bandits, and outlaws wander, in need of severe discipline; these are ancient fears whispered into the ears of nineteenth-century frontier generals who ordered genocide, forced confinement, and mass displacement. Since then, the sepia-toned fantasies of White cowboys pacifying Indigenous peoples have been replaced with apocalyptic images of smugglers, gang members, and rapists overrunning the border. The new generals pick at the scars and are compelled to deliver compliance once again, this time by twenty-first-century means.

ORGANIZATION OF THE BOOK

It is easy to feel overwhelmed when faced with the metastasizing collection of law enforcement surveillance technologies. To examine a single data system means pulling a thread that could unravel indefinitely, weaving in and out of an avalanche of other interconnected data systems, each with its own acronym. The federal government constantly develops new data repositories to store data, applications to process data, and information-sharing mechanisms to transfer information. Some of them are discontinued abruptly or slowly die out from lack of use, and yet others takes their place. It seems impossible to keep up with the pace of change. Consequently, I have chosen to forgo any attempt at a comprehensive overview of the immigration surveillance apparatus in favor of in-depth deconstructions of a select few databases and information-sharing programs. My aim is to identify the historical and contemporary logics of state surveillance, control, and horror, as well as their existential implications. Here I provide a brief outline of the book's organization.

Borderland circuitry relies on mass digital data repositories that store large volumes of information. Chapter 2 traces the development, deployment, and modification, from the 1980s to 2018, of two key federal immigration data systems: the Enforcement Integrated Database (EID), a data repository that is accessed through a set of applications called the Enforcement Case Tracking System (ENFORCE), and another data system called TECS (not an acronym). The volume and diversity of information in EID and TECS has substantially expanded over the years. Chapter 2 follows the growth and exchange of information between these two data systems and the resulting augmented information exchange between Immigration and Customs Enforcement (ICE) and CBP.

Chapter 3 examines how interoperable gang databases move racialized, unreliable, and at times falsified information across law enforcement jurisdictions to form a set of regional gang surveillance circuits centered primarily in the Southwestern and Western United States. Beginning in the early 2000s, California connected the CalGang Database to other gang databases in Washington State, Arizona, Texas, Nevada, and the Baltimore/Washington, D.C. area. These regional circuits connect—through EID, TECS, and the ICE-Gangs Database—to federal agencies, enabling law enforcement to target immigrant and native-born Latino, Black, and Asian youth who fit the profile of gang member or affiliate.

In chapter 4 we meet the attorneys who confront the gang labels ricocheting between databases as they guide immigrant youth through the Deferred Action for Childhood Arrivals (DACA) application process. Gang allegations, discretionarily applied by immigration officers and pulled from other law enforcement jurisdictions via the TECS system and local gang databases, can quickly transform deportation protection into an expedited deportation action. Administrative programs like DACA not only dispense benefits but also act as enforcement, intelligence gathering, and surveillance mechanisms under the auspices of gang enforcement.

ICE officers draw on the information in EID, TECS, and gang databases to perform risk assessments on apprehended noncitizens. Chapter 5 enters immigration detention centers to examine automated risk assessment tools. ICE leadership present automated technology as an antidote to human inefficiency, inadequacy, and bias. However, subjugating politics are programmed into automated technology, providing technological cover for the wretched brutality that occurs as a standard part of immigration enforcement. Ultimately, ICE deploys automated programs and discretionary decision-making in such a way as to expand the negative labeling practices that sweep immigrants into borderland circuitry.

In chapter 6 I introduce an information-sharing program that enables the US government to share data from EID and TECS with local and state law enforcement agencies. Federal immigration officials enlist local and state agencies in the surveillance of "criminal aliens" and alleged gang members, further ensnaring immigrants in the very criminal justice processes that may have affixed them with a negative label in the first place, continuing the cycle of enhanced surveillance, criminalization, and enforcement.

In addition to stretching inward through domestic programs, borderland circuitry stretches outward through international information-sharing agreements that target immigrants from Mexico, Central America, and the Caribbean. In chapter 7 I show how in sending criminal history information and gang allegations back with deported immigrants, the US government aggravates global precarity.

The conclusion provides an overview of borderland circuitry and considers how it enables the expansion of racialized labeling practices, the destruction of land for border militarization, the emergence of authoritarian governance, and corporeal horror against immigrants and racial others. The appendix offers a detailed explanation of my methodological approach and describes the disturbing difficulties I encountered in retrieving information that should be publicly accessible.

NOTES ON LANGUAGE

I use the term *criminal alien* throughout this book to refer to a noncitizen who has had contact with the US criminal justice system because it is the term used by the federal immigration enforcement apparatus that constitutes the subject of my analysis. Nonetheless, I take issue with the term through an analytical lens that is critical both of criminalization via a systematically biased criminal justice system and of the othering processes endemic to the construction of one as an "alien." I do not use quotations around the term for stylistic reasons; I find it frustrates the flow of the writing when used with great frequency. Nonetheless, wherever it appears, the reader should understand that it is, like all legal categorizations, the product of a process of power that I seek to interrogate.

Since the 1980s US immigration enforcement agencies have increasingly prioritized immigrants with criminal records for detention and removal, illustrated by the steep increase in criminal alien deportations since that decade.[48] The substantial rise in criminal alien deportations was enabled by the creation of the "aggravated felony" category, which describes crimes that qualify immigrants for deportation.[49] Since Congress established the category in 1988 to include murder, drug trafficking, and firearms trafficking, immigration statutes have progressively expanded the range of crimes that qualify as aggravated felonies to include crimes of moral turpitude, misdemeanors, convictions resulting in a sentence of at least one year, and several violations that do not include violence.[50]

While the definition of a criminal alien may appear straightforward at first, it is in practice a constantly moving target. As outlined earlier, immigrants have come to be labeled criminal aliens for violations of the criminal code that are less and less severe.[51] The criminal alien category has progressively expanded to encompass greater proportions of the immigrant population, thus enabling enforcement against greater numbers of people.[52]

I employ the term *alleged gang member* to describe people accused of gang membership, association, or affiliation by a law enforcement, government, or other agency (for example, a private or charter school). I use the term *alleged* to emphasize the problematic nature of gang labeling, which is often based on overly broad and vague criteria that are infused with racial stereotypes. Like the definition of criminal alien, the exact definition of *gang member*, *associate*, or *affiliate* is quite elastic, allowing for its application to broad groups of people of color.

While the Trump administration escalated federal attacks on alleged gang members, Democratic administrations, most notably the Obama administration, institutionalized the vilification of alleged gang members in immigration policy.[53] To carry out these policies, federal gang enforcement in large part relies on information sharing with local law enforcement agencies that are more up-to-date on local gang intelligence.[54] Thus, cross-jurisdictional gang surveillance assumes a central role in the current configuration of racialized immigration surveillance.

I use the term *subjugation*, as in "racially subjugated groups," to refer to the social, economic, and political domination of a racial group over other racial groups. The use of the term *subjugation* emphasizes that race is "a verb not a noun," to quote Carby.[55] Racialization is an ongoing process by which meaning is attached to physical and cultural characteristics. Racial categories are not inherent but instead are made by people, dependent on context, and thus can shift with movement across time and space. For example, Italian and Irish immigrants who in the nineteenth century were racially excluded have today largely assimilated into Whiteness. Moreover, at any one time the racial categorization of a given person may vary in different parts of the world or even in different regions of the same country. *Subjugation* makes clear that racialization is not simply about difference; it is a practice of domination and subordination. People are assigned racial differences in order to cast them into a power hierarchy.

Finally, drawing from Singh's definition, I consider the primary objective of *police* to be the "management and disposal of racial outsiders," not the reduction of crime or the augmentation of public safety.[56] Furthermore, in keeping with Didier Bigo's conceptualization, I employ the term *policing* broadly, to describe a collection of agencies that perform social control, surveillance, and enforcement functions on multiple jurisdiction levels, including local police departments, county and state law enforcement, immigration and border control authorities, and intelligence services.[57] Thus, in addition to local police, I consider immigration enforcement, border control, and homeland security agencies to be rooted in frameworks of White supremacy that ultimately drive the people in these agencies to target, assault, confine, and forcibly move racial outsiders.[58]

I finished my first book under the sound of Los Angeles Police Department (LAPD) helicopters after the police murders of Michael Brown and Tamir Rice. I wrote the first draft of this book just northeast of the Los Angeles Convention Center, which became a makeshift National Guard outpost after the police murders of Breonna Taylor, George Floyd, and so many others. By the end of May 2020, soldiers were installed at gas stations throughout the city as the LAPD launched tear gas and rubber bullets into Black Lives Matter protesters. It was a violent summer. Violent. I continued to write as the violence continued. In March 2021, the LAPD aggressively cleared houseless people and their allies out of the Los Angeles neighborhood of Echo Park and arrested journalists in the process, dispensing with even cursory overtures to democratic principles. Through it all, it has been glaringly obvious that law enforcement of various stripes is a source of, not a solution to, chaos and violence.

While much criminological scholarship takes for granted the widespread belief that the police have been established to reduce crime and increase public safety, I take as my foundation a historically realist examination of policing, which reveals law enforcement organizations to be institutions born in and continually dedicated to the maintenance of racial hierarchy, an objective that requires ongoing indoctrination punctuated regularly by brutal shows of force. The crime control function of law enforcement is residual, and the use of digital technology by governments to accomplish racial terror is only the latest iteration in a long tradition.

2 You Cross a Border and the Feds Build a Database

I WANT YOU to imagine this. Everything is at its peak. It is the crown of summer. The time is nearing the precipice of midday, and the sun is suspended at around 103 degrees. It is too early in the year to hope that a late afternoon summer storm may blow in, and so you just have to endure the sky's ruthlessness. You can drive north across this border into San Diego County from Tijuana, or into Douglas from Agua Prieta, El Paso from Juarez, or Brownsville from Matamoros. But I want to bring you to my land for this exercise. I want you to imagine driving into Nogales, Arizona, United States, from Nogales, Sonora, Mexico, collectively known along the border as Ambos Nogales. *Ambos*—both Nogaleses—are entangled, embattled lovers. This part of this border is one of the busiest and most militarized land crossings in the world. On maps the Tohono O'odham Nation Reservation goes right up to the demarcated international boundary, but the people span the border. Their mobility, land, and ceremonies are increasingly threatened by Border Patrol occupation.[1]

A lot of people are surprised at how the land looks here along the border: fewer cacti than imagined, more sweeping brush, aspens, and mesquite trees. On both sides of the international boundary you will see reefs of green foliage, thorns, and brown sand, interspersed with obsidian volcanic rock. You will see people whose green uniforms say, "Customs and Border Protection." Increasingly the skin of the people in the green uniforms is brown.[2] This fact is irrelevant. Regardless of the demographics of the people in the uniform, the mission is the same: to forcibly control the movement of racialized groups.[3] Increasingly the mission relies on surveillance: on the knowledge of who and where people are, where they have been, and where they are going. Control depends on knowing detailed information about people in order to categorize them in ways that render them conceptually foreign and dangerous, making them eligible for multiple modes of detention, violation, and forced transport.

In between the flora and the uniforms, the land is speckled with 160-foot surveillance towers. You can drive with a seemingly endless view of the horizon for miles and then suddenly confront these sparkling, bone-white castles shooting up into the sky, barnacled with satellite dishes and infrared cameras. The US government uses this border as a laboratory to test technology and warfare tactics that are later exported to other borders around the world—Jordan, Israel, Guatemala, Kenya—and vice versa. The towers on Tohono O'odham land were built by the Israeli arms company Elbit Systems, which claims its products are "field-proven" on Palestinians.[4] Even if you are a US citizen, be careful of the towers; sometimes at their base, Border Patrol officers set up a checkpoint where they engage in both immigration and domestic police work. In fact, between 2013 and 2016, about 40 percent of seizures by the Border Patrol at these checkpoints consisted of small amounts of marijuana being carried by US citizens.[5]

Today, in a common occurrence, the line of cars waiting to cross north into the United States stretches farther than the line idling southbound toward Mexico. Imagine that you are at a full stop;

perhaps you are the driver, drumming impatiently on a cloth-covered steering wheel. You are not part of the Trusted Traveler Program that provides preapproved members with an accelerated screening process.[6] If you were, you might be moving right now or even already over the border into the United States. After all, the mission of Customs and Border Protection (CBP) is not only to keep "terrorists and their weapons out of the U.S.," but also to facilitate "lawful international travel and trade."[7] Hopefully CBP considers you part of the latter.[8]

You might wonder in annoyance why more lanes are not being opened; there must be at least a dozen, but you see only three booths open. Your timeline stretches out in front of you. There is so much waiting involved in border and immigration control: waiting in lines to cross borders, waiting years for applications for lawful permanent residency to be considered, waiting for an asylum interview. By making you wait at these temporal borders, power makes itself known. You are not in control of your time, and you must forfeit control to those who regulate entrance to the kingdom.[9]

You absentmindedly sing along to the radio while noticing the signs that admonish crossers to control any pets in the presence of the contraband sniffing dogs and their handlers, who meander up and down the line of gleaming white SUVs, pickup trucks, and old two-door sedans. Perhaps you dread the moment when you will be forced to roll down your window, either because of the 103-degree punch that will break the air-conditioned refuge of your vehicle, the questions about to be dispensed to you by a border guard, or both. You think about how vulnerable a body is out here, the intense mortality of it all.

If you look like a person that a CBP officer might racially profile as an immigrant or a threat—two categories that immigration authorities often conflate—you might be particularly nervous about the impending screening. In light of recent reports of CBP officers searching, questioning, and taking photographs of journalists, lawyers, and activists who critically cover border issues, you might also be anxious if you have publicly stated or published something that reflected similar sentiments.[10] You now understand, viscerally, the authoritarianism and the cruelty of those who guard borders. You understand the fear and what it is intended to do to you.

You consider these tangled lines of thought as your car sits alongside other cars at the port of entry, one of several locations where an individual can attempt to lawfully enter the United States by presenting themselves and their luggage for screening.[11] Finally you pull up to the booth and a CBP officer leans over to ask the purpose of your visit to the United States. The officer will also take a look in your car and request that you produce official documentation. The CBP officer queries the TECS Platform to check your information against criminal and immigration databases and watch lists.[12] License plate readers simultaneously scan your car to check law enforcement databases for matches to stolen vehicles.[13] A CBP officer runs a density meter over the body of your car looking for indications of hidden contraband.[14] If there are no incriminating results, then the CBP officer will continue the inspection process to determine your admissibility to the United States. Subsequently, your information will be stored in a TECS subsystem, most likely one called the Border Crossing Information System.[15]

However, if something during the primary inspection process piques the CBP officer's interest, the officer may direct you to a secondary inspection station in which you will undergo a more extensive screening. More questions will be asked, more databases queried. A CBP officer may create a TECS Subject Record on you to indicate that you are an enforcement interest.[16] Ultimately the CBP agent will decide to either grant or deny your entrance into the United States or to detain you.

Either way, your name and information will go into TECS alongside hundreds of thousands of others. TECS is a huge, broad system, a writhing, multitentacled thing that according to the Department of Homeland Security (DHS) contains "every possible type of information from a variety of Federal, state and local sources, which contributes to effective law enforcement."[17] The types of information and the categories of people on whom information is held are too great in breadth to comprehensively review here, but they include violators, suspected violators, and victims of violations of federal laws, including those pertaining to immigration, tax, or drug violations; individuals detained by CBP; and those whom CBP considers to pose a potential threat to the United States.[18] CBP also stores biographic information in TECS on people who are not suspected of violations, including information gleaned from routine screenings of both US citizens and noncitizens traveling across US borders, and biometric information including iris scans, to which people may be unaware they are being subject.[19]

TECS is thus a mammoth *data repository*, a place to store information that has been collected about people directly by CBP officers or information about people that authorities have imported into TECS from other data systems. More than a single data repository, TECS is a conglomerate of several subsystems, or modules, that store different types of information.[20] Information on passengers for an international flight, for example, will go into a different TECS module than information on those suspected of drug trafficking. Nonetheless, information maintained under the larger TECS umbrella could be used for investigative purposes later on and be shared with other agencies.[21]

In addition to serving as a series of data repositories, TECS performs two other vital functions. First, it is a *targeting system* that includes analytical tools to screen travelers and cargo, both coming into and going out of the United States.[22] In other words, TECS performs automated risk assessments on people and objects in place of the less efficient practice of a having a human review all traveler information. Risk assessment thereby emerges as a keystone of border management that tags business and tourist travelers as "low risk" while regarding as "high risk" those who cross borders because of economic need or violence in their home countries. Authorities thus construct a border that is selectively permeable, allotting mobility to White men from first world countries while denying it to other border crossers racialized as "migrants" or illegitimate and dangerous travelers.[23]

The second vital function of TECS is as an *information-sharing environment*, meaning that someone with access to TECS can both search the TECS system and use the TECS platform to search other systems like the National Crime and Information Center (NCIC) Database, an important index of criminal justice information maintained by the Federal Bureau of Investigation (FBI) that is available to law enforcement, across jurisdictions, throughout the United States.[24] TECS interfaces with dozens of other data systems in what Emma Knight and Alex Gekker identify as an "interfacial regime."[25] Thus the TECS Platform facilitates *interoperability* and information sharing among law enforcement agencies. John Palfrey and Urs Gasser broadly define interoperability as "the ability to transfer and render useful data and other information across systems, applications, or components."[26] Interoperability helps databases talk to one another.

The US government prioritized interoperability initiatives after the attacks on September 11, 2001, to increase collaboration between federal, state, local, tribal, and international law enforcement agencies.[27] Interoperable data systems now constitute the "connective tissue" that ties together a web of decentralized federal immigration and law enforcement agencies and situates federal agencies within larger national and transnational surveillance infrastructures.[28] TECS information is also shared for non–law enforcement purposes. For instance, when United States Citizenship and Immigration Services (USCIS) officers conduct background checks on immigrants applying for citizenship or benefits, they will check records in TECS (more on this in chapter 4).[29]

Although the buildup of the southern border picked up pace in the 1990s, opportunistic politicians used the September 11 attacks as a justification to accelerate and heighten border militarization and immigration restrictions. This is one reason the line of cars in which you wait is so long. The contemporary, post–September 11 mode of immigration enforcement is defined by *securitization* frameworks wherein federal law enforcement agencies and political actors present immigration as a dire national security issue requiring urgent and severe action. In the processes of securitization, government officials associate immigrants from certain regions, including Mexico, Central America, and the Caribbean, with the threats of terrorism, transnational gang activity, human trafficking, and drug trafficking. Consequently, the US government has deemed immigrants from these countries to be high risk and thus eligible to be subjected to greater scrutiny when attempting to enter the United States.

Securitization requires a two-pronged approach, depending on enhanced enforcement both at the border and in the interior of the United States.[30] Two key surveillance systems, which are the focus of this chapter, undergird border control and interior immigration control practices: TECS and the Enforcement Integrated Database (EID). Over time, TECS and EID have come to include an increasingly broad range of information on an equally broad range of surveillance subjects, which sets the foundation for the expansive labeling of people as criminal or dangerous and initiates the tracking process. The linking together of TECS and EID allows this information to flow between the borderlands and the interior of the country in a way that makes possible contemporary immigration enforcement.

TECS IS NOT currently an acronym, but it used to be. When it was originally developed by the United States Customs Service in the mid-1980s, the individual letters stood for "Treasury Enforcement Communications System."[31] At the time the Customs Service, housed under the Department of the Treasury, was charged with the collection of duties and tariffs on imported goods, a task that is inevitably tied to immigration screening because imported goods by definition cross borders.[32]

After September 11, 2001, Congress restructured government agencies, nesting the enforcement and administrative functions of the immigration system under the newly created DHS. The DHS agency CBP is dedicated to border enforcement. Another DHS agency, Immigration and Customs Enforcement (ICE), investigates and enforces immigration laws in the interior. Yet another DHS agency, USCIS, is an administrative arm responsible for immigration and naturalization adjudication functions and immigration services. When someone applies for immigration benefits or to change their immigration status, USCIS officers handle the application. The creation of DHS as a consolidation of immigration, customs, border inspection, border patrol, and transportation security is remarkable in its reframing of these federal tasks as specifically driven by terrorism detection and prevention.[33]

As part of the restructuring, the Customs Service was transferred from the Department of the Treasury to the newly established DHS and renamed Customs and Border Protection.[34] The new agency name and new home department came with a new mission, that of preventing terrorists and terrorist weapons from entering the United States while expediting legitimate travel and trade. Following CBP, TECS also moved out of the Department of the Treasury and into the DHS, where it was christened "TECS (no longer an acronym)," or referred to in government documents as "the system formerly known as the Treasury Enforcement Communications System," in the tradition of "The Artist Formerly Known as Prince" but with more xenophobia.[35]

This iteration of TECS is what you confront in your car under the sweltering sun at the port of entry. However, the type of crossing that anti-immigration commentators most loudly decry is frequently accomplished on foot between ports of entry. Entering without inspection is what is known in the language of immigration enforcement as "unlawful" entry. CBP agents enter information into TECS on people they catch crossing between ports of entry too.[36] Because most of these people will initially be detained by CBP and then have their detention transferred to ICE, their information also must be transferred from CBP to ICE.

Table 1 Evolution of TECS and Agency/Departmental Homes

Date Range	Department	Agency	System
1980s to early 2000s	Treasury	Customs Service	Treasury Enforcement Communications System
Early 2000s to ~2010	Homeland Security	Customs and Border Protection	TECS
~2010 to current	Homeland Security	Customs and Border Protection	TECS Modernization

To facilitate information exchange between CBP and ICE, DHS introduced a portal that connects CPB officers and TECS data to the EID, a system that forms the backbone of the inquiry in this book. EID is a data repository, accessed through a collection of applications called the Enforcement Case Tracking System (ENFORCE), which maintains information on federal investigation, arrest, booking, detention, and removal operations.[37] For the sake of very simplistic conceptualization, one could think of TECS as the primary data system used by officers at US borders, therefore mostly supporting border enforcement, and the EID/ENFORCE system as primarily accessed by ICE field personnel and immigration detention workers to support interior enforcement, including detention and removal.

And so the border bleeds toward the center, carrying fingerprints, criminal records, maps of irises, and much more to the banks of multiple interior enforcement agencies. The combination of TECS and EID/ENFORCE feeds border surveillance into interior surveillance systems and thus expands border-like controls beyond the physical territory of the border. Like rivers on a cartographer's map, the invisible circuitry wriggles across the landscape, following people—both

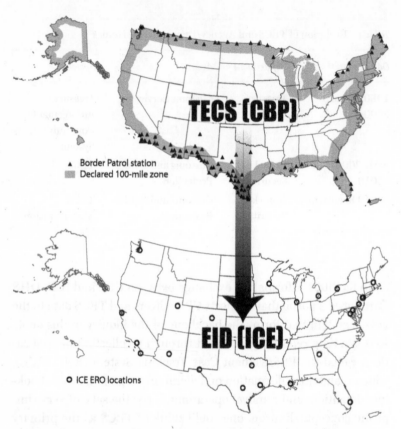

Map 1. Information transferred from Border Patrol to ICE field offices. When individuals are transferred from CPB to ICE custody, their information is transferred from TECS to EID. *Credit:* Nat Case, INCase, LLC.

citizens and noncitizens—as they scatter across the country. You drive north, away from the border, and the border follows.

LIKE TECS, EID has worn multiple faces. First, there was the Deportable Alien Control System (DACS), which first became operational in 1984 under the Immigration and Naturalization Service (INS) and was primarily accessed by immigration enforcement agents, deportation officers, detention removal assistants, and clerical staff to track immigrant detainees between detention centers and to centralize case status and disposition information.[38]

When the INS, which was housed under the Department of Justice, was dissolved as part of the post–September 11 restructuring of immigration agencies, DACS landed under the care of ICE. The new stewards noticed that the data system was ill suited to the contemporary landscape that centered anti-terrorism objectives and required increased information sharing and risk assessment capacity.[39] Consequently, in September 2007 ICE initiated the replacement of DACS with ENFORCE, a collection of applications through which immigration enforcement personnel could track an individual from the point of investigation to case completion across DHS components.[40] By 2009 ENFORCE was ICE's primary administrative case management system for removals.[41]

Shortly thereafter ICE developed EID, a data repository accessed via the ENFORCE applications by ICE, CBP, and USCIS. The Virginia-based private contractor Dev Technology Group and another tech company, SRA International (featured more in the next chapter), helped to develop and manage ENFORCE applications.[42]

The information that immigration authorities maintained in DACS from the 1980s through the early 2000s was initially relatively narrow because they primarily conceived of DACS as a case management system that assisted in deportation or detention efforts "by providing management with information concerning the status and/or disposition of deportable aliens."[43] However, as DACS has morphed into EID, it has come to constitute more than a case management system; federal law enforcement has reframed the system as both a surveillance system and an investigative tool that broadly supports law enforcement activity. As a result, there has been a substantial increase in the range of people and information that can fall within its purview.

THE REORGANIZATION OF information infrastructure during this period has several major implications. First, a *broader range and*

Table 2 Evolution of EID/ENFORCE and Agency/Departmental Homes

Date Range	Department	Agency	System
1980s to mid-2000s	Justice	Immigration and Naturalization Service	Deportable Alien Control System
Mid-2000s to ~2010	Homeland Security	Immigration and Customs Enforcement	Enforcement Case Tracking System
~2010 to current	Homeland Security	Immigration and Customs Enforcement	Enforcement Integrated Database

greater number of people are eligible to have their information maintained in the database than before, forming the contours of a broad-based surveillance system. For example, federal authorities define ENFORCE and EID as systems that process "records pertaining to the investigation, arrest, booking, detention, and removal of persons encountered during immigration and criminal law enforcement investigations and operations conducted by DHS."[44] Compare this to the far less ambitious objective of DACS, which was to maintain information on "aliens alleged to be deportable by INS."[45]

In the leap from DACS to ENFORCE to EID, the range of individuals whose information can legally be maintained in information systems broadened from people alleged to be in violation of immigration statutes to persons *encountered* during investigations and operations. This change in criteria expanded the potential database population to include immigrants not in violation of immigration statutes as well as US citizens who had contact with agents and officers during investigations and operations. Because regulatory guidelines define the data systems as supporting law enforcement investigations—and not solely immigration case management—noncitizens and citizens who are allegedly implicated in violating immigration laws or simply encountered in the course of investigations may be documented. Sociologist Sarah Brayne argues that one characteristic of this type of dragnet surveillance, in which surveillance is focused on nearly everyone and not only "suspicious" people, is that the threshold for inclusion "primarily operates below legal thresholds of reasonable suspicion and probable cause."[46] Information in databases is then retroactively called upon to build a case against someone only *after* they come under suspicion.

Second, the *types of information* that can be maintained on people in the data systems are expansive and include subjects' employment, educational, travel, and health history; familial and nonfamilial associations; physical characteristics such as scars, marks, and tattoos; and information about DHS agents' encounters with individuals in the course of law enforcement activities. ENFORCE applications also process biometric information on suspects in the form of fingerprints, DNA, and photographs.[47] Law enforcement agencies now possess the technological capacity to feed their information-gathering compulsion, however marginal the information may appear at the point it is gathered. More than having the passive capacity to do so, law enforcement agencies at multiple jurisdictional levels are actively incentivized to get as many people's information into data systems as possible.[48]

Third, boundaries—between criminal and immigration records as well as administrative and enforcement data—are weakened, blurred, and confounded. The data systems are fed and accessed by a range of agencies that fulfill both *enforcement- and nonenforcement*-related functions. Some information collected by administrative immigration agencies, like USCIS, will make its way into enforcement databases, like EID/ENFORCE and TECS, and vice versa. Consequently, not only has the number of people and types of information in systems expanded, it has expanded in ways that tie together criminal and immigration records and at times frame immigrants as criminal.

This criminalization has been facilitated by the expansion and standardization of criminal history information in immigration records. With EID, immigration authorities began to import comprehensive criminal history information, including arrests, charges pending, charges dropped, convictions, wants/warrants, presence of false IDs, supervision history, gang history, drug history, and dispositions.[49] As the amount of criminal history information increases to include not only convictions but also charges that may have ultimately been dropped and allegations like those pertaining to gang affiliation that do not require an arrest, there are increased opportunities for immigrants to be labeled criminal or dangerous based on questionable information.[50] Sociologist Sarah Lageson argues that the rise of broken windows policing has been key here because the practice leads to arrests and the creation of records for petty crimes. However, many cases that are initiated as a result of broken windows policing are later dropped and not prosecuted.[51] If one were to include only conviction information in a database, these dropped petty cases would not show up on a given individual's record. However, when the universe of information is expanded to include arrests that do not result in prosecution, unadjudicated information will show up as a liability on someone's record.

Fourth, the *information sources* have expanded. Much of the information in data repositories is not collected directly from people but rather pulled from other data systems, or *secondary sources*. Law enforcement agencies collect information from undercover operatives, surveillance technology, confidential informants, visa and immigration benefits applications, travel documents, international partners, employers, schools, individuals making bond arrangements, law enforcement databases, and commercially available databases (i.e., newspapers, registries, social media).[52] This has led to the growth in "big data policing" and "big data surveillance," or the fast processing of large amounts of data from previously separated, but now consolidated, data sources.[53]

To some extent, authorities' data collection tasks have been made easier by the rise of what surveillance scholar Bernard Harcourt terms the "expository society," wherein large numbers of people are willing to expose their own information on social media platforms that surveilling agents then easily collect.[54] Nonetheless, much of the information collected by immigration enforcement personnel is invasive, nonconsensual, and undetected by the surveillance subject.

Fifth, and last, *information is more often collected, mined, analyzed, and maintained by private entities* contracted by government agencies rather than by the government agencies themselves. Knight and Gekker argue that in "turning to private industry to build America's modern security apparatus, securitization was never treated as a political issue but rather as a technical problem," thus depoliticizing surveillance and cleansing it of its racialized and brutal reality.[55] Furthermore, by relying on outside data brokers, law enforcement can evade privacy laws. For example, organizations can hide their contracting work with ICE by routing it through third-party contractors, as Google did in an unsuccessful attempt to avoid controversy when it contracted with ICE to provide Google Cloud technology for surveillance along the US-Mexico border in 2018.[56]

Journalist Todd Miller demonstrates that "revolving doors" between private industry and government cement a "border-industrial complex," with former government officials working in the private homeland security corporations and consulting companies that are contracted by the federal government.[57] In turn, these border security corporations feed the campaigns of politicians who are friendly to border militarization. For example, between 2006 and 2018, Lockheed Martin, General Dynamics, Northrop Grumman, Raytheon, and Boeing contributed $6.5 million to members of the House Homeland Security Committee and $27.6 million to members of the House Appropriations Committee.[58]

Academic institutions, which are increasingly privatized as public funding declines, support border militarization by developing surveillance technology and products. One such endeavor is the Borders, Trade, and Immigration Institute, which includes the University of Houston, University of Arizona, University of Texas–El Paso, University of Virginia, West Virginia University, University of

North Carolina, University of Minnesota, Texas A&M, Rutgers University, American University, Texas A&M, the Middlebury Institute of International Studies, and the Migration Policy Institute.[59] In early 2020, the Institute's University of Houston site began to field test drones with thermal imaging for use in hunting contraband and humans.[60]

THE ALTERATION OF one component necessitates the alteration of neighboring ones, like dominoes falling in perpetuity. TECS is undergoing yet another costume change because its current platform has not kept up with the modifications of data systems around it, interrupting interoperability and compromising system security.[61] Palantir, Amazon, Booz Allen Hamilton, Northrop Grumman, and a host of other contractors have been entrusted to accomplish the modernization of TECS, a task at which Raytheon failed several years ago before ultimately losing the contract.[62]

The outcome of TECS modernization for CBP is the new and improved TECS Platform. For ICE, Palantir has delivered the Investigative Case Management (ICM) system, which will interface with the TECS Platform so that ICE and CBP can continue to share information as well as interface with many other data systems. ICM is heavily dependent on secondary information, as its "primary function is to aggregate information from external databases."[63]

ICM was initially slated to be used primarily by only one subsection of ICE called Homeland Security Investigations, an investigative arm with the authority to enforce a broad range of federal criminal laws, some of which are only peripherally related to immigration. Money laundering, intellectual property theft, cybercrime, human rights violations, transnational gang activity, and antiquity theft are a few of the things that fall under the scope of Homeland Security Investigations.[64] The breadth of its mission means that the information in ICM will also be broad, much like the information in TECS and EID/ENFORCE. The information in ICM may become broader yet, as more recently, ICE's Office of Removal Operations has begun to use it for civil immigration matters and deportation.[65] ICM may very well eventually come to be ICE's data system of choice.

I FIND IT increasingly difficult to remember a pre–September 11 airport, when we could walk right up to the gate to welcome or say goodbye to someone; I know I participated in this now-lost ritual, but I cannot remember it. Sense memories of the old border are similarly dissolving in my brain, and I grieve the patchwork of holes left behind. I am writing to remember, writing as it slips away.

Several years ago my mother told me a story, a memory, of an older US-Mexico border, one that existed when I was a child, before there were so many private contractors vying to modify databases, before those databases were so gargantuan, before most were interoperable; when the wall was shorter and flimsier and the people who lived in the borderlands more often took wire cutters to it, sometimes to cross for nothing more than a drink with fellow fronterizos on the other side; and before the border flung its circuits far and wide, when it was only on the cusp of transforming itself into code. As my mother remembers, I was very young then, four or five years old, and we were crossing back over to the United States through the Nogales port of entry on foot after spending a day in Nogales, Sonora. In the chaos of customs, my mother looked down to see an empty space where I should have been standing. I imagine her, curls bouncing wildly, earrings jangling, leather sandals smacking, pushing through the throngs in a panic, shouting my name into the thick air. After a few minutes she found me hanging onto a metal turnstile, gleefully swinging back and forth, into and out of Mexico, into the United States and back again. A Mexican officer, who appeared to be no more than a teenager, stood nearby holding an assault weapon, only mildly interested in my presence.

This was in the 1980s and early 1990s, the era of a more porous border. Of course this is not to deny that since its inception, the border has always been, by definition, a mechanism for race-based exclusion where some pass more easily than others. It was always the "1,950 mile-long open wound / dividing a *pueblo*, a culture, / running down the length of my body," identified by Anzaldúa.[66] Even as I grieve my vaporizing memories of the old border and come to terms with the newly expansive technological borders, I understand that things were not *good*, especially for people who, unlike me, had to cross over a deadly landscape for survival under the crosshairs of border guards. I judge my grief against José Emilio Pacheco's condemnation: *"Who could feel nostalgic for that horror?"*[67]

Though the border of my childhood was horrific in many ways, I think there was more room for playfulness among people who lived in the borderlands then. For example, between 1979 and 2007, residents of Naco, Sonora, and Naco, Arizona, used the barbed-wire border fence as a net in volleyball games. But the switch to taller metal beams ended the cross-border tournaments. Even if the metal beams were short enough to allow for volleyball, it is likely that a Border Patrol agent, outfitted as if in an active war zone, would quickly intervene to break up the game.[68] And so the border town of Naco, named for the Opata word for prickly pear, along with so many other towns along the border, has become hypermilitarized. Crossing now requires a more extensive screening process with more extensive documentation, backed by higher walls and a widespread surveillance infrastructure; the brutality is more efficient and systematized and does not allow for a quick lunch with brothers and sisters on the other side.

The border becomes ever more hardened physically as it becomes more fluid digitally. The US government continues to turn to private contractors to modify TECS and EID/ENFORCE into increasingly more monstrous surveillance systems that undergird the tracking, assessment, and investigative functions that are foundational to borderland circuitry. Through interconnected data systems developed by private industry, myriad law enforcement agencies impede the movement of individuals both domestically and internationally, with a particular focus on people deemed criminal aliens or gang members. For now we leave the Arizona-Mexico border for California and other parts of the United States, to map how federal databases, including TECS and EID/ENFORCE, have become plugged into regional gang databases, creating internal borders with catastrophic consequences for criminalized youth of color.

3 California Cops Become the Tip of the Spear

A SPECTACLE OF neon is nestled between the verdant slopes of the Hollywood Hills. A contrived quasi-indoor, quasi-outdoor setting, CityWalk is a family-friendly simulacrum of the Vegas strip. People of all ages peruse the Bubba Gump Shrimp Company, Hard Rock Café, and Abercrombie and Fitch. An employee costumed as Marge Simpson or a Jurassic Park raptor might make an appearance. Omnipresent pop music and the echo of disembodied voices mingle with an announcement about purchasing tickets to the King Kong ride in 3D. This is the epitome of the sanitized theme park bemoaned by critical urban scholars like Mike Davis and Bernard Harcourt, a highly controlled space riddled with surveillance cameras and private security to facilitate mass consumerism.[1] In the desert you have to move slowly and watch the sky, but here you can hurry from one diversion to another, and the smog obscures the skyline anyway.

Set against the edge of CityWalk is a building with a conference room in which twenty members of the CalGang Executive Board convened in late January 2006 to discuss another type of surveillance: that of allegedly gang-affiliated people whose information is held in the CalGang Database (hereafter referred to simply as CalGang). About six hundred miles northwest of the Nogales port of entry, CalGang administrators are working with ICE to build their own internal borderlands in California and across the Unites States, where people are criminalized, rendered foreign, detained, and forcibly moved.

In CalGang, law enforcement maintains information on thousands of alleged gang members and associates in California. At one time the database held over 250,000 names.[2] CalGang is fed by local law enforcement "node" agencies, who are responsible for their respective corners of the CalGang universe.[3] Around the conference table that day in January 2006 sat node representatives from the Alameda County Sheriff's Office, California Department of Corrections, the California Department of Justice, California Youth Authority, Fresno County Sheriff's Office, Kern County Sheriff's Office, Los Angeles Sheriff's Department, Los Angeles Police Department (LAPD), Orange County District Attorney's Office, San Bernardino Sheriff's Department, San Diego Police Department, San Jose Police Department, Santa Barbara Police Department, State Chiefs of Police Association, and Sonoma County Sheriff's Department. Also present were representatives from the California Office of Emergency Services and the California Attorney General's Office.

For some reason, nearly from the point of its inception, the administration of CalGang settled in Sonoma County, a place better known for its vineyards than its violent street gangs. Sonoma County Sheriff's Department lieutenant Jay Farmer was integral to the founding of both of CalGang's administrative bodies, the Cal-Gang Executive Board and California Gang Node Advisory Committee.[4] The CalGang Executive Board was chaired by Dennis Smiley, a detective sergeant for the Sonoma County Sheriff's Department.[5]

In the middle of this sea of law enforcement sat Kathy Wendt, representing SRA (Systems Research and Applications Corporation) International, Inc., an information technology services and solutions company that counted among its clients the US Departments of Defense, Homeland Security (DHS), and Justice. SRA personnel had contracted with the US government since the 1970s to provide multiple services, including intelligence work, visa screening, asset forfeiture tracking, monitoring the Immigration and Naturalization Service's (INS's) and later Immigration and Customs Enforcement's (ICE's) worksite enforcement efforts, and support for the TECS data system.[6]

Early in the development of CalGang, the California Department of Justice had enlisted the Irvine-based firm Orion Scientific Systems Inc., which also provided technical assistance to the Central Intelligence Agency and National Security Administration. In 2004, Orion was purchased by SRA, and the merged corporate entity developed the GangNet System to provide the technological infrastructure for CalGang.[7] This winding trail of contracts and mergers is how SRA representative Wendt found herself surrounded by uniforms in a conference room on the third floor of a building overlooking the midday neon glow of Universal CityWalk.

There were several important items to discuss at that day's Cal-Gang Executive Board meeting. The acting assistant secretary of ICE had just signed a memorandum of understanding with the California Department of Justice to exchange gang intelligence information. As a result, SRA was hard at work developing a new ICE information system, called ICEGangs, which would mirror CalGang in its design and connect directly to CalGang.

However, as we will see, ICEGangs never quite caught on. Rather than serving as a national repository of immigrant gang members, it simply allowed for information exchange between ICE and law enforcement in only one state, California. After ten years of minimal use, ICEGangs just sort of died out. This chapter is dedicated to a postmortem of the ICEGangs Database, a quest to reconstruct its interoperable birth, sudden death, and the disproportionate toll it took on immigrants and youth of color in California and other select regions of the United States. By reconstructing the inadequacies of

ICEGangs, we can better understand its mirror image: the databases that federal law enforcement prefers for tracking surveillance subjects.

Nonetheless, the current absence of ICEGangs cannot erase its decade-long presence. This chapter provides a historical and cartographic mapping of how California innovated and then exported a starkly racialized and brutal regime of gang enforcement to other parts of the United States and even internationally. The way in which the ICEGangs Database connected federal immigration authorities to local law enforcement in certain hotspots casts a shadow today; it institutionalized a model of information sharing and profiling that continues to terrorize immigrant communities and communities of color throughout the nation. Furthermore, this massive cross-jurisdictional information-sharing operation ultimately relied, and continues to rely, on street-level officers who document youth of color as gang members based on racist stereotypes, questionable criteria, and fabricated information. A cop decides someone is a gang member and writes it on a card; the card gets input into a database, which feeds into another database; and eventually, with little oversight, at the other end someone is given a decade-long gang enhancement on their criminal conviction or fast-tracked to deportation.

THE PASSAGE OF the Street Terrorism Enforcement and Prevention (STEP) Act in 1988 was a watershed moment; it provided a template for defining gangs; criminalized alleged participation in a street gang; and meted out punishment, including gang enhancements, for gang affiliation.[8] In California the STEP Act grew in lockstep with the spread of gang databases. One of the earliest computerized gang databases, and quite possibly the first of its kind, was the Los Angeles County Sheriff's Department's Gang Reporting, Evaluation, and Tracking System, or GREAT, developed in 1987.[9]

GREAT quickly became a statewide database, and by 1993 the California Department of Justice, in concert with local law enforcement agencies, began the search for a software developer who could create a better version. At this point, the California Department of Justice contracted Orion Scientific Systems Inc., which, as described earlier, was later purchased by SRA. SRA then developed the Gang-Net System, the software on which CalGang runs. By 1998, CalGang had been deployed statewide.

CalGang administrators adopted a slightly modified version of the STEP Act definition to characterize a gang as "a group of three or more persons who have a common identifying sign, symbol or name, and whose members individually or collectively engage in or have engaged in a pattern of definable criminal activity creating an atmosphere of fear and intimidation within the community."[10] Cal-Gang administrators then established that an individual must satisfy at least two of the following criteria to be entered into CalGang: admits to being a gang member, is known to have gang tattoos, has been seen associating with other documented gang members, has been seen frequenting gang areas, has been seen wearing gang dress, admits to being a gang member during an in-custody classification interview, has been arrested for offenses consistent with usual gang activity, has been seen displaying gang symbols and/or hand signs, has been identified as a gang member by a reliable informant/source, or has been identified as a gang member by an untested informant.[11]

Police officers use Field Interview cards to record information on suspected gang members and associates, including their personal information, physical description, clothing, social media accounts, contacts, and vehicles, to later be transferred to gang databases. Law enforcement can document someone as a gang member on a Field Interview card without arresting or charging them for any crime.[12] Thus, even though officers often do not necessarily document criminal behavior on Field Interview cards, this type of intelligence gathering can eventually turn into evidence that results in punishment. Brayne notes that Field Interview cards are "fundamental building blocks" for data-driven policing.[13] For example, every time someone comes into contact with the LAPD and a Field Interview card is filled out, one point is added to that person's "chronic offender" score.[14]

Although there is no explicit language about race in the STEP Act's definition of a "gang" or in the CalGang criteria for gang membership, gang profiling functions as a racialized legal proxy that allows police to target people of color without adequate cause or evidence. Repeatedly, local and state gang databases have been found to be rife with misinformation, fabricated evidence, and unjustifiable entries on mostly Black and Latino men.[15] For example, in 2015, the CalGang population was 64.9 percent "Hispanic," 20.5 percent Black, and 93.1 percent male.[16] On the federal level, prosecutors apply the Federal Racketeer Influenced and Corrupt Organizations Act (RICO) overwhelmingly to street and prison gangs associated with racial minority groups rather than White motorcycle gangs or White supremacist groups.[17] In 2020, the Salt Lake County district attorney charged Black Lives Matter protesters with gang enhancements for their participation in First Amendment–protected activity, with a potential sentence of five years to life.[18]

Although often overlooked, gang labeling along the West Coast targets Asian/Pacific Islanders as well.[19] In 1980s California, police accelerated gang profiling and enforcement in Chinese, Vietnamese, Filipino, Laotian, and Cambodian immigrant neighborhoods, establishing Asian gang task forces and specialized Asian gang units.[20] A 1995 ACLU lawsuit that ended in a settlement claimed that the Garden Grove Police Department profiled young Asian Americans as gang members based on their ethnicity and attire. The settlement included provisions to rein in gang labeling by requiring that Field Interview cards only be completed in the case that police have reasonable suspicion of criminal activity and that there exists a process for people to contest their field interview information.[21] Nevertheless, police continue to profile and harass Asian/Pacific Islander youth based on accusations of gang involvement.[22]

Scholarship and government audits suggest that the disproportionate effects of gang enforcement stem from overly broad labeling practices by law enforcement that are "devoid of hallmarks of due process," infused with racial stereotyping, and easily sweep in broad groups of neighbors, family members, and friends who live in heavily policed areas.[23] Gang-labeling criteria provide a given law enforcement officer on the street great latitude in whom to label; police have considered Los Angeles Dodgers gear, Virgen de Guadalupe tattoos, and oversized red or blue clothing to be indicative of gang affiliation. As a result, officers can use gang allegations to justify targeting and harassing people whom they do not otherwise have a legal basis to detain.

The power of gang profiling lies in its elasticity, in law enforcement's ability to expand or contract the definition to fit the situation at hand; it allows police to target a broad range of people of color in public spaces. The breadth and vagueness of the criteria create an environment in which gang allegations are both everywhere and nowhere, constituting a constant threat that terrorizes and disciplines racialized groups. Thus gang profiling is part of a larger assemblage of racialized practices throughout history that have sought to push people of color out of public space, heavily regulate their presence in public space, or prevent them from crossing multiple types of borders.

GANGNET DATABASES IN different jurisdictions can link to one another to form regional and national webs of information exchange, which SRA envisions will one day form the foundation for a national gang repository.[24] Once GalGang, which runs on GangNet software, was established in the late 1990s, CalGang administrators secured agreements with other local and state law enforcement agencies that also used GangNet. Each agreement gave CalGang users and partner agency users reciprocal "read-only" access, meaning that a CalGang user could search and view, but not modify, information in an another agency's database. At the other end, an officer in the partner agency would similarly be able search and view information in CalGang but not modify any information.

In 2004 CalGang reached an agreement for mutual read-only access with the Las Vegas Metropolitan Police Department.[25] In short succession in 2011, CalGang administrators also signed agreements with the Arizona Department of Public Safety, the Spokane Police Department, and the Washington-Baltimore High Intensity Drug Trafficking Area Program.[26] By 2010, one-third of ICEGangs users were located on the West Coast.[27]

Although the Arizona Department of Public Safety agreement was signed in 2011, CalGang Executive Board meeting notes claim that as many as sixty-nine agencies in Arizona were already connected to CalGang by 2007.[28] Similarly, CalGang Executive Board meeting minutes in 2008 document fifty-eight agencies participating from the Washington-Baltimore High Intensity Drug Trafficking Area Program and its users as having entered more than six thousand gang members into the system, even though a formal agreement was not signed until 2011.[29] Thus, rather than initiating information exchange, a memorandum of understanding seems to cement already occurring practices. Both CalGang Executive Board meeting notes from 2012 and an SRA proposal to the US government from 2010 state that CalGang connected to Customs and Border Patrol (CBP) as well as law enforcement in New Mexico. However, memorandums of understanding do not appear to exist for either of these partnerships.

CalGang administrators pursued federal agencies as well. In 2006 they signed an agreement with the Bureau of Alcohol, Tobacco, Firearms, and Explosives (ATF) to track alleged gang members and firearm exchange. According to CalGang Executive Board meeting minutes, approximately three hundred ATF users accessed CalGang, and there were 2,307 alleged gang members in the ATF system about whom CalGang users could access new information.[30] CalGang administrators also signed an agreement with the Federal Bureau of Investigation (FBI) for the purpose of accessing the FBI's Violent Gang and Terrorist Organizations File with a specific focus on information pertaining to alleged gang members from El Salvador.[31] Finally, CalGang administrators signed the information-sharing agreement with ICE.

Map 2. CalGang information-sharing agreements. *Credit:* Nat Case, INCase, LLC.

Through CalGang, California law enforcement engaged in information sharing with local law enforcement in Washington State, California, Nevada, Arizona, Maryland, Washington, D.C., and if internal ICE and CalGang communications are reliable, New Mexico. The result is a system of regional circuitry that targets non-citizen and American-born Latino, Black, and Asian/Pacific Islander (API) youth whom officers choose to profile as gang members or affiliates in the American West, Southwest, and to a lesser extent, mid-Atlantic region. These regional circuits are then plugged into federal agencies including the FBI, ATF, ICE, and possibly CBP.

Previous research indicates that immigration agents rely heavily on local law enforcement to identify gang members because local police possess "highly localized geopolitical knowledge" and more up-to-date surveillance information than do federal agents.[32] Jeff Sessions, during his stint as US attorney general, referred to local law enforcement as "the tip of the spear" in the war on gangs.[33] Interoperable databases facilitate this *jurisdictional buoyancy*, wherein gang labels float up from local to federal law enforcement. Once gang-profiled people of color in the targeted geographic areas are listed on local gang databases—databases subjected to little oversight and fed information by largely unchecked officers—they enter a fast track to state-level gang databases and ultimately, federal enforcement.

THE JEWEL IN the crown of CalGang interoperability was the connection to ICEGangs. Access to ICEGangs enabled local law enforcement in California to learn the immigration status of the suspected gang members and associates in CalGang. In return, access to Cal-Gang provided ICE with information on potential enforcement targets as well as on those already in immigration custody.[34]

The ICE agreement was inaugurated in 2006, an important temporal marker; this is the point in time at which the Deportable Alien Control System (DACS) began its transformation into the Enforcement Case Tracking System (ENFORCE) and the Enforcement Integrated Database (EID). TECS also underwent significant modification at this time, during which DHS officials noticed that TECS was deficient in its capacity to store gang intelligence information. Consequently, they sought to develop a separate, but connected, database dedicated to gang intelligence gathering to supplement information in TECS.[35] DHS and ICE personnel looked to other law enforcement agencies for inspiration and found it in California when they landed on CalGang and the underlying GangNet system as the most promising model to replicate.

ICE subsequently dispatched a representative to the CalGang Executive Board who was welcomed as a voting entity. Soon enough, an official agreement was penned, ICEGangs went into development, and SRA established the SRA International ORION Center for Immigration and Customs Enforcement to provide technical training and support for ICEGangs.[36]

Since ICEGangs and CalGang were created by the same developer with interoperability in mind, the systems looked a lot alike. The criteria for entry were very similar. An individual had to fit at least two of the following criteria to be entered into ICEGangs as a gang member: has gang-related tattoos; associates with other alleged gang members; frequents "notorious" gang areas; displays gang signs or symbols; has been arrested with other gang members on two or more occasions; has been identified as a gang member in written or electronic correspondence; has been seen wearing gang-style clothing; has been identified as a gang member through documented reasonable suspicion; or has been identified as a gang member by a reliable source, untested informant, jail staff, or prison staff. Individuals could also be entered into ICEGangs if they had convictions at the federal or state level that imposed punishment or civil consequences for gang-related activity or if they admitted membership to a law enforcement officer. ICEGangs users entered individuals as gang "associates" if they socialized with allegedly active gang members.[37]

ICE defined a "gang" based on the STEP Act and CalGang designations, as a "formal or informal group, club, organization, or association of three or more persons that has as one of its purposes the commission of criminal activity either in the United States or outside the United States, has committed two or more criminal acts on separate and distinct occasions, and the members of which may share a common identifying sign, symbol, or name."[38]

ICE required its officers and agents to enter data into ICEGangs on alleged gang members and associates within seventy-two hours after encountering them in the field. Like their counterparts in local police departments, ICE officers used Field Interview cards to record information to be later transferred to the ICEGangs Database.[39] Each ICEGangs record had to have a corresponding TECS record.[40] Programmers then scraped and entered additional data remotely.[41]

It is clear that the ICEGangs Database was underutilized and, like most gang databases, contained racialized and unreliable infor-

mation. Most of its subjects were identified as male (75 percent),
2 percent were identified as female, and 22.8 percent did not have a
gender recorded. "Descent" was recorded as Mexican for 44 percent
of people. The countries with the next highest representation were
El Salvador (7 percent) and the United States (just over 1 percent).
The presence of people with the United States as their country of
origin suggests there were US citizens listed in what was supposed
to be an immigration gang database. Nearly 40 percent of the data
in the "descent" category is missing. Forty-seven percent of ICE-
Gangs subjects were alleged to be associated with street gangs, just
under nine percent with prison gangs, and about one percent with
motorcycle gangs. Information was missing for 42 percent of subjects in this category. ICE profiled a large proportion of the alleged
gang members under its purview as belonging to either Sureños
(nearly 25 percent) or MS-13 (nearly 17 percent). Eighteenth Street
and Latin Kings each had about 4.5 percent of the share of people
in ICEGangs attributed to them. The remaining ICEGangs subjects
were spread across an additional 831 distinct gangs or subsets.

The criteria according to which ICE personnel determined gang
affiliation are striking and reinforce the questionability of gang-
labeling criteria. Over 66 percent of entries were not justified with
any criteria, and the next highest percentage, nearly 19 percent of
entries, was logged as "self-admitted." The next most common criteria were "convicted of violations" (about 3 percent of entries),
"affiliates with gangs" (about 2.5 percent), and "gang tattoos" (a little
over 2 percent). Thus, most subjects in ICEGangs did not have jus-
tifying criteria listed or were listed as self-admitted; a criterion that
has proven controversial in other gang databases. For example, self-
admission is listed as the only qualifying criterion for 90 percent of
people in Chicago's gang database, which scholars suggest indicates
law enforcement abuse of discretion.[42]

The vast majority of the entries were made by personnel within
either ICE's Office of Intelligence or ICE's Detention and Removal
Headquarters. The rest of the entries were made by personnel at

ICE field offices, service processing centers, and intelligence units throughout the country but concentrated in California and Texas. Additionally, Los Angeles Sheriff's Department officers stationed at Mira Loma Immigration Detention Center directly accessed ICE-Gangs and made entries.

Notably, the attaché in Kingston, Jamaica, made entries into ICE-Gangs as well. Todd Miller writes that attachés have been central to the post–September 11 expansion of the border through their influence in shaping the border control practices of other countries. (Miller also recounts an official from the office of the attaché in Mexico claiming to be able to "sense" who was a gang member.) Attachés work in US embassies and consulates around the world in an advisory capacity. As of this writing, US Customs and Border Protection operates attaché offices in twenty-three countries, where in-house specialists "inform and advise the U.S. Ambassador or Consul General on CBP programs and capabilities."[43] ICE has sixty attaché and assistant attaché offices around the world.[44] Miller argues that US attachés train foreign security forces to fortify their borders, American style, with the ultimate goal of preventing migrants from reaching the United States. ICEGangs, CalGang, and the local, state, and federal law enforcement agencies that use them are links in a layered border strategy in which US immigration and homeland security agents repel migrants at multiple points around the globe.

THERE WERE SIGNS of trouble with ICEGangs early on that never let up. Initially, rough connectivity forced CalGang administrators to conduct data dumps with ICE rather than continuous, real-time information exchange.[45] Additionally, ICE agents did not appear to make good use of the ICEGangs platform. For example, at the point when ICEGangs was discontinued, there were 14,896 subjects in the nationwide database; for comparison, around the same time, the statewide CalGang Database contained information on about five times as many people.[46] ICEGangs users consistently filled in only nine out of ninety-one possible categories in the database.

Although the shared GangNet software offered connections to numerous law enforcement agencies, during the lifecycle of ICE-Gangs, ICE established its information-sharing agreement with Cal-Gang only. Consequently, noncitizens who were classified as gang members in California and a few other geographic areas entered a fast track to immigration enforcement, but the dream of a cross-jurisdictional national gang repository through GangNet software never fully materialized.[47]

Peter T. Edge, then executive associate director of Homeland Security Investigations, declared that the ICEGangs Database would be discontinued in October 2016, severing the memorandum of understanding with CalGang. Edge reasoned, "There is no substantial evidence to indicate that the system is effective in helping to combat transnational gangs."[48] The lack of evidence-based support is an underwhelming rationalization considering that anti-gang programs continue all the time in the face of proven inefficacy. It is more likely that ICEGangs was underused because it was redundant. Improvements in EID and TECS offered enhanced capacity for immigration authorities to collect, access, and share gang-related information. ICEGangs was a comparably inadequate vehicle both for recording and sharing gang-related information. The Edge memo concludes: "Barring greatly expanded connectivity to state and local gang data on a large scale, the use of ICEGangs should be discontinued."[49] A 2016 internal ICE document detailing the schedule to retire the system bluntly states that ICEGangs was discontinued because "the application is rarely utilized and not cost-effective."[50]

Thus, despite flirting with gang databases, ICE ultimately appears to prefer to flag noncitizens as gang members in more general immigration databases—and it is doing a lot more flagging of late. ICE stated in its 2018 *Enforcement and Removal Operations Report* that it identifies known and suspected gang members by checking against information in other federal law enforcement databases as well as through interviews with immigrants and information received from law enforcement partners. ICE reported that "removals of known and suspected gang members increased by 162 percent in FY2017, more than doubling from the previous year. These critical removals increased again in FY2018, rising by 9 percent from FY2017."[51] Even if US government officials had not euthanized ICEGangs in favor of other systems, it likely would have been doomed by political threats looming in California.

"THAT WOULD BE the end of CalGang. . . . It won't exist." On June 21, 2016, Sonoma County Sheriff's sergeant and CalGang Executive Board chair Dennis Smiley explained to the California State Senate Public Safety Committee the consequences of passing California Assembly Bill 2298. Sergeant Smiley was seated with the CalGang node administrator for the Fresno Sherriff's Office, Joel Cobb, before a half-circle of committee members in the state Capitol in Sacramento, California. Deputy Cobb hunched forward, broad and imposing, both elbows on the table. Sergeant Smiley was more relaxed yet confident throughout the proceedings, leaning softly on his left elbow.[52] They both predicted a doomsday scenario for policing.

The law enforcement entities that had administered and used CalGang for nearly two decades were finally under examination, and they did not like it. Two years earlier, in January 2014, California Senate Bill 458 had gone into effect, requiring that local law enforcement agencies provide written notice to persons under eighteen years of age and their parents or guardians in the event that they were designated as a gang member, associate, or affiliate in a shared gang database.[53] California Assembly Bill 2298, the legislation before the committee, proposed to expand the notification requirement to adults, thus extending notification and appeal rights to any person added to CalGang regardless of age.[54]

Sergeant Smiley stressed that CalGang could only be accessed by law enforcement agencies when they conduct criminal investigations. Deputy Cobb added that CalGang data cannot be used against someone to block their access to any type of social benefits. Neither of these statements is true. As an immigration attorney explained later in the hearing, and as I explain in the next chapter, being documented as a gang member or associate in a gang database can result in denial of immigration benefits and the initiation of deportation proceedings.

Along the chamber wall, a series of men with light skin and dark hair as well as one pale blonde woman lined up to voice opposition to the bill. Matthew Siverling, representing the Association for Los Angeles Deputy Sheriffs, the Los Angeles Police Protective League, and the Riverside Sherriff's Association, backed up the shaky claim that records are only accessed in response to a criminal complaint and added that CalGang cannot be accessed through background checks. Wearing suits ranging in color from light beige to brown to grey to deep black, the men and woman voiced opposition on behalf of the California State Sheriffs Association, California District Attorneys Association, California Police Officers Association, California Statewide Law Enforcement Organization, Fraternal Order of Police, and California Police Chiefs Association.

It was of no use. The bill got enough votes to move out of the public safety committee and would eventually become law, going into effect on January 1, 2017. An additional piece of legislation, California Assembly Bill 90, later topped off the reform efforts in 2018, establishing the Gang Database Technical Advisory Committee, transferring oversight and administration of CalGang from local node agencies to the California Department of Justice, and prohibiting information sharing from CalGang and other shared gang databases in California for immigration enforcement purposes. Had ICEGangs not already self-destructed, AB90 would have mortally wounded it by cutting off its main information supply in CalGang.[55]

And yet even in its pared-down form, CalGang remains a beast. Despite the discontinuation of ICEGangs, gang labeling in the immigration system continues unabated. CalGang reforms did not initiate the downfall that law enforcement representatives envisioned. Rather, people now receive notification letters when they are added to CalGang, and if they can pay for or secure pro bono legal representation, are often able to successfully contest their designation. However, it is much more difficult to appeal a designation without legal assistance.

In January 2020 an appeal by the parent of a minor added to CalGang uncovered that LAPD officers fabricate information in order to ensure that individuals fit the requisite criteria to be entered into CalGang.[56] Shortly thereafter a whistleblower revealed that the LAPD required officers to meet quotas by filling out a certain number of Field Interview cards each day.[57] The number of officers implicated in the fabrication scandal multiplied until California's attorney general temporarily barred police from using CalGang records generated by the LAPD, which constitute a quarter of all CalGang records.[58]

CalGang is therefore being weakened not because inordinate police resources are monopolized by the notification process, as law enforcement spokespeople predicted, or because notification letters are undermining confidential investigations. Rather, CalGang is being compromised because of the compromised officers who make use of it. Databases ultimately depend on racialized and fraudulent information from officers on the ground; no amount of technological innovation or slight policy reforms can change that.

ICEGANGS AND CALGANG interoperability, the ultimate demise of ICEGangs, and the implementation of CalGang oversight revealed certain truths about law enforcement strategies, one being the common routes along which information travels. Federal law enforcement agencies, including immigration enforcement, are eager to plug into gang surveillance circuitry primarily concentrated in the American West and Southwest, and increasingly mid-Atlantic, regions, with distinct criminal justice implications for US-born Latino, Black, and API youth and immigration consequences for gang-profiled immigrant youth.[59]

A second takeaway is that federal law enforcement agencies prioritize centralization. Rather than maintaining information on alleged gang members in a separate ICEGangs Database, immigration authorities prefer to tag individuals with the gang member label and multiple other labels in larger databases like TECS and EID. It is possible that local and state law enforcement will follow a similar pattern. As CalGang continues to be undermined and delegitimized, police departments may opt instead for centralized systems that have effective gang intelligence subsystems or gang-flagging mechanisms. The LAPD's Palantir system, for example, has this capacity and already ingests the same Field Interview card information that goes into CalGang.[60]

Finally, law enforcement agencies seek to maximize interoperable information sharing between local, state, federal, and as I show later in this book, international, law enforcement partners. Software developers and law enforcement agents envision a seamlessly functioning national and even international web of interconnected data systems. The extension of CalGang access to the attaché in Jamaica reveals the law enforcement impulse to push the borders of gang surveillance across not only US state borders but also nation-state borders. However, as the glitches between CalGang and ICEGangs information sharing illustrate, the practical accomplishment of advanced levels of interoperability is often trickier than planned.

The discontinuation of ICEGangs has not stopped the flow of information from California law enforcement to federal immigration authorities. It is time to meet the attorneys who work with immigrant youth in Southern California who have been labeled gang members. Their stories provide a qualitative look at the damage done by gang labels that make their way from local police to immigration officers and threaten to expel immigrant youth to the other side of US borders.

4 A Lawyer Watches a Wreck Unfold

THERE ARE THREE brothers. Or rather, there were. The eldest has been murdered. The middle brother is listed on CalGang as an alleged gang member or associate. He knows this because he received a letter from the Los Angeles Police Department (LAPD) informing him that he had been added to the database. His parents fear that law enforcement may have profiled the eldest's death as gang related, causing a domino effect in which the middle and youngest brother were also labeled as gang involved. They have come to an upper floor in a conspicuously tall office building near downtown Los Angeles to see if Chris, an attorney who specializes in gang allegations, can help them.[1]

LA is a low-slung sprawl such that an eighth-floor view makes one feel omnipotent. You can see any number of accidents and near accidents from up here: a garbage truck nicking a sports car during a lane change, three-car pileups, a narrow miss on a risky left turn. All day, glancing out of the full-length window to the left of his desk, Chris can watch the quotidian bedlam of the city unfold in silence.

He looks down at the paperwork in front of him, similarly characterized by banal chaos; gang labeling is a mess. The eldest brother
in the family at hand is gone, but the other two brothers can still be
helped.

Chris writes to the LAPD requesting more information on the
criteria by which the middle brother has been labeled so that he
can better understand and if appropriate, contest, the designation.
The LAPD responds that, despite the notification letter, the middle
brother is not listed on CalGang. Sitting in his office's conference
room at the end of the day, Chris explained to me, "It's not clear to us
whether they got a letter from us and they were like, 'Not worth it,'
or if they got a letter from us and they reviewed it and they were like,
'Who added this kid to a database? This is ridiculous, he shouldn't
be on here.'" Chris also inquires about whether the youngest brother
is listed as a gang member or associate in CalGang. He is not.

Some scholars have conceptualized gangs in epidemiological
terms, characterizing the spread of membership and violence as if
it were a virus.[2] Notwithstanding the disturbing and racially loaded
exercise of comparing alleged gang members (a group that is often
composed largely of people of color) to drivers of disease, the meta-
phor also misses the mark. If there is a viral analogy to be made
here, it is with the metastasizing of wanton gang labeling through
interoperable databases. The questions faced by gang-labeled youth
in heavily policed neighborhoods are strikingly similar to those faced
by populations threatened by a pandemic: Have I been infected with
a gang allegation (i.e., has law enforcement infected me)? How do
I know if I have it? How can I find out if I have it? Once I have it,
how do I keep my family from contracting it? How do I keep my
loved ones safe? Because I might have it, should I stay inside and
avoid social contact? Because someone I know might have it, should
I keep my distance from them? This is how a gang allegation worked
in 2006 when California law enforcement gathered around a table at
Universal CityWalk Hollywood to construct internal borderlands for
alleged gang members, and it continues to work the same way over a

decade later when Chris tries to unhook the two surviving brothers from the system of gang surveillance. He has done this repeatedly for other people. Only a half dozen years or so into his legal career and the pattern around gang profiling is already clear: it is a dangerous mess, all of it.

There is an overwhelming amount of death and suffering, and beneath it is a thriving surveillance industry consisting of interoperable databases, huge contracts, informal as well as sanctioned horizontal collaboration among regional police, and vertical collaboration between local and federal law enforcement. The magnitude of this operation, the private contracts, and the technological innovation give the information that flows through these databases a veneer of legitimacy. However, the criteria for categorizing an individual as a gang member or an associate are incredibly broad and hinge on racist policing practices. Nonetheless, once unreliable gang allegations are entered into gang databases, they become sanctioned. Racial profiling by police on the streets is transformed into an authoritative account that later justifies detention and deportation. This is how bias becomes hard data and how racism becomes law.

Because of the chaotic nature of gang labeling, it represents a constant yet unpredictable threat. Like living under the boot of an abusive person, youth of color can never be sure when the capricious blow will fall or from where it will come. Gang labels can appear out of nowhere, undermining the future opportunities of a young person with promising prospects. In other cases, people fully expect gang labeling to become an issue for them, but it never materializes. As just described, people have received CalGang notification letters only to later be told the information is incorrect by law enforcement once they have legal representation.

For immigrants, gang labels carry particular types of precarity. While ICEGangs has faded away and the CalGang reforms covered in the last chapter have instituted some measure of accountability, the gang labeling of immigrants continues. Between 2016 and 2018 I spoke with attorneys and advocates who work with immigrant youth in Southern California to assess the effects of gang labeling. What I found were people attempting to navigate a terrain in which the ground could fall away at any moment.

To clearly illustrate the immigration consequences of gang labeling, or even potential gang labeling, I focus on gang allegations that occur during the application process for the Deferred Action for Childhood Arrivals (DACA) program. In order to obtain DACA, applicants must undergo a detailed background check. Because gang allegations do not require that the accused be arrested, charged, or convicted of a crime and often do not require notification, attorneys and DACA applicants face uncertainty about the information maintained by government agencies. Consequently, attorneys and DACA applicants are forced to engage in a twisted scavenger hunt in which they gather clues to whether or not the government considers the applicant to be gang involved.

THERE ARE A number of ways in which immigrants come to be classified as gang affiliated. Immigration authorities may classify someone as a gang member if they find that another agency, such as local police, schools, or a social service provider, considers the individual in question to be a gang member. In county jails, state prisons, and federal prisons, inmates are housed according to gang affiliation, purportedly in order to ensure inmate and personnel safety. Immigration detention facilities assess detainees for gang association during the intake process and house detainees according to alleged gang affiliation, called Security Threat Group status.[3]

In 2017 a Department of Homeland Security (DHS) special agent admitted to classifying immigrants as gang members at the point of initial arrest in order to ensure they would be ineligible for bail.[4] In 2018 a US district judge found that Immigration and Customs Enforcement (ICE) had falsely claimed a DACA recipient was gang affiliated in an attempt to deport him.[5] Across the country, pro bono attorneys who represent immigrants facing gang allegations have found that when they demand evidence for the allegation, ICE drops the claim without explanation. In one case, the government insisted an immigrant was a gang member "because the government databases said so."[6] But most immigrants in the deportation system do not have attorneys to demand that evidence be presented. Instead, the government claims an immigrant is gang affiliated and can then deport them without having to provide proof.

Immigration attorneys and advocates repeatedly express frustration with the way unfounded gang allegations launched by immigration agents and government attorneys result in exorbitantly high bond, denial of bond, and deportation. Luis, an immigration attorney in Southern California, explained how the lack of procedural protections for immigrants in immigration hearings aggravates the spread of gang allegations:

> If you have unreliable, random, low-level police officers [making gang allegations] and then now it's in the file somewhere, and then now they can use that to keep somebody locked in and detained or raise somebody's bond and make it unaffordable for a family to help them out, I think that's a big deal that should be looked at. Immigration laws are such that you can use hearsay evidence, so immigrants I feel like are especially vulnerable to a gang allegation because, first of all, they lack resources. Secondly, you can use hearsay evidence. You can use basically anything and immigration attorneys, if they're nonprofit attorneys, they don't have resources to fight back.
>
> And a gang allegation—it can be an allegation—can really affect someone given that they would be a threat to the community. I got someone released on bond a few weeks ago. And even in just that one hearing, I saw the gang allegations come up over and over again. Maybe some of them were legitimate, but to me that's irrelevant. How can someone just use a gang allegation to satisfy their burden on the government's side? You shouldn't be able to allege something and then have an impact on a case that much. It's our job as advocates to object to that but if a judge is willing to listen to that, then there's little I can do.

Although most public and scholarly attention has been paid to gang labeling at the point of apprehension or deportation, exemplified by

Luis's anecdote, gang profiling also occurs in the administrative arm of the immigration system, frequently through US Citizenship and Immigration Services' (USCIS) assessment of asylum claims, DACA applications, and eligibility for immigration benefits. In assessing applications to change citizenship status, for example, USCIS officers conduct interviews with applicants, during which they may question applicants about their relationship to gang activity and alleged gang members. Although I employ DACA as a useful example of gang labeling during an administrative process, the gang-labeling dynamics that occur within the DACA application process provide broader insight into how immigration authorities conceptualize and target alleged gang members, criminalize immigrant youth more generally, and transform unfounded allegations into sanctioned evidence.

ON JUNE 15, 2012, JANET Napolitano, then secretary of the DHS, released a memorandum announcing the development of DACA via executive action. The memorandum instructed immigration officers to exercise prosecutorial discretion with respect to unauthorized immigrants who had arrived in the United States as children.[7] Under DACA, eligible participants receive a renewable two-year stay from deportation and legal employment authorization.[8] In November 2014, President Obama announced a series of executive actions intended to expand DACA protections to additional groups of unauthorized immigrants. An accompanying DHS memorandum, "Policies for the Apprehension, Detention and Removal of Undocumented Immigrants," described the "highest priority to which enforcement resources should be directed," including immigrants who have participated in street gangs.[9]

Prospective DACA recipients submit an application to United States Citizenship and Immigration Services (USCIS), which asks, "Are you **NOW** or have you **EVER** been a member of a gang?"[10] The DACA application specifies "gangs" in its language, a departure from lines of questioning in most other affirmative settings in which questions are framed more broadly, asking if someone has been a member of a group that has engaged in harm and persecution. That USCIS decided to craft a question that explicitly inquires about gang affiliation implies that the agency profiles the eligible DACA population as susceptible to gang involvement.

Nicole is a young juvenile justice attorney who frequently represents people accused of gang affiliation. Over lunch in Little Tokyo on a predictably sunny Los Angeles afternoon, we talk about the mosaic of horrors happening on the border: Border Patrol agents' unlawful denial of asylum seekers, family separation, the travel ban. We talk about missing the border even while realizing its horror, and we talk about the borders that follow, specifically the long searching finger that reaches out to try to pull DACA recipients back to a border they crossed long ago. Nicole recounts to me how immigration authorities constructed DACA in such a way as to cement gang profiling in administrative immigration processes:

> DACA was the first time that USCIS point blank asked anything about gang activity. Before—and this is true right now of the U-VISA, the U-VISA never asks about gang affiliation—just says stuff like, have you ever been a member of a group who has used force or violence against another individual? So it's very broad as to how it is defined. But DACA was the first instance that we ever saw them explicitly question about gang activity. [. . .] DACA was the first time that we noticed this is going to become a problem.

The inclusion of a question explicitly about gangs further embedded the racially coded and unreliable practice of gang profiling in immigration administration.

As part of the standard DACA background check, USCIS personnel run each applicant's name against TECS and two other federal databases, the Automated Fingerprint Identification System (IAFIS) and the Automated Biometric Identification System (IDENT). At times, USCIS also contracts with private companies, including Pacific Architects and Engineers, to assist with criminal background checks, verification, and vetting.[11] A special adjudication team handles DACA

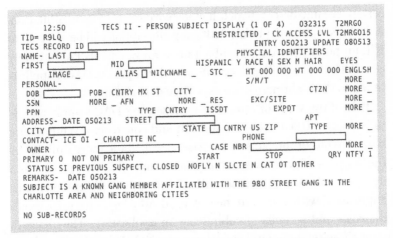

```
   12:50          TECS II - PERSON SUBJECT DISPLAY (1 OF 4)   032315  T2MRG0
TID= R9LQ                            RESTRICTED - CK ACCESS LVL T2MRG015
TECS RECORD ID [          ]                      ENTRY 050213 UPDATE 080513
NAME- LAST [       ]                           PHYSCIAL IDENTIFIERS
FIRST [       ]        MID [     ]     HISPANIC Y RACE W SEX M HAIR    EYES
       IMAGE _      ALIAS □ NICKNAME _   STC _   HT 000 000 WT 000 000 ENGLSH
PERSONAL-                                        S/M/T                  MORE _
   DOB [        ]    POB- CNTRY MX ST   CITY                     CTZN   MORE _
   SSN             MORE _ AFN          MORE _ RES     EXC/SITE          MORE _
   PPN                    TYPE CNTRY    ISSDT         EXPDT             MORE _
ADDRESS- DATE 050213   STREET [           ]                     APT
   CITY [       ]                  STATE □ CNTRY US ZIP     TYPE      MORE _
CONTACT- ICE OI - CHARLOTTE NC                        PHONE
   OWNER [                    ]              CASE NBR [        ]        MORE _
PRIMARY O  NOT ON PRIMARY              START        STOP       QRY NTFY 1
   STATUS SI PREVIOUS SUSPECT, CLOSED  NOFLY N SLCTE N CAT OT OTHER
REMARKS- DATE 050213
SUBJECT IS A KNOWN GANG MEMBER AFFILIATED WITH THE 980 STREET GANG IN THE
CHARLOTTE AREA AND NEIGHBORING CITIES

NO SUB-RECORDS
```

Figure 1. Sample TECS record used in USCIS DACA screening training. Recreated verbatim for image quality. *Credit:* Nat Case, INCase, LLC.

applications that indicate "criminality" as a result of the background check, including those pertaining to "known or suspected gang members" and applicants who have been "associated or affiliated with a gang member." The protocol of the adjudication teams clearly leans toward an assumption of guilt in the case of any gang allegation. For example, according to the protocol, adjudication teams "should not be asking for the evidence supporting the reason behind the finding of known or suspected gang membership."[12]

If the adjudication teams have reason to believe that a DACA applicant is gang affiliated, but there is "insufficient evidence to deny the request based on the requestor's actual gang membership," the teams are instructed to vet the case thoroughly.[13] Thus, the teams assessing DACA applications are procedurally encouraged to intensively screen and discretionarily deny an applicant with a gang allegation, yet are restricted in their ability to approve an applicant with gang allegations.

Information pertaining to denied DACA applications is not supposed to be shared with ICE for enforcement purposes except in certain circumstances, which include suspicions of gang affiliation. A declined DACA applicant with gang allegations will be referred to ICE for potential enforcement action as an Egregious Public Safety case.[14] Thus, gang allegations can turn the hope of a DACA application into the nightmare of an expedited deportation.

Part of the work of attorneys representing DACA applicants is to introduce USCIS to the applicant and construct a sympathetic narrative out of the facts of the case, a task made more difficult by the vagaries of gang allegations. Since gang affiliation results in a declined DACA application and referral to ICE for enforcement, applicants, with the guidance of legal attorneys, have to weigh the costs and benefits of submitting an application. They have to struggle with three vital questions: the "if," the "where," and the "what now?"

FIRST, THERE IS the *if* of gang labeling. When an attorney begins to work with a young person, together they have to figure out if that young person has been labeled a gang member or associate. Chris described the typical bind of working with DACA applicants who are concerned they may have been documented as gang affiliated:

> For people affirmatively adjusting status, they typically are worried they have been labeled a gang member and that may come up why they try to adjust status through the visa process, or they know for sure they are labeled because law enforcement has told them, or there has been allegation in some other context, or they have labeled family. So, in anticipation of that we are trying to figure out what they can do before they apply to protect against allegations. Most often, we are anticipating allegations because of direct contact with local law enforcement where they have verbally communicated something like that to them [. . .] or because this is an experience of their family or their community.

There is a lot to unpack in Chris's statement. First is the intimation that gang allegations are often *buoyant*, making their way to ICE from local and state law enforcement jurisdictions. While immigrants are also labeled by ICE and DHS agents in the field and in detention, in the context of administrative immigration processes like DACA the risk of labeling is highest from local police, who have consistent contact with youth of color on the streets and therefore the most opportunities to profile immigrant youth as gang members.[15] Another point Chris makes is that attorneys are cognizant of a confluence of factors related to appearance, place, and social networks that make a prospective applicant a potential target for gang allegations. For example, an applicant's tattoos, when combined with their race, may conform to stereotypes about the appearance of gang members. Furthermore, if a prospective applicant's family, friends, or neighbors have been labeled, legal advocates are wary of the applicant being designated guilty by association.

Because the DACA-eligible population is young, mostly Latin American born, and concentrated in major urban areas—a population commonly stereotyped by law enforcement as gang involved—racialized gang allegations were likely to become a salient issue in eligibility determinations. Of the 690,000 people enrolled in DACA as of September 2017, more than nine out of every ten were born in Latin America; two-thirds were twenty-five years of age or younger; and three-quarters lived in twenty US metro areas, with the greatest concentration in the Los Angeles/Long Beach/Anaheim metropolitan area. Youth from El Salvador, Guatemala, Honduras, and Mexico, in particular, risk being profiled as gang members based on racial and xenophobic stereotypes.[16]

Because of many DACA applicants' roots in Latin America, attorneys anticipate potential allegations of affiliation with transnational gangs, usually MS-13 or 18th Street. ICE training materials portray certain gangs as imported by immigrants. For example, an ICE National Gang Unit Operation Community Shield training Power-Point presentation claims that the 18th Street gang consists of "80% illegal aliens from Mexico/Central America."[17] However, because DACA youth have grown up in the United States, legal advocates are also prepared to respond to allegations of involvement with small, local street gangs that are confined to one city and about which local police are more likely to have knowledge than federal agents.

The uncertainty around gang labeling is largely a function of two key components. First, the criteria for the gang membership categorization can be satisfied largely by an officer's discretionary assessment based on visual cues. An officer can determine an individual has met the criteria based on their observed clothing, tattoos, neighborhood context, and social network. While an arrest or conviction for a gang-related crime will certainly appear in the DACA screening process, allegations of gang membership do not require a conviction, arrest, or charge. Second, law enforcement has rarely been required to notify people of their placement on the database.

Consequently, legal advocates and prospective DACA applicants have to guess whether a prospective applicant has been labeled based on how closely they fit the profile of gang-labeled youth and any other indications from law enforcement, including street harassment by local police. Legal advocates describe the composite profile of a potentially gang-labeled applicant as a young person of color who grew up in heavily policed areas in which gang profiling is common, which in cities like Los Angeles represents a large group. However, even if police have verbally communicated to the applicant that law enforcement considers them to be a gang member, it is not clear if the accusation has been documented in writing in such a way that it would emerge during a DACA background check, which introduces more uncertainty into the process.

So attorneys have no choice but to go searching. They try to access anything that may signal whether or not their clients have been gang labeled. They seek out school records, call local police departments, and put in requests with CalGang administrators.

The 2014 reforms requiring law enforcement to notify people when they are added to CalGang have helped to clarify the "if" in some cases. While preparing to apply for DACA, some immigrant youth received notification letters informing them that they had been added to the database. Chris explained:

[Legislation] went into effect January 1, 2014 or something like that and about 8 or 9 months later, LAPD started issuing letters and that's when I started getting people referred. [. . .] Really it was 2016 when clients themselves who were experiencing both things at once, the immigration—either reapplying for DACA or applying for the first time—and the fear of gang labeling started happening.

However, the notification requirement is not retroactive and therefore, does not benefit those already listed on CalGang before the law went into effect. Even with the postreform restrictions on sharing CalGang information for immigration enforcement purposes, someone's being listed as a gang member on CalGang will likely still come out during an administrative background check for benefits and services.

Related to uncovering if a DACA applicant has been labeled as a gang member is figuring out from where USCIS officers may pull the allegation. Because gang allegations can stick to people over a long period of time, following them through multiple institutions, their origin can become maddeningly obscured and therefore uncontestable.

NICOLE, THE JUVENILE justice attorney with whom I ate Japanese food, has found a clue. After she was unable to come up with any other proof that her client might have been labeled a gang member, she asked a probation officer to run a check. "Something told me that I should just check in," Nicole tells me, "He did have juvenile adjudications, but that did not bar him from applying. I asked his probation officer[,] who looked him up and confirmed, yes, he's already been classified as a gang member. [. . .] We decided not to risk it in filing the DACA application." She has located a clue, and so Nicole and her client advance a step further in this fucked up game. They encounter the next stage: after confirming the existence of the allegation (*the if*), applicants and their advocates try to decipher the origin of the allegation, to search for the *where*, often to no avail.

After years in nonprofit work, Luis opened his own small immigration law practice out of a beige stucco building off a main thoroughfare in Northeast Los Angeles. When we meet to talk further about some of his cases, he makes me the strongest coffee I've ever tasted, a pool of deep onyx in a thick porcelain mug. In a steady, gentle voice, Luis explains how overwhelmed he feels when he begins to look for the source of gang allegations: "There are federal guidelines about what constitutes a gang member. There's state guidelines. There's multiple gang databases. So it's unclear. It's unclear where they got their information from. They just said, we believe that this person is a gang member." Nicole had mentioned something similar during one of our earlier conversations: "I've never had an instance where an ICE agent or trial attorney has said, 'I'm pulling out this [Field Interview] card that was given to me.' They just say, 'I have basis to believe this individual is gang-involved' without providing much evidence, which is also frustrating because in immigration court anything goes."

When Nicole says that "anything goes," she is alluding to the fact that people in immigration court are not entitled to the protections that people receive in the criminal justice system, such as compulsory legal defense, protections against self-incrimination, and restrictions on hearsay and illegally obtained evidence.[18] This is because the US Supreme Court has declared deportation and immigration dentition to be a civil remedy, not a punitive action.[19] By contrast, the criminal justice system dispenses punishment. Consequently, there are theoretically greater process protections. It is important to note that criminal protections are inadequate in practice. Police regularly violate constitutional rights.[20] Due to case overload, public defenders are too frequently unable to adequately defend the accused, and defendants are regularly pressured into plea deals in which adjudication is altogether bypassed.[21] Nonetheless, protections are not present, even in theory, in the immigration system.

Despite the definition of immigration proceedings as nonpunitive, contemporary immigration enforcement produces outcomes that are strikingly punitive in nature.[22] Immigration officers engage in activities that mirror criminal investigation, including conducting stops of suspects, arrests, questioning, and interrogations, yet do so according to relatively relaxed procedural requirements.[23] There are few opportunities to challenge procedural violations or inaccuracies when they do occur.[24] Nicole, Luis, and Chris are all working in a space where the permissive framework of the immigration system collides with the permissive framework of gang policing, in which people are categorized without evidence or adjudication. Though this makes no sense in terms of practical logic, it does make sense when situated within the logic of American White supremacy and the historical mosaic of horrors that constitutes the immigration system. The racism of the criminal justice system and the immigration enforcement system intersects in ways that are particularly harmful to Black immigrants. For example, Black immigrants are far more likely than other immigrants to be detained and deported for criminal convictions.[25]

Another immigration attorney, Sofia, noted that ICE records will simply state that an immigrant is a "known or suspected gang member" and list the source as "database" without specifying which database, let alone which officer decided the classification based on which evidence. Rather than looking out onto traffic, Sofia's office windows face into another, larger room, one filled with stacks of papers, and busy paralegals and law students. Recently returned from court, she removes her dark blue blazer and places it on the back of her chair. As we watch the flurry of movement in the next room, Sofia tells me that regardless of whether the accusation came from local police, probation, school records, social media scraping, or a federal agent, the allegation's presence in a database imbues it with an authority that is difficult to counter. The objectivity of the information is conferred by the fact that it is extracted from a database, enabling the immigration enforcement and administration regime to use technology to sanction racial profiling by making it into a neutral data point.

Because granting or denying DACA is a discretionary decision, USCIS does not have to justify rejections, and applicants often never discover why they have been labeled or from where the label originated. Although attorneys attempt to trace the life of a gang label to its source, the "paper trail always dead-end[s] somewhere into the black box of law enforcement privilege," as one attorney, Matt, characterized it.

In winnowing down possible sources, many attorneys found that most gang allegations they encountered originated with local law enforcement and were subsequently shared with federal law enforcement. For example, one of Chris's clients, a DACA recipient, was picked up by ICE and accused of gang membership with no further explanation. Upon inquiry, Chris learned that the client was not in a gang database. Chris's best guess was that he had been documented as a gang member or associate on a Field Interview card during a police stop more than five years earlier. Somehow, the information from the card did not make it into a gang database but did make it into the hands of ICE.

Nicole separately noted similar situations. "We see this in the DACA context a lot," where a young person has "been stopped and questioned but never formally arrested" and yet, USCIS or ICE has accused them of gang involvement. She reasoned that allegations in these cases must come from a local agency because "these are kids to young adults. So they've never been involved in any type of intense federal crime or anything that would put them on the FBI radar or have even been on the ICE radar before."

OUTSIDE CHRIS'S WINDOW, the rush hour traffic picks up and the sliver of a half-moon emerges above the mountains. He lays everything out: the DACA application, the letters from LAPD, school records, and declarations. At some point in a case, attorneys and applicants confront the *what now?* Attorneys are hesitant to pursue an application in the presence of any indicators of gang labeling because a declined DACA applicant with gang allegations is referred to ICE for enforcement action. The risk of proceeding is just too great. In select cases, however, attorneys still try to move forward with an application by attempting to contest law enforcement labeling at the local and state levels and presenting documentation to USCIS to effectively counter the accusation. Unfortunately, the requirements for proving a lack of gang affiliation are a farcical trap.

Sofia is also making final case decisions in her own tall building not far from Chris's office. Leaning back in her chair, Sofia exasperatedly describes how easily gang allegations stick: "All they have to do is create a negative inference of that or make a suggestion, and then I think it becomes our burden to prove that someone is not part of any sort of gangs." This reminds me of how Chris described the difficulty of unsticking the classification: "It's the same problem posed to them that every individual faces, which is how do I show you that I am not this thing? How do I prove that negative to you?" To prove gang membership, law enforcement officers try to prove the presence of something—associations or gang-related tattoos, for example. These criteria are incredibly questionable, but they at least represent *something*. By contrast, what would an accused person present to prove *non*membership? Sworn statements by neighbors attesting to the fact that they have never seen the person in question with alleged gang members? What evidence could a gang-labeled individual possibly put forward to prove their innocence?

The protocol for the DACA adjudication teams dictates that USCIS is supposed to conduct an interview with applicants suspected of gang membership or association. If, after the interview, the requester has not established by preponderance of the evidence that they are not a gang member, the adjudication teams are instructed to deny the DACA application because "the requestor has not met the burden of showing he or she does not pose a threat to public safety."[26] The DACA assessment process, and the process of gang labeling more generally, is thus at odds with legal standards that are supposed to be foundational to the American legal system but are often elusive for non-White people. The burden of demonstrating the validity of an allegation by a preponderance of evidence is flipped; no preponderance of evidence is necessary to sustain an allegation, but it is required to contest the allegation.

Again, the attorneys and applicants have no choice but to try. Again, they go searching. They gather supportive declarations from credible experts and refute the validity of law enforcement's gang-labeling criteria and assessment tools. In an attempt to present elusive evidence of nonmembership, attorneys request letters from local police departments or CalGang administrators that confirm a given client is not listed on any gang database. However, police departments never go so far as to say that someone is *definitively not* a gang member. Even with the strongest documentation, attempts at appeal are likely to be unsuccessful since the decision to grant DACA is a discretionary one with vague standards. The process appears to be not only fixed but also illogical to the point of disorientation. Attorneys and applicants are on a playing field where the rules are both stacked in their disfavor and opaque.

In the worst-case scenario, in which a DACA application is denied under the auspices of an Egregious Public Safety threat, the information is turned over to ICE to follow up for enforcement purposes. The denied applicant will likely be documented in TECS as a noncitizen who poses a public safety risk and will possibly be detained and deported.

Additionally, even the potential of a gang allegation can be damaging because it dissuades people from applying for key benefits to which they are entitled. Recall Nicole's words after a probation officer confirmed that her client was listed as a gang member in a database: "*We decided not to risk it in filing the DACA application.*" Based on a process that lacks basic due process or even logic, DACA applicants at risk of gang profiling forgo work permits that enable them to avoid exploitative employers and relief that provides deportation protection. The outcome is increased precarity for large segments of young people in the United States.

It is important to note that successful DACA applicants also have their biographic and biometric information entered into federal data systems. In addition to its wonderful benefits, DACA is a surveillance program that tracks a population who otherwise may have remained unknown to the US government.[27] Thus, the exposure risk from applying for DACA is not limited to declined applicants. This is the double bind of subjugation: coming out of the shadows can confer life-sustaining benefits or, on the contrary, may ultimately expose one to the brutal machinations of state violence. DACA, then, is a humanitarian program that further entrenches state violence against migrants.[28]

While DACA confers renewable two-year work authorization and temporary discretionary relief from deportation, it does not confer citizenship. If the DACA program is discontinued, the US government will possess the information of hundreds of thousands of undocumented people with only an Obama-era policy on information-sharing restrictions guarding the breach between the administrative (USCIS) and interior enforcement (ICE) arms.

Even if the program is retained, DACA applicants are not safe from unfounded gang allegations and enforcement. In 2017, a DACA recipient in Washington State was taken into custody by ICE and stripped of his DACA status based on ICE's claim that he was a self-admitted gang member.[29] Additionally, investigative reports have uncovered that ICE can access DACA information despite the guarantee that information on DACA applications is not shared with ICE except in instances of Egregious Public Safety threats.[30]

The hardening of gang allegations from unreliable or fabricated information into authoritative data through their presence in databases is central to state violence against immigrants, particularly those from the Global South and US-born people of color. The clean output of "Known or suspected gang member. Source: Database" conceals the process that leads to allegations, a process that is shot through with equal parts incoherence, absurdity, and nefarious racial stereotypes. The borders have multiplied, and their undertow is strong.

WHEN NOT TALKING to attorneys about DACA and gang classifications, I spend my days trying to observe how gang allegations work in immigration court, but instead end up getting thrown out of one Los Angeles immigration courtroom after another. Though I am away from the US-Mexico border, I am beginning to see the formation of internal borderlands through gang policing, particularly on the West Coast.

Nonetheless, my border arrives to me in the form of a manila envelope at the end of a long day of questioning by court security. Inside the envelope are newspaper clippings from my dad about goings-on in Southern Arizona. I turn it upside down, and the contents float down onto my desk, the thin paper fluttering. When dispatches from the border arrive at my door, I wait until the day almost disappears, when the sky is a strange color, orange-ish like before a tornado, and I can act as if time does not exist. It is a sort of ritual to steel myself against the hurt. Then I pick up the first article from the pile and let the border in.

I read that at the request of DHS, thousands of active duty troops and National Guard troops will be sent to the US-Mexico border. Some of them will spend their days unspooling a sixth layer of concertina wire between the towns of Nogales, Sonora, and Nogales, Arizona, further breaking apart the lovers. Others will block northbound lanes at ports of entry, and still others will join Border Patrol agents as they stalk across the land. I am not going to tell you when exactly this occurred because it could be many dates. Whenever it is politically expedient, soldiers are released onto our streets and dirt trails. The borderlands live in a time warp. There is no future and no past, only a repetitious present.

Another clipping gives an update on a legal case against a Border Patrol agent who shot and killed someone. Again, the time warp: I have not read this specific article before, but in another sense, I have read this article many times. "Border time" condemns me to read this same article in perpetuity.[31] I set the clipping aside and pick up another.

Something good; there is a super bloom across Southern Arizona. Golden poppies, creamy desert evening primrose, lupine stalks, tiny rock daisies, and scarlet ocotillo flowers burst forth in sweeping fields or hang vertically off mountain ridges.

On to the next. Chad Wolf is at the border. He is aggressively hair gelled, as usual, and wearing dark aviator sunglasses and a navy blue windbreaker with DHS insignia on the left breast.[32] He is welcomed by Martha McSally, the unelected sitting senator who was not chosen by the electorate yet still made it to the Senate via appointment by Arizona governor Doug Ducey. The congressional district in which part of my family lives was represented for a time by McSally. During the 2018 election cycle, she got big money from border security contractors Raytheon, Northrop Grumman, Lockheed Martin, Boeing, General Dynamics, BAE Systems, and Elbit Systems. It was perfect symbiosis then that McSally spent the majority of her congressional career peddling legislation that brought more agents, technology, weapons, dismemberment, and death to the borderlands.[33]

With McSally as his guide, Wolf will tour border wall construction and Border Patrol stations in the Tucson sector. He will see how the contractors extract millions of gallons of groundwater near sacred Quitobaquito Springs and use it to mix concrete for The Wall: between 1.7 and 3.7 million gallons for every five miles.[34]

DACA represents but one location where gang allegations have been used to identify, criminalize, and deport immigrant youth. Gang hysteria has also been advanced as a justification for restrictions on asylum, an engorged Border Patrol budget, and the need for The Wall. During the Trump presidency, Trump and then attorney general Bill Barr spoke incessantly about dark-skinned, tattooed men and children, including unaccompanied minors, overflowing the border with an unmeasured lust to victimize American (read: White and suburban) women and children, then getting to stay in the United States through asylum. Chuck Grassley is demanding information from USCIS, convinced that gang members are being awarded DACA protection.[35]

While on the border, Wolf also has gangs on the brain. He gives an exclusive interview to Fox News about an "'exciting' plan to go after the gangs fueling the flow of illegal migrants, weapons and drugs across the southern border." People (migrants) get thrown together with weapons and drugs as things to be "eliminated." The exciting plan is going to require a lot more government money.[36] Nevertheless, as water is sucked from the borderlands to lay the foundation for a gang-repelling wall, other problems are brewing for Chad Wolf in a detention center far away.

5 ICE Rigs an Algorithm

JOSE VELESACA HAD lived in New York City for over a decade when he was arrested by agents in Immigration and Customs Enforcement's (ICE's) New York field office on January 30, 2020. He was then transferred to the Orange County Correctional Facility in the Southern District of New York, a facility that contracts with ICE to provide bed space for immigrant detainees, where he was ordered held without bond. A couple of months after his arrest, Jose became one of the lead plaintiffs in a case entitled *Velesaca v. Wolf et al.*, his name set against that of the then unlawfully acting US secretary of homeland security, Chad Wolf. In *Velesaca*, Jose represented a class of people arrested by immigration officials in the New York City area and detained without individualized risk assessment.

There was an individualized assessment tool, called the Risk Classification Assessment, available to the immigration detention workers who did Jose's intake. Immigration officers are supposed to use the assessment, which pulls information from the Enforcement Integrated Database (EID) and TECS, to evaluate the public safety and flight risk

posed by an apprehended immigrant and recommend either detention, release on bond, or release as part of an alternatives to detention
(ATD) program. However, starting in June 2017, ICE programmed
the algorithm to recommend the detention of nearly everyone who
entered the facility.[1] Thus, while the information on Jose and others
may have technically been analyzed by the Risk Classification Assessment, immigration officers were only going through the motions; the
decision to detain had already been determined in advance.

In order to prioritize enforcement resources, immigration agencies have adopted risk management strategies that parallel those
developed earlier in the criminal justice system.[2] In 2010 ICE esti-
mated that it had the resources to remove less than 4 percent of
the projected undocumented population and therefore needed to
selectively target certain groups of immigrants for enforcement.[3]
Risk assessment tools became particularly pronounced in the immigration enforcement system as a result of the Obama administration's directive to prioritize immigrants for enforcement according
to public safety risk. Risk assessment occurs at various points in the
enforcement process, including at the initial point of identifying
people for apprehension, as part of immigration detention intakes,
during bond hearings, and in the course of asylum and visa interviews.[4] This chapter focuses on risk assessments used by ICE to
determine enforcement targets and to conduct detention intakes.

Immigrants who do not have criminal records or who have very
minor records are nonetheless prioritized because they have been
deemed a flight risk, public safety risk, or part of a security threat
group in which they are suspected of gang or terrorist group affiliation. As outlined in the last several chapters, the expansion in the
information that is available for assessment, including suspicions,
allegations, and charges that have not been adjudicated, creates
ample opportunities for authorities to label immigrants as dangerous through risk assessments.

Immigration authorities have also attempted to automate risk
assessment. Surveillance scholars have previously uncovered how

automated data-driven efforts that are portrayed as objective and neutral by municipal criminal justice stakeholders and social service providers nonetheless reproduce inequality.[5] In this chapter I follow parallel threads in the immigration system by focusing on two programs—ICE Level analysis and the Risk Classification Assessment—that automate data collection and processing. It is imperative that anyone interested in immigration enforcement know about both programs. Equally important, the way in which immigration authorities have developed and deployed automated ICE Level analysis and the Risk Classification Assessment provides insight into how, in replacing human with machine analysis, ICE leaders claim they have found a faster, more efficient, less error-prone, unbiased approach to classifying immigrants as dangerous.

This is a façade. Human biases remain embedded in the procedure, organizational culture, and design of technological tools. Far from being neutral, ICE has built automated tools in such a way as to grow the numbers of "dangerous" immigrants who require detention under the legitimating veneer of technology. They have done so by assessing risk based on gradually broader factors like unadjudicated accusations, charges, and suspicions, until by 2017 ICE ultimately just programmed the Risk Classification Assessment to recommend compulsory detention.

IN JUNE 2010 THEN director of ICE John T. Morton released a civil enforcement priorities memorandum, which directed field personnel to specifically prioritize noncitizens "who pose a danger to national security or a risk to public safety," including those who had participated in organized criminal gangs.[6] In the memo, Morton directed ICE personnel to refer to offense levels, or ICE Levels, to organize criminal history information into severity tiers.[7] Level One, the highest enforcement priority, includes noncitizens convicted of aggravated felonies or two or more crimes each punishable by more than one year. Level Two includes noncitizens convicted of any felony or three or more crimes each punishable by less than one year.

Level Three covers noncitizens convicted of crimes punishable by less than one year. ICE officers were directed to use ICE Levels in the field to further fine-tune frontline enforcement activities, targeting first noncitizens in Levels One and then in Level Two for apprehension, followed by Level Three.[8] Information to calculate ICE Levels comes from TECS and the National Crime Information Center Database (NCIC).[9]

The ICE union initially refused to follow the new discretionary guidelines, prohibited members from attending training on the guidelines, and even lodged a vote of no confidence against Director Morton.[10] Scholars have found that law enforcement organizations are not a single homogenous entity; rather, personnel positioned in different subsections of law enforcement organizations tend to exhibit varying behavioral patterns, including in how they respond to technological innovation and surveillance directives.[11] The ICE union revolt against Morton is a clear demonstration of the disconnect that can occur between leadership and line, a theme that recurs throughout this chapter.

Nonetheless, ICE officers eventually relented and, however resentfully, began to record ICE Level classifications in EID's Enforcement Case Tracking System (ENFORCE) modules by manually entering and analyzing criminal history information and then selecting the appropriate ICE Level from a drop-down menu.[12] However, Department of Homeland Security (DHS) and ICE leadership identified the manual analysis of ICE Levels as vulnerable to data entry errors, inefficiency, and inconsistency.

Humans are agonizingly imperfect. We get tired and miss a word here, accidentally add an extra digit there. Down the line, this imprecision costs time to rectify. For example, ICE regretted that "users are manually selecting the ICE Level and could make an error."[13] Furthermore, one ICE officer might interpret information, and therefore assess an immigrant's risk level, differently than another ICE officer. ICE leadership clarified that the risks posed by ICE officers' humanness was "temporary in nature because ICE plans to automate the

ICE Level calculation. This improvement will minimize the possibility of user error in identifying the correct ICE Level based on available criminal history data."[14]

David Lyon argues that most surveillance innovations are introduced for reasons other than social control, with efficiency being a primary motivator.[15] Like many organizations, immigration enforcement agencies seek to increase efficiency by *automating* the tasks associated with information consolidation, surveillance, and risk assessment. Automation involves the replacement of manual acts with automatic processes to varying degrees. Systems can be fully automated and therefore absent human intervention after the design stage, or semiautomated, wherein a human role is maintained.[16]

While some scholars and law enforcement practitioners argue that automated technology can reduce bias in policing practices, others argue that social inequality is imbedded in automated technology in the design stage.[17] Whether automated or manual, the process of categorization still constitutes a means of *social sorting* wherein surveillance is not simply a practice of collecting information but also becomes a practice of assigning worth, often based on long-standing axes of social inequality.[18] Immigration surveillance reflects and reinforces racial inequality within the United States, with focused efforts to exclude non-White immigrant groups through categorizing them as dangerous.

Shortly after Morton's memo, ICE introduced the "automated solution," the promise of a machine future juxtaposed against a present of imperfect flesh.[19] Unlike humans, the automated solution does not come to work hung over, sleep deprived, or distracted by heartbreak; does not require rest, wrist braces, or back surgeries. And so, by 2012, the automated solution had nudged its human predecessors out of the task of ICE Level calculation. Instead, the ENFORCE program began to automatically pull criminal history information, analyze it, and sort noncitizens into ICE Levels.[20]

ICE officials touted the degree to which automation minimized the human risk of data entry errors and increased the speed at which enforcement priorities could be identified.[21] Imperfect interpretation of information would also be eradicated by replacing human data analysts with preprogrammed business rules to algorithmically analyze criminal history information and map it onto ICE Levels.[22] ICE personnel quickly became "human interference," themselves a risk in the business of risk assessment.[23]

Despite the promises of objective machine processing, the way in which immigration personnel programmed ICE Level automation provides an example of the subtle expansion of categorizations of immigrants as dangerous. Although in the June 2010 directive ICE Levels were classifications assigned to immigrants *convicted* of a criminal offense, when programmed into ENFORCE, ICE Levels included *charges* as well. The ICE Level could be raised to indicate more serious crimes if an individual had multiple lower-level charges.[24] Even if ICE Levels are automated, the rules are still made by people in the programming stage, and in this case, people designed the rules in such a way as to construct more immigrants as dangerous. Nevertheless, ICE has pursued automation on the grounds that it is not only efficient and accurate, but as I delve into next, also *unbiased*.

LONG BEFORE HE was the lead plaintiff in a class action lawsuit against Chad Wolf and other government officials, Jose Velesaca came to the United States from Ecuador, successfully bypassing several layers of US borders in Central America and Mexico along the way. Like many people who live in the United States without official documentation, Jose has children and other family members who are US citizens.[25] When, many years after his border crossings, he was detained by ICE and taken to a detention facility, he bumped up against a class of workers both "precarious and powerful," reviled as human rights violators by some while celebrated as protectors and public servants by others.[26] Detention center workers exert considerable power over detainees, and some reportedly express that power in the form of torture, sexual assault, and other forms of abuse.[27] Yet they have almost no control over any other part of the immigration process outside of the detention center and, as mapped throughout this chapter, may be moving toward obsolescence in select areas. Employees consistently find ICE to be an unpleasant work environment; based on an employee satisfaction survey of 305 federal agencies, ICE ranked 299th in 2016 and 288th in 2017.[28] It breaks a person to break other people.

ICE justifies the mass detention of immigrants, including Jose, by claiming that they are flight or safety risks and therefore cannot be granted release to await a hearing date. To make custody recommendations, ICE officers rely heavily on secondary information, particularly criminal history information.[29] Consequently, ICE has repeatedly modified EID and the associated ENFORCE applications to increase the amount of criminal history information the data system can hold and analyze.

The Risk Classification Assessment, deployed nationwide in 2013 as a new ENFORCE tab, automates decisions about whether a noncitizen should be detained, released on bond, or subject to an ATD program pending the adjudication of their case.[30] Previous to the modification, ICE performed risk assessments manually with paper forms at the time of booking.[31] In the course of a Risk Classification Assessment, ICE officers may ask a detained individual as many as 178 questions, resulting in an intake process that can last several hours.[32] ICE officers enter interview information into structured data fields (ICE officials view unstructured free narrative text as more susceptible to errors and less efficiently processed).[33] The Risk Classification Assessment then automatically generates a custody recommendation based on the structured interview information, criminal history information pulled from other databases, and information from other "unspecified" sources.[34]

The Risk Classification Assessment produces a recommendation that is then reviewed and either accepted or refuted by the ICE officer conducting the assessment and a supervisor. A supervisor can override the automated recommendation by entering an explanation into the allotted place in the system.[35] In the case that

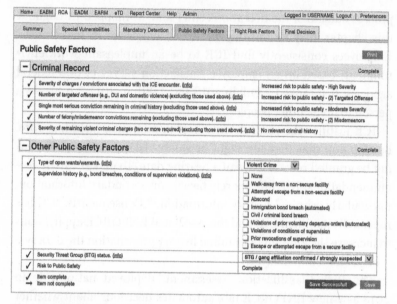

Figure 2. Sample Risk Classification Assessment form in ENFORCE. Recreated verbatim for image quality. *Credit:* Nat Case, INCase, LLC.

continued custody is recommended and accepted, the Risk Classification Assessment also recommends a detention custody classification level of Low, Low/Medium, High/Medium, or High. Noncitizens whom ICE personnel identify as subject to mandatory detention are still assessed in order to produce a detention security level.[36]

Similar to justifications for automated ICE Level assessment, ICE officials have claimed that automated risk assessment increased accuracy by minimizing human data entry errors and increased efficiency by enabling ICE personnel to more quickly process detention intakes.[37] Additionally, ICE officials have argued that "automation of certain portions of the custody decision process helps to ensure the consistent application of ICE's custody policies and guidance and to reduce the risk that decisions will be made arbitrarily and based on factors other than those permitted by law and policy."[38] In other words, automation will help to ensure that assessment tools do not capture the subjective beliefs of ICE personnel; rather, people are merely the conduit through which messages about danger flow.

The problem with humans goes beyond that of aching joints. People are also infused with subtle prejudices, deep-seated assumptions, and subconscious compulsions. According to ICE's line of thought, because automation reduces the human role, it also reduces bias (i.e., racial bias, stereotypes about country of origin) in assessments of immigrant danger. The automation-as-solution-to-bias position may well be a response to ongoing challenges to the legality and legitimacy of immigration enforcement. As detention and deportation rates have exploded, social movement leaders have challenged the moral validity of immigration enforcement practices, and legal advocates have launched racial profiling litigation and other challenges to restrict detention and deportation.[39] Brayne traces the same process within the Los Angeles Police Department (LAPD), a department that turned to technology to rebrand itself in the wake of decades of high-profile civil rights violations, corruption, and a federal consent decree.[40] Immigration enforcement officials similarly lean on automated technology to erase the organization's history of abuse and legitimize the enterprise of immigration enforcement as a race-neutral, objective endeavor. In practice, things are far more complicated.

THE REPORTS COMING out of the DHS Office of Inspector General are not good. The Office of Inspector General, tasked with oversight responsibilities for DHS agencies including ICE, conducts audits and inspections with an eye toward "economy, efficiency, and effectiveness."[41] The latest Office of Inspector General audit of ICE's Risk Classification Assessment finds all three virtues—economy, efficiency, and effectiveness—lacking, concluding that the tool is "time consuming, resource intensive, and not effective in determining which aliens to release or under what conditions."[42]

The inspection revealed that of 228,095 Risk Classification Assessment decisions made between July 2012 and December 2013, the tool made no recommendation for 18.4 percent of cases, thus requiring personnel to make a custody decision.[43] Furthermore, the report concluded, "When the system does make a recommendation, ERO officers routinely override the recommendation," in this case, 21.9 percent of the time.[44] When the Risk Classification Assessment recommended the release of LGBT detainees in particular, ICE officers overrode the recommendation 60 percent of the time, choosing instead to detain them.[45] Transwomen are held for up to twice as long as the average detention stay.[46]

Legal scholars Mark Noferi and Robert Koulish provide further insight into how discretionary overrides by ICE personnel can increase negative classifications and consequently, detention rates. In a study of the Risk Classification Assessment, the authors present the case of a twenty-six-year-old Salvadoran man who, despite having no criminal history, was classified in the Risk Classification Assessment process as a safety concern primarily because an ICE officer strongly suspected him of gang membership during an interview. Noferi and Koulish conclude that the classification of this man as dangerous "may not be because of anything he did, but because he matches the profile of MS-13 gang members of similar age," and thus "the tool classifies him as medium safety risk and high flight risk, and recommends detention in medium/high custody."[47]

Although one purpose of risk assessment is to reduce the detained population by reserving detention for the highest risk individuals, Noferi and Koulish find an overuse of immigration detention with risk assessment.[48] The authors echo critical criminologists' concerns about risk assessment tools that are functionally biased yet legitimized by the sanitizing effect of scientific language, stating that "the facial neutrality of actuarial decisions (whether correct or not) may further the political legitimacy of over-detention, and increase the likelihood over-detention will continue."[49] Focusing specifically on parole, punishment scholar Robert Werth argues that assessment and classification techniques are overly broad because they assess not *if* someone is dangerous but rather *how*, operating so as to preclude the possibility of a subject who is not inherently danger-ous to some degree.[50]

The inspection authors have advised ICE to find a way in which the tool could be implemented to more effectively utilize resources with fewer overrides; they recommend less human interference so that assessment tools become more fully automated rather than semiautomated.

NOT EVERYONE AGREES that humans are the problem. While ICE caved on ICE Level automation, it was more stubborn when it came to the Risk Classification Assessment. ICE officials resisted the DHS Office of Inspector General's analysis, stating; "Some overrides are not only expected, but even desirable. Supervisors must main-tain the ability to exercise discretion and the [Risk Classification Assessment] requires written justifications in cases where recom-mendations are overridden."[51] ICE officials stressed that the Risk Classification Assessment produces a custody *recommendation*, but only an ICE officer can produce a final custody *determination*.

Surveillance researchers argue that automation complacency and automation bias encourage decision makers to place an exces-sive amount of trust in automated systems, "even when they sus-pect error or malfunction."[52] In the case of immigration custody decisions, automation complacency and bias would lead risk-averse personnel to uncritically follow the automated Risk Classification Assessment recommendation.[53] However, the Office of Inspec-tor General's critique of the Risk Classification Assessment is that officers do not demonstrate *enough* automation complacency; they do not have enough trust in the automated recommendations and instead, in acts of gross inefficiency, take the time to override them. In this sense, the findings here are more in line with Brayne's conclu-sions about "algorithmic secrecy," in which automated technologies remain opaque even to those deploying them; as a result, frontline officers may become suspicious and question the efficacy of data-driven tools, opting instead to rely on their own experience.[54]

Judith Almodovar, an ICE acting assistant field director, explained in a deposition for *Velesaca v. Wolf et al.* that "the RCA [Risk Classification Assessment] system is just a tool that we use. It can give whatever recommendation it gives. But at the end of our review that—our decision is what counts. So we can overturn the RCA recommendation at any time."[55] In communicating with ICE detention personnel, ICE leadership has similarly claimed that despite the introduction of automated systems, officers, agents, and supervisors would maintain control over the tool. For example, the then executive associate director of enforcement and removal operations described the Risk Classification Assessment to ICE removal personnel in a memorandum in the following manner:

> RCA [Risk Classification Assessment] provides an initial recommendation on whether to detain or release an alien, custody classification level if detained, or level of community supervision if released. While RCA generates recommendations based on the data provided, ERO officers and agents may always record disagreement and override RCA's recommended action. The final decision rests with the ICE Supervisory Detention and Deportation Officer. The RCA scoring methodology is configurable, and will evolve based on the feedback provided by ICE officers, agents, and supervisory officers.[56]

In this memo, ICE leadership portrays the Risk Classification Assessment as a relatively passive tool that will provide assistance to ICE personnel, who retain final discretion on detention decisions and whose feedback will shape future modifications to the tool. Internal project briefings repeatedly emphasize that the "automated solution" will still "enable the officer to execute discretion at all times throughout the Risk Classification Assessment process."[57] Specifically, "the solution will electronically calculate an alien's Risk to Public Safety ensuring consistency and accuracy," while maintaining "the current operational process for an officer to make a decision outside of guidelines."[58] Brayne, again, finds a similar dynamic among LAPD captains and sergeants, who "implemented data-driven policing by highlighting—rather than minimizing—their officers' experiential knowledge," emphasizing that they are "seeking to 'supplement' officer knowledge and experience with data."[59]

In the guts of training manuals and pedantic bureaucratic memos, people and machines vie to be the active subjects. As information systems move toward greater automation, the systems threaten to assume the active role. People cease to access, process, and analyze information. Rather, *EID retrieves* information from other databases. *EID populates* the information into the appropriate ENFORCE tab. *Business rules analyze* data to produce ICE Levels. *The tool classifies* an immigrant as a gang member.[60] Those who originally programmed the business rules, who set the process in motion at each detention intake—the immigration enforcement workers themselves—have started to disappear, at least rhetorically. ICE leaders push back against this pattern a bit, but they are admonished by oversight bodies to give themselves over to automation. ICE is in the business of disappearing people, often from work sites, their children left waiting at schools and day care, alone and scared, for a pickup that does not come. As automation advances across professions, will ICE officers and agents find themselves disappeared from their jobs, too?[61]

THE RISK CLASSIFICATION Assessment is not the only tool detention personnel use to criminalize immigrants. Chris, the car-crash-watching attorney from the last chapter, tells me about a detention facility in Southern California: "There's this guy there who is in charge of security for suspected gang members and he has what he calls a Security Threat Group Roster and he decides who goes on the roster. He has a survey and it's got a score. Like, if you score over five points, you're labeled as a gang member. It's got a set of questions that he goes through." I am intrigued.

When I get hold of the assessment instrument that "this guy" uses to determine detainees' gang involvement, I am struck, first, by the Corrections Corporation of America (CCA) stamp across the bottom, suggesting that the form is perhaps used throughout CCA detention centers, and not just by this one guy. Second, I am struck by the pseudoscience of the instrument. It opens with a straightforward question asking if the detained person has ever been a gang member or associate, followed by more specific questions about which gang they belong to, how long they have belonged, if they have contact with the group outside of detention, and if they receive financial support from outside the detention facility. The questionnaire instructs detention staff to ask about the leadership structure and function of the gang, and there are multiple sections for the interviewer's narrative comments. The assessment tool also dedicates a lot of room to documenting tattoos: where they are on the body, when and where the person in question got them done (streets or prison), and detailed descriptions of the body art.

Next, there is a nine question, forty-seven-point rating system to confirm a detainee's status as a gang member or associate. Each question is worth four or five points and asks about the detainee's self-admission, tattoos, possession of paraphernalia or contraband, contact or communication with other suspected gang members, and presence in photographs with suspected gang members, as well as whether the detainee has been identified as a gang member or associate via intelligence information from other agencies or through direct conformation by law enforcement, and if there are photographs of the detainee with other alleged gang members or associates. A score of nine or lower earns someone "suspected gang member" status and ten or higher anoints someone as a "confirmed gang member."

I wonder how many self-styled gang experts walk the halls of detention centers, inputting suspicions about detained immigrants' gang involvement into either the Risk Classification Assessment or some other assessment tool that functions more under the radar. I think of all the people who have been kept in the mire of detention centers because of a classification. I follow the classification down the line and think of all the people who have been denied bond and asylum claims based on gang allegations, who have been made deportation priorities, and have been pushed back across borders,

returned to their home countries with the gang label permanently
stamped on them.

I KNOW, MY position seems impossible. I find virtue in neither the
discretion of an immigration agent nor the mechanistic determinations of automated programs. This is because humans are the problem, and the machines do not eradicate the heart of the chaos, only
threaten to obscure it. For all the talk of a data system "ingesting"
information, it does not eat anything on its own. People feed it. They
create the stomach and the mouth in the first place. They put a col-
lar on it, stroke it, and tell it where to hunt.[62] What is (intentionally)
lost in the technical and passive language is that humans still run the
show, and it is a horror show. Reports abound of immigration detention centers where people are packed into small concrete rooms without water or hygiene products and subjected to sexual abuse, torture,
and nonconsensual medical procedures.[63] An automated program
does not bear the responsibility for any of this horror, but people do.

ICE, like most law enforcement agencies, has an enforcement
compulsion, and it bends technology to fit this compulsion. In the
immigration enforcement context, the law enforcement mission is to
increase the pool of surveillable, detainable, and deportable immigrants, so the enforcement tools, human and nonhuman alike, are
calibrated to enable the negative categorization of broad swaths of
the population. The repetitive, dry language of technological procedure merely weaves a legitimating cloak. Granted, this concept,
that "all technologies are human activities," that the program is programmed, is not a new one.[64] However, it is necessary to continue to
break open, pull apart, and demystify automated technological tools,
particularly in the arenas of immigration detention and homeland
security, where surveillance systems are hyperobscured.

ICE gets so much out of floating in the middle ground, justify-
ing decisions with automated technology while also making ample
use of overrides to discretionarily detain people. The agency gets to

simultaneously lock up large numbers of people and deflect responsibility for those decisions onto technology. Automated ICE Level calculation and the Risk Classification Assessment provide a veneer of technical legitimacy while ICE expands the negative categorization practices that sweep immigrants into borderland circuitry.

One political implication is that anti-immigrant talking heads can claim there has been an increase in the population of criminal aliens, when what has actually occurred is a change in how immigrants are categorized. The expanded categorization of immigrants as dangerous has led to expanded enforcement against immigrants who do not have criminal convictions but instead have pending charges and unadjudicated allegations, like those of gang involvement. According to ICE's 2018 *Enforcement and Removal Operations Report*, compared to 2017, "arrests of convicted criminals remained relatively level," yet "administrative arrests with pending criminal charges increased by 48 percent. This continues the upward trend seen in FY2017, where arrests with pending charges increased by 255 percent over FY2016."[65] ICE now lumps together immigrants with pending criminal charges and those with criminal convictions and calls them collectively "aliens with criminal histories" or "aliens" who demonstrate "criminality."[66] This represents a departure from previous reports, which refer to "non-criminal" and "criminal aliens," ICE defining the latter as "an alien with a known criminal *conviction*."[67]

By the time Jose Velesaca was brought into the hellish conditions of immigration detention, ICE had removed the "release" recommendation from the Risk Classification Assessment entirely. While ICE personnel could still override recommendations, the only default option programmed into the Risk Classification Assessment was to detain, making it a tool to assess detention security level only. As a result, after the 2017 removal of the "release" recommendation only 3 percent of people assessed as low risk were granted release, compared to roughly 47 percent from 2013 to 2017.[68] ICE personnel continued to maintain a role by conducting the intakes, which came to constitute more of a standardized information collection mechanism than an individualized predictive assessment tool.

CHAD WOLF IS at the border again. A US attorney for the Southern District of New York represents him in *Velesaca v. Wolf et al.* so that he can be in the desert. He is far away from the detention center where the rights of Jose Velesaca were violated but close to the town of Eloy, where the largest employer is CoreCivic. The private corrections corporation operates four facilities in Eloy, bearing names like Saguaro Correctional Center. CoreCivic is actually Corrections Corporation of America; it rebranded itself after a long list of infractions occurred in its detention centers and tarnished its original name.

This time, Wolf is in a flak jacket. There he stands, posing for photos in a bulletproof vest while behind him stretch acres of tranquil desert. Below the sound of cameras flashing, there is only the soothing coo of a mourning dove or the scurry of a lizard toward the protection of a prickly pear. It is always revealing what political figures choose to do when they visit the southern borderlands. As president, Bill Clinton went to an old Mexican restaurant in South Tucson and ate a bean tostada, birria taco, chile relleño, chicken enchilada, and beef tamale. George W. Bush examined an outdoor poster board display, constructed ad hoc by CBP to showcase examples of the surveillance technology and weaponry used along the border. It looked like a surreal science fair in the middle of open desert. Wolf, still attired in flak, jumps on an ATV and revs the engine as he races along the border, the bars of bollard fencing creating a kaleidoscopic effect in the background.[69]

The saguaros nearby could use the bulletproof vests. In addition to dodging the dynamite that contractors are exploding to clear the way for a wall and being co-opted in the naming of prisons, a historic drought has made saguaros erupt in unprecedented "side blooms." Saguaros usually bloom white flowers on their crowns in May, but distress has caused them to reactivate, in autumn, older budding sites located further down their trunks. The ecologists count the

ivory petals and are stymied, the meteorologists forecast flooding
that never arrives, and hydrologists pump dry rivers with reclaimed
water in an attempt to resuscitate the underground aquifers.[70]

The deaths in the desert continue. The deaths at the hands of
local police and federal officers continue. The rhetoric around gangs
continues. Secretary of Homeland Security Kirstjen Nielsen claims
that the family separation policy is necessary because MS-13 is using
children to disguise themselves as families at the border. The only
way to stop the march of gangs is to rip the children away and knife
the water-guzzling Wall through more land and more people, fill the
detention centers and databases to the brim, then build more. The
appetites are bottomless.

Mark Morgan, the acting director of ICE, says that unaccompanied children are either current or soon-to-be MS-13 members. How
can he tell? The eyes. He's been to the border, gone into the cages,
looked into the eyes of children in detention, and he *just knows*.[71]
Politicians keep showing up in the borderlands, but it remains Mar-
tian to them. This place holds none of their love stories, so they only
know how to break it. In a flash of hard clarity, I understand there
may not exist a repair that can touch the depth of this damage.

6 We Make Our Own Maps

On October 13, 2016, a Mexican immigrant left the routinized horror of California's Adelanto Detention Facility and walked into the Mojave Desert, a land speckled with extraterrestrial Joshua trees. Adelanto is an immigration detention facility that is privately operated by GEO Group, a corporation that Immigration and Customs Enforcement (ICE) pays $124 per bed per day to guarantee at least a total of 1,455 beds for detainees. Additional beds cost ICE an extra 44 bucks each. The US government is GEO Group's biggest customer. Both the technological and brick-and-mortar infrastructure of immigration enforcement is increasingly developed and managed by private contractors.[1]

I do not know the name of the person who made it out of Adelanto in October 2016. I do not know what brought them across the border into the United States, which borders they crossed, how many they crossed, or when they reached the first layer of US borders. Perhaps they passed by people sitting in their cars at the Nogales port of entry or crossed paths with a California police officer punching information into the CalGang Database, information that would soon be routed to ICE. Maybe, once in Adelanto, they sat for hours answering screening questions as part of the Risk Classification Assessment, only for the inevitable "detain" recommendation to pop up.

I know not what this person hoped for the future or who was waiting for them. What I do know is that after being released from detention, they made their way out of North America's driest ecosystem and kept moving westward until they reached the coastal city of Oxnard as the stars shifted above. Twenty-four hours later, a message from ICE reached Oxnard-area law enforcement, informing them that an immigrant with an assault conviction on their record had recently taken up residence in their seaside city.

On the other side of the country, an unidentified immigrant from Jamaica was released from the Essex County Correctional Facility. This person crossed the Hudson River and settled in the Bronx, the city lit up like stars laid upon the earth. That same day, ICE notified New York City law enforcement that a Jamaican immigrant with a 1299 (robbery) conviction on their record had been released from immigration detention and was now in their jurisdiction. A little later, ICE released an Iraqi immigrant from detention in New Orleans and sent a message to law enforcement in Prairieville, Louisiana, warning of their imminent arrival.

These immigrants are being monitored under the Law Enforcement Notification System, LENS for short. LENS enables ICE to share information, mostly from the Enforcement Integrated Database (EID) and the National Crime Information Center (NCIC) Database, with local law enforcement agencies when a noncitizen who has been convicted of a violent crime, a serious crime (defined by Department of Homeland Security [DHS] to include misdemeanors), or a sex offense is released from ICE custody into US territory. When a noncitizen who meets one of the qualifying conditions is booked out of ICE custody, LENS automatically pulls information from federal databases and sends it to the law enforcement agency

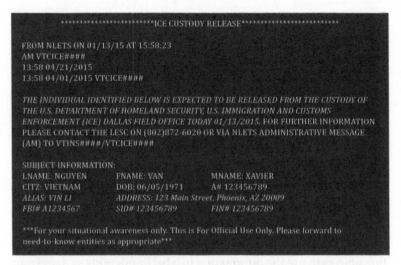

Figure 3. Sample LENS notification with simulated data from US Immigration and Customs Enforcement, *Law Enforcement Notification System (LENS) Fact Sheet.* Recreated verbatim for image quality. *Credit:* Nat Case, INCase, LLC.

where the individual is released and where the released individual intends to reside, if different.[2] Like ICE Levels and the Risk Classification Assessment, LENS is an automated program, requiring minimal human assistance when functioning properly. And like the initiative between CalGang and ICEGangs, it increases interoperability and information exchange between multiple levels of law enforcement.

It is by virtue of their criminal record that these immigrants are being tracked and their information cross-jurisdictionally shared. People who have been labeled "criminal" are treated differently in the immigration system just as they are treated differently in multiple institutional and social spaces. DHS and ICE frequently use accusations of criminality to justify surveillance, mandatory detention, solitary confinement, prioritized deportation, and overly aggressive policing.[3] The "criminal alien" label also allows law enforcement to more freely collect and use an individual's biometric and biographic data. For example, when the Trump administration announced in 2019 that it would collect DNA information from all people in federal immigration custody, DHS justified the invasive move based on the supposedly "criminal aspect" of asylum seekers.[4]

Thus far, we have followed the flow of captive information and bodies from the border into the interior of the United States, and from local police to federal law enforcement. We have seen the amount of information and the types of information in data systems expand considerably. In the process, we have also seen the gang member label wash over an increasingly broad range of people, percolate up through jurisdictions, and enable the surveillance and control of racialized youth. Furthermore, as authorities deploy data systems to absorb more information, there are more opportunities for immigration officers to use the information to label immigrants as dangerous and then justify detention, deportation, and surveillance. In the last chapter we ventured into detention centers to observe the process by which immigration officers use data from surveillance systems to conduct risk assessments. Here we will see how the digital categorization of a person as threatening not only enables authorities to do more with someone's body—confine them for long periods, restrain them, forcibly move them—but also allows authorities to act more liberally with their information. I trace the circulation of negative classifications back down from the federal to the local level as LENS brings information into the interior of the country, tracking immigrants once they exit detention.

I AM BACK at Sofia's glass-lined office. She is thinking about Oxnard too because that is where one of her clients, let's call him Alex, has been profiled as a gang member. While in immigration detention, Alex has become a confidential informant and is seeking asylum based on the claim that gang members in his home country will kill him for ratting should he be deported. A local police department wants to wire him, and he is game. The purpose of the wire is to record a murder confession from someone with whom Alex is in detention. But according to Sofia, ICE wants no part in it, because it knows that there is something colloquially referred to as a "snitch visa," or, in official language, an "S" classification that makes informants eligible for permanent resident status. Acting as an informant broadens Alex's options for staying in the United States. Sofia believes ICE does not care about how Alex might be able to help the local police department with their murder investigation. ICE just wants him deported as soon as possible, and an S classification would disrupt that objective. This is one example of the many ways in which the interests of ICE and local police diverge at times.

While some local police departments resist active collaboration with ICE out of concerns about discouraging immigrant communities from reporting crime and cooperating with police investigations, others enthusiastically work with ICE through 287(g) programs or joint task forces. Some police departments sit in a contradictory middle ground, both reaching out to immigrant communities while discretionarily arresting undocumented immigrants and turning them over to ICE.[5] Still others find themselves in the position apparent in Alex's case: expected to turn over to ICE undocumented people who are in police custody but unsatisfied with the cooperation they receive from ICE in return.

Many people have likely heard of debates around local law enforcement cooperation with ICE in the context of the Secure Communities program. In the pre–Secure Communities era, when a local law enforcement officer arrested and booked someone, they ran the fingerprints through Federal Bureau of Investigation (FBI) databases, including the NCIC Database, to check for criminal history. While immigration alerts can appear in an NCIC check, the onus is on local law enforcement to contact immigration authorities when the alert appears. By contrast, Secure Communities makes use of interoperable technology to automatically run fingerprints through both FBI and DHS databases such that immigration authorities are automatically flagged to the presence of unauthorized immigrants. There is no need for a local law enforcement officer to actively contact ICE about a deportable immigrant.[6]

The post–Secure Communities booking process drastically increased immigration authorities' awareness of noncitizens in police custody and resulted in an explosion of deportations during the Obama administration.[7] It is an easy way to identify large numbers of people for apprehension and deportation that does not require steep increases in local police acting as "force multipliers."[8] Secure Communities also bypasses the need to station large numbers of immigration agents in jails to identify unauthorized immigrants in person, as was originally done in the Criminal Alien Program.[9]

LENS is, in a way, the mirror image of Secure Communities. It is built on the same idea—to exchange information on so-called criminal aliens between local and federal law enforcement—but works in the opposite direction by pushing information from the federal to the local level. In reporting documents, fact sheets, and newsletters, immigration authorities frame LENS as a resource for local law enforcement agencies to more effectively conduct investigations by "narrowing the pool of potential suspects when a violent or serious crime is committed in their jurisdiction and there are few leads in the investigation, or if the particulars of a crime being investigated are similar to circumstances surrounding the violent or serious crime for which the individual was previously convicted."[10]

This approach fits into many local police departments' focus on targeting "chronic offenders" as perpetrators of a large proportion of crimes. For example, the LENS objective described earlier is strikingly similar to the letter that the Los Angeles Police Department (LAPD) sends to individuals who "indicate a propensity to engage in at-risk behavior" warning: "When certain types of crimes occur in areas we have connected to you, we will investigate the crime to determine if there are any patterns or similarities related to your past practice."[11] LENS indirectly enlists state and local law enforcement in immigration control, increasing the cross-jurisdictional surveillance of immigrants when ICE is unable to keep them in custody or immediately deport them.

The US government originally framed Secure Communities as a voluntary program. After jurisdictions across the nation refused to participate, DHS clarified that locales actually did not have the discretion to opt out. Resistance at the local level and frustration at the federal level have continued in various forms. The Trump administration threatened to withhold federal funding from police departments, cities, and states with sanctuary policies that prohibit cooperation between local public agencies and federal immigration authorities.[12] The administration even tried to disqualify police departments in sanctuary cities from applying for funding to support gang enforcement efforts.[13]

Programs like LENS provide local law enforcement with a method to partially skirt "sanctuary" or "safe city" orders in which states or cities place restrictions on information sharing and collaboration between local police and ICE. While sanctuary provisions prohibit local law enforcement from entering into agreements with federal immigration officials or from directly performing immigration enforcement functions, it is unlikely to keep them from signing up for LENS notifications if they are motivated to do so, because ICE contends that the notifications only provide state and local law enforcement with an "awareness" of criminal aliens in their jurisdiction. Specifically, "These notifications are intended as *situational awareness* messages only, which do not direct or require law enforcement agencies to take action, but rather help inform agencies that have an interest in an alien in connection with a pending investigation or prosecution, for parole or other forms of supervision, or for public or officer safety purposes."[14]

Nationwide deployment of the LENS program occurred in September 2015, at which time LENS notifications were sent to state law enforcement partners. These partners were mainly state identification bureaus and fusion centers, which then distributed the information to local law enforcement agencies.[15] Between August

2015 and August 2016, DHS issued roughly one hundred notifications per month. After August 2016, local law enforcement agencies (including police on university and college campuses) were able to subscribe to receive LENS notifications directly, without going through a state-level agency per the previous protocol.[16] As a result, LENS notifications to state and local law enforcement agencies increased sharply, to about four hundred cases per month beginning in September 2016. This abrupt increase was followed by a general trend of increasing cases through September 2017 (the last available data point), which had the highest reported count of LENS notifications at 625.[17] Each year, the LENS program expands substantially.

ON SEPTEMBER 20, 2016, ICE released a Vietnamese immigrant from a detention center in Florence, Arizona. This person was most likely apprehended in the Tucson sector, consistently one of the highest-volume areas for unauthorized border crossing along the US-Mexico border. After they were released from Florence, they traveled back south to an area on the far northwest side of Tucson that abuts the Interstate 10 freeway. The next day, ICE released a notification to Tucson law enforcement informing them of the Vietnamese immigrant's arrival.

The Tucson sector and indeed, the entire length of the US-Mexico border, has become a crossing point not only for Mexicans and Central Americans but for people from all over the world, who see it as the most viable place of entry.[18] In the 1990s, the Clinton administration radically increased the number of crossings in the Tucson sector, and therefore the deadliness of crossing, by beefing up Border Patrol in areas with more moderate climates like the Tijuana-San Diego region. As a result, border crossers pivoted to less-patrolled, more remote, rugged, incredibly hot terrain like the Sonoran Desert around Tucson.[19]

Similar strategically planned mass deaths happen elsewhere, too. For example, European powers have externalized border controls to militarize Algerian migration routes, pushing migrants into the Saharan Desert. Thus, Harsha Walia reminds us that migration routes are organized and intentionally established by the state, often for murderous ends.[20] Although the Tucson sector is now far more patrolled, it remains deadly. Many still see it as the most promising crossing point and worth the risk of heat stroke or hypothermia, depending on the season.

There is a particular historical cruelty in a Vietnamese immigrant being detained at the US-Mexico border. Large-scale Vietnamese immigration to the United States began after the horrors of the Vietnam War, during which the US military created the "McNamara line," an electronic system on the border between North and South Vietnam that employed seismic technology and heat detection to surveil the Viet Cong. In 1970, the Border Patrol used this same technology to introduce motion sensors to the US-Mexico border, a profound development that ushered in the early militarization of the southern border.[21] US imperialism abroad established a perilous migration circuit and then militarized it with technology forged in war.

On the same day that ICE released the notification to Tucson law enforcement regarding a Vietnamese immigrant, a Cuban immigrant was released from an Aurora, Colorado, detention facility also run by GEO Group. The Cuban immigrant trekked across the country to Tampa, Florida, where law enforcement had already received a LENS message from ICE notifying them of the immigrant's arrival. Both of these individuals were released under orders of supervision (OSUP), part of alternatives to detention (ATD) programs that condition release on continued surveillance in the form of an electronic ankle monitor, periodic reporting to an ICE officer, and restricted travel. Both of these people also ended up in two of the most popular destinations for LENS notifications, Arizona and Florida.

LENS notifications are not evenly distributed across geography. It is important to remember that local and state law enforcement agencies sign up to receive these notifications, meaning that LENS receivers have courted the notifications. Thus, a jurisdiction with large proportions of LENS notifications indicates that law

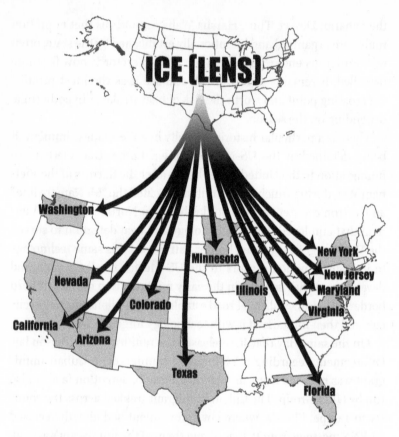

Map 3. Most common LENS notification destinations, 2015–2017. *Credit:* Nat Case, INCase, LLC.

enforcement agencies in those areas actively want to engage in the surveillance of immigrants. Over the three years for which data is available, thirteen states, in varying order each year, occupied the top ten spots for receipt of LENS notifications: California, Texas, New Jersey, New York, Florida, Arizona, Virginia, Minnesota, Maryland, Washington, Illinois, Nevada, and Colorado. California, New York, Texas, Florida, Arizona, New Jersey, and Virginia were in the top ten in all three years for which data is available.

Table 3   LENS Notifications: Top Ten Receiving States

2015*		2016		2017**	
State	*% of Total*	*State*	*% of Total*	*State*	*% of Total*
CA	32.44	CA	28.08	CA	25.40
NY	14.12	FL	9.53	AZ	8.43
TX	8.97	AZ	7.81	FL	7.43
FL	6.87	TX	7.39	NV	4.37
AZ	4.77	NY	5.71	TX	6.46
MN	3.05	NJ	3.6	VA	3.95
NJ	2.86	WA	2.63	CO	3.08
VA	2.48	MN	2.14	NY	3.03
IL	1.72	VA	2.10	NJ	2.42
MD	1.53	IL	1.99	MN	2.20

Data from analyzed FOIA requests.
*Data starts in March.
**Data ends in September.

Each year, law enforcement agencies in California receive by far the largest share of LENS notifications (at least a quarter of all notifications). Although Los Angeles represents the most popular receiving city in California, its proportion of LENS notifications never surpasses more than 4 percent of the national grand total for LENS notifications in any given year. Rather than LENS notifications being concentrated in a few large cities, the notifications were dispersed nationally across 246 cities in 2015, 810 cities in 2016, and 1,128 cities in 2017. In other words, although thirteen states dominate as primary LENS notification recipients, it is not because one or two large cities within those states receive an overwhelming number of notifications. Instead, dozens or even hundreds of cities spread across each state receive LENS notifications, which add up in the aggregate, and the number of cities that subscribe to receive LENS notifications increases each year.[22]

Table 4   LENS Notifications: Top Ten Receiving Cities

2015*		2016		2017**	
City	% of Total	City	% of Total	City	% of Total
Brooklyn, NY	4.01	Phoenix, AZ	3.90	Las Vegas, NV	4.79
Los Angeles, CA	3.63	Los Angeles, CA	3.75	Phoenix, AZ	3.75
Adelanto, CA	3.24	Miami, FL	3.12	Los Angeles, CA	2.61
New York City, NY	2.48	Houston, TX	1.31	Miami, FL	2.02
Miami, FL	2.29	Bronx, NY	1.01	Houston, TX	1.38
Phoenix, AZ	2.29	Dallas, TX	1.01	Tucson, AZ	1.04
San Diego, CA	2.29	Brooklyn, NY	0.86	Dallas, TA	0.96
Houston, TX	2.10	Mesa, AZ	0.79	Denver, CO	0.84
Bronx, NY	1.91	New York City, NY	0.79	Santa Ana, CA	0.84
Garden Grove, CA	1.91	San Diego, CA	0.79	Sacramento, CA	0.79

Data from analyzed FOIA requests.
*Data starts in March.
**Data ends in September.

The post–September 2016 spike in LENS notifications was particularly pronounced in Nevada, where notifications increased from 48 between March 2016 and December 2016 to 364 notifications between January 2017 and September 2017. Most of Nevada's increase is attributable to Las Vegas, where 20 LENS notifications were received between January 2015 and December 2016, compared to 235 between January 2017 and September 2017. By late 2016, a pattern had emerged in Nevada in which people released in Pahrump went to Las Vegas or Henderson, or in the reverse, were released from the Las Vegas/Henderson area and traveled immediately to Pahrump. The increase brought Nevada to fourth place overall for frequency of LENS notifications received in 2017. The other state that appears for the first time in the top ten states for receipt of LENS notifications after the 2016 spike is Colorado, which experienced an increase from 53 LENS notifications between March 2015 and December 2016 to 151 notifications from January 2017 to September 2017, largely attributable to Denver.

THERE IS A small town in western Oregon that sits along the South Yamhill River. It is there, as July 2017 winds down, that a Salvadoran immigrant arrives after leaving the Houston Contract Detention Facility on an OSUP. ICE sent a LENS notification to law enforcement in the area shortly thereafter. That same summer, two immigrants— one from Somalia, the other from Laos—left a detention site not far from the Elk River in Minnesota. They then traveled to other Minnesota cities, where LENS notifications were released to law enforcement the same day.

In 2017 ICE released LENS notifications pertaining to immigrants from 119 countries, including, with relative frequency, those from El Salvador, Somalia, and Laos. However, as most of the US immigration enforcement firepower is directed at Mexican nationals, it is perhaps unsurprising that the majority of LENS notifications target people from Mexico. Over the course of 2016, ICE released notifications to law enforcement agencies around the country on 983 Mexican immigrants released into US territory. Between January and September of 2017, ICE upped its output to released notifications on 2,213 Mexican immigrants.

LENS notifications concentrate on people traveling particular migration circuits, with a heightened focus on immigrants with Mexico as their country of origin, followed by those from Cuba. People from Guatemala, Honduras, and El Salvador consistently receive a relatively high proportion of LENS notifications. Jamaica and the Dominican Republic have a presence in the top countries of origin for LENS notifications in some years, though the proportion of notifications is between just 1 and 3 percent of the total. In select years, Somalia and Sudan also garner between 1 and 3 percent of LENS notifications. Laos, Cambodia, and Vietnam are also consistently represented as countries of origin in LENS notifications.

Table 5   LENS Notifications by Country of Origin

2015*		2016		2017**	
Country	*% of Total*	*Country*	*% of Total*	*Country*	*% of Total*
Mexico	24.81	Mexico	36.93	Mexico	45.11
Cuba	12.79	Cuba	13.15	Cuba	11.15
Vietnam	7.82	El Salvador	5.75	El Salvador	6.52
China	5.53	Vietnam	5.30	Guatemala	5.14
Laos	4.96	Guatemala	4.81	Honduras	3.81
El Salvador	3.82	Honduras	3.83	Vietnam	3.36
Somalia	2.86	Laos	2.89	Laos	2.14
Jamaica	2.48	Jamaica	1.95	Jamaica	1.20
Dominican Republic	1.91	Cambodia	1.73	Cambodia	1.16
Guatemala	1.72	Suden	1.05	Somalia	1.08

Data from analyzed FOIA requests.
*Data starts in March.
**Data ends in September.

The groups who are most frequently the subject of LENS notifications are those who have been stereotyped as threatening and are targeted by immigration and criminal justice enforcement efforts. Mexican, Central American, and Caribbean immigrants constitute groups toward whom US immigration authorities have historically dedicated large proportions of enforcement resources and, particularly since the 1980s, have targeted under various criminal alien, drug interdiction, and anti-gang initiatives.[23] Beginning in the 1980s, American media outlets and politicians framed Cuban exiles as criminal and targeted them for mandatory detention.[24] Immigrants from Laos, Cambodia, and Vietnam are also targeted under similar anti-gang, anti–drug trafficking, and other criminal alien enforcement programs.[25]

Two African countries that were targeted with relative frequency—Somalia and Sudan—were both included in the Trump administration's Muslim ban in 2017, and both countries have been targets of US immigration surveillance regimes since the attacks of September 11, 2001. In recent years there has been a steep increase in Somalian migrants being detained by Mexican authorities at the Mexican border with Guatemala and Belize, in no small part as a result of the US government's assistance in militarizing Mexico's southern border.[26]

Immigrants who are the subject of LENS notifications have been convicted of at least one crime. At this point, it is undeniable that police target Black and Brown people; that Black and Brown people are more likely to get convicted and are given longer sentences than White people; and that once someone has had contact with the criminal justice system, they are more likely to become caught in its tentacles repeatedly. The immigration system is a racialized system in its own right, with immigration agents in the field targeting phenotypically non-White people for identification and document checks.[27] LENS is a crystallization of the racialized intersection between the criminal justice and immigration systems and the surveillance bureaucracies in which both are couched.[28] LENS subjects are cycled between criminal justice and immigration oversight, each exchange further ensuring their lives will be made more precarious.

For those being tracked by multiple law enforcement agencies, the border seeps inward, snaking northward into big cities and small towns in Arizona, California, Colorado, Nevada, Minnesota, Virginia, and New York. The connections between each violent agency form dark constellations over the land. Over the past few decades, the immigration surveillance bureaucracy has increasingly encroached into the interior of the country via internalized or intraterritorial enforcement wherein migrants are subjected to law enforcement practices that are "analogous to the control exercised at the physical border itself."[29] ICE pursues interior enforcement more aggressively today than in the past, when immigration control focused more on stopping people at the border. As a result, immigrants, including long-term permanent residents, have come to live under an "eternal probation" model, confronting enhanced surveillance and marked expansion in the reasons they may be deported regardless of how long they have made a home in the United States.[30]

Internalized enforcement increases the points of contact through which immigrants can be identified for detention and deportation. These points are further inflated by cooperation and technological interoperability between immigration agencies, local police, and state law enforcement, creating a formidable surveillance web. It is through these everyday rituals carried out by a network of law enforcement officers, sometimes spectacular, at other times mundane, that people are made into suspects, made criminal and illegal, and rendered foreign and precarious.[31]

There are the more obvious ways in which internalized enforcement delivers precarity: gang labels that make one ineligible for immigration benefits, raids and checkpoints that uncover missing documents, leading to detention and deportation. Then there are the subtler ways that geographically internalized enforcement enters the body. Building on a Foucauldian perspective, Saher Selod, for example, finds that the feeling of being surveilled, added to watch lists, and constantly tracked, while remaining unsure of the specifics, leads Muslim American men to intense feelings of vulnerability, anxiety, hypervigilance, and self-policing.[32] This dynamic is also evident in the way alleged gang members who are US born, including those listed on the CalGang Database, avoid public spaces and gatherings for fear of being harassed or arrested by police.

"The police and Immigration and Customs Enforcement (ICE) are not only in immigrant neighborhoods but also in the minds of undocumented people," write researchers at the UCLA Dream Resource Center, a project for and by undocumented youth in Los Angeles. The "Pol[ICE]" get in your head.[33]

I USED TO go just before sunrise to the border, most often near the Buenos Aires National Wildlife Refuge, where a jaguar roamed in the 1990s. Winter dawn on that open plain was physically almost unbearable. Desert cold slices to the bone like little else. But I would look over that land and think that if I could just stay there forever, I would require nothing else: no other person, no life's work, nothing. In the borderlands, in this place made deadly by politicians who rarely set foot here, in a place where the land held so much blood, I rarely thought about death.

When the wall building really began to flourish, I stopped my sunrise walks that brushed up against the line. Others I knew stopped crossing with as much regularity too, or stopped crossing altogether, after stricter travel document requirements were instituted by Congress in the mid- to late 2000s. Even many of those who could get a passport, a passport card, or a border crossing card that allows the holder to travel up to fifty-five miles inland within the border zone stopped crossing.[34] From a proper distance, I bid the people who continued to cross farewell as they set off for Nogales, Sonora.

I stayed in the borderlands but out of eyeshot of the actual thing, which is why, despite the way it is embedded in me, I have never walked up to and laid my hand on the newest metal fencing or repurposed landing strips. For some reason, I fear that if I touched it, I might disappear. Yuma's sand dunes, California's canyons, the Rio Grande Valley's wide rivers—places that were not so long ago declared "unfenceable"—are now, at great expense, getting fences and walls—useless barriers since the land is so rugged in these areas that it is nearly impossible to cross on foot anyway.[35]

Though I stayed away from The Wall, for a while I stayed close enough to the border that I regularly bumped into groups of uniformed Border Patrol agents getting lunch in Southern Arizona cities, and I navigated the Border Patrol checkpoints splattered across the landscape. If I flew out of Tucson, I saw Border Patrol agents at the airport, right next to the Transportation Security Administration (TSA) agent who checks your ticket against your ID, and when I flew into Tucson, they were there at the gates waiting for people to deplane. I constructed a reliable mental map of where I might be intercepted by them. I knew that I could head down from Tucson to Tubac without trouble but that coming back north would mean getting stopped off Interstate 19. I knew that if I drove from Tucson to Las Cruces, I would not hit a checkpoint for a while but would get stopped on the westbound return from Las Cruces to Tucson. Although checkpoints can appear unexpectedly, on an unassuming back road or major highway, for most of my life there was a general consistency to their placement, in part because a good number of them are permanent. I avoided those routes when possible. Doing so remains part of a standard day in the borderlands.

Although the legal stakes are clearly different, people of color who are US citizens are subjected to policing and harassment by immigration officers and feel the weight of racialized internal enforcement. Through the concept of policeability, Gilberto Rosas describes a system of racialized management that is directed at both noncitizens and citizens and carried out by a network of coercive state agents, including Border Patrol, customs agents, and local police officers. In the southern borderlands, Latinos are particularly vulnerable to this type of policing, in which "illegality" refers to both a lack of immigration authorization and racial (non)belonging regardless of citizenship status.[36] Rosas is speaking of actions taken by coercive state agents that are both within and outside of the law; racial management relies on legal and extralegal coercion carried out by civilians or state agents or civilians *and* state agents who commit racialized vigilante violence together.[37] This is why in the borderlands you make a map; survival depends on it.

The Trump years upset the normal rhythms of Border Patrol deployment and expanded their power geographically even more inward. Whereas line officers in ICE and Customs and Border Protection (CBP) openly bristled at Obama's directives to prioritize "criminal" and "dangerous" groups of immigrants for enforcement, Trump gave these agencies free rein to go after anyone. Many agents rejoiced and bared their teeth.[38] Agents began to patrol farther north, pushing into Phoenix. During this time, a friend in Flagstaff called to tell me that agents had popped up in Northern Arizona. Shortly thereafter, a group of Border Patrol agents drove from San Diego to east Los Angeles to arrest a young immigration activist.[39] I saw more sheriff's vehicles patrolling Maricopa County, too. My mental map was obliterated, and I felt lost and scared driving in places I knew well enough to navigate with my eyes closed. I had nightmares with embarrassingly simplistic symbolism. I dreamed that I awoke to find my potted cacti destroyed, the flesh hacked and the pottery in shards. I dreamed that the desert flowers tattooed on my body faded and then disappeared. This is how it gets inside of you; this is what it is supposed to do to us.

ICE AND BORDER Patrol make their own maps. If you forget how close you are to the border in California, the Border Patrol will surely pull out a map that shows LA, Oxnard, and all of California's major cities are well within with the one-hundred-mile border zone that rings the entire contiguous United States. The agents will remind you of the exceptional power they have within this zone. Large parts of Washington State, where CalGang law enforcement partners dwell, are within the border zone, and it completely covers CalGang partners in Baltimore and Washington, D.C. It completely covers New York State and Florida and bites off chunks of Louisiana, Alabama, and Georgia.

If you have forgotten, for a moment, the border breathing down your neck, ICE will remind you that it is there, inside the country and inside your body, even outside of the one-hundred-mile border zone, in places you do not think of it being. Do you realize how close you are to the border in Denver and Vegas, in Illinois and Virginia? Interoperable surveillance technology collapses space and folds it toward the edges so that the border meets you on the Yamhill River in Oregon and the Elk River in Minnesota.

Unlike natural tributaries, the informational ones flow in both directions. And so, finally, we arrive at the last component of borderland circuitry: information-sharing partnerships between the US government and foreign partners to surveil and police people beyond US territory or, in other words, the "offshoring of American law enforcement" in circuits that flow through the United States, Mexico, Central America, and the Caribbean.[40] I have one more map to show you.

7 A Border Bleeds Out

In 2007, MEMBERS OF Georgetown Human Rights Action, a student group at Georgetown University Law Center, set out across Guatemala to find gang-labeled deportees on the other side of the deportation process. They met a man, to whom they assigned the pseudonym Pedro, upon his arrival at a Guatemala City air force base after his deportation from the United States. Pedro had lived most of his life, since he was a small child, in the United States. Pedro's 2007 deportation was his second, triggered after he was detained trying to cross the Texas border. He had first been deported from the United States back to Guatemala in 2001. Georgetown Human Rights Action researchers described Pedro's 2001 arrival:

> As Pedro left the Guatemalan airport, the police stopped him, told him to remove his shirt in the middle of the street, and interrogated him because of several visible tattoos. Pedro asserted that he had no gang affiliation and explained to the police that he worked in the United States in gang suppression. After further interrogation Pedro pleaded to speak with the U.S. Embassy. The police told him that now

that he was in Guatemala, nobody could help him. After an argument, the police arrested Pedro, took him to a jail in Villa Nueva, and continued his interrogation.

When Pedro refused to cooperate with the police in Villa Nueva, an officer arrived and began to beat him. Pedro asserted that he knew nothing about gangs in Guatemala, and the incensed officer then broke a soda bottle and slashed Pedro's upper arm and thigh. He lay bleeding in a cell for fourteen days, until the police put him in the back of a pickup truck, robbed him, and dumped him on the side of the highway. Fearing for his life, Pedro immediately began to make arrangements to return to the United States.[1]

Pedro's experience of being targeted as a suspected gang member and criminal after his deportation from the United States is echoed in the findings of scholars who study Central American migration. In another example, between 2006 and 2008 immigration scholar Susan Coutin conducted interviews in Southern California and El Salvador with Salvadoran migrants. Two of her interviewees, Francisco and Marcus, described to her the harassment they faced from police and the public on their return to El Salvador after having been deported from the United States:

MARCUS: I just get pulled over. All the time. Just getting arrested. Because the way I look. The way I dressed. The way probably I talk . . .

FRANCISCO: They call us gang bangers.

MARCUS: It's not usual to them here. . . . I used to get just disrespected from the police. Just pulled [over] from that. With not proper words. Just, "What the fuck are you doing here?"

FRANCISCO: We got beat up by the cops. Me and my two brothers [who were also deported]. They told us, "We don't want you deported guys here."[2]

In the realm of US policy, deportation has often been represented as an end point. Policymakers and political commentators have scapegoated immigrants for neoliberal economic collapse and presented the removal of immigrants as the solution to a range of societal ills. Once deported, they are no longer in the country and thus no longer a concern. However, for migrants deported from the United States, the arrival back in their home countries marks one point in a trajectory in which being labeled as a gang member or criminal alien is consequential. Individuals classified as gang members by US law enforcement may be subjected to violence by gangs, vigilantes, and government death squads as well as face social stigmatization and labor market exclusion, which in turn may once again necessitate migration.[3] As migrants are rejected or hunted by authorities from multiple countries, they take on a sort of statelessness, a fronterizo-like state of in-between.

The authors of the Georgetown Human Rights Action report and other scholars identify the mass deportations following the passage of the 1996 Illegal Immigration Reform and Immigrant Responsibility Act (IIRIRA) as a critical factor in aggravating the spread of gang violence in Central America. American-made gangs, such as MS-13 and 18th Street, capitalized on the post–civil war culture of fear and a weakened economic structure that left youth without many options in late twentieth-century Guatemala and El Salvador.[4] Similarly, destabilization caused by US-backed coups created conditions for the growth of *maras* in Honduras.[5]

Officials in Central America and the Caribbean have also used the late 1990s increase in deportations to blame deportees for rising crime rates and instances of violence that are likely unconnected to gangs or deportees. As is the case in the United States, gangs provide Central American government officials and the general public with a scapegoat, or as Elana Zilberg characterizes it, a "ritual repository" into which societal fears are hastily packed.[6] A singular focus on gangs allows officials to sidestep questions of direct state complicity, such as evidence that state security forces engage in criminal collaboration with gangs and participate in extrajudicial killings of suspected gang members, and structural causes of violence including government corruption and ineptitude, economic disparity, and legal inequality.[7]

Whatever the actual relationship between deportation and violence, representatives from Central America and the Caribbean have
sought to better identify returning citizens who have been classified
as criminal aliens or gang members during their time in the United
States. In response to demands from Latin American and Caribbean
authorities for photographs, criminal history information, and fingerprint data on criminal aliens, by 1997 the US government agreed
to provide at least three days' advance notice of a criminal alien's
return to their country of origin, accompanied by criminal conviction information. Despite these reforms, representatives from several countries, including Jamaica and Honduras, criticized the US
government for providing only the criminal history information
that was directly related to the incident that incited removal from
the country. Latin American and Caribbean representatives wanted
historically comprehensive, detailed criminal records from US local,
state, and federal law enforcement agencies.[8]

US policymakers and law enforcement have in turn sought criminal history information and surveillance tools to track previously
deported alleged gang members and drug traffickers in case of their
return to the United States. Over the years, US authorities have met
repeatedly with representatives from Mexico, Central America, and
the Caribbean to discuss collaborative anti-gang efforts, including
the development of shared training academies and cross-national
biometric databases.[9] The Criminal History Information Sharing
(CHIS) program, the focus of this chapter, is one of several initiatives
that grew out of data-sharing negotiations between the US government, the Mexican government, and governments in Latin America
and the Caribbean in the post-IIRIRA era. CHIS enables the surveillance of migrants, like Pedro, who have been labeled criminal or
dangerous in the United States and who travel the common migration route between the United States and Central America. Through
CHIS, Immigration and Customs Enforcement (ICE) extracts
information from databases, including the Enforcement Integrated
Database (EID) and TECS, and shares it with law enforcement in

other countries, some of whom in turn relay information back to US authorities.

MY BORDERLAND IS big blue sky splintered by aircraft. I grew up on silence and sonic booms. Hunks of metal streak through the air above me, flying out of Davis-Monthan Air Force Base to the east of Tucson and Barry M. Goldwater Air Force Range (a bombing range) to the west. There are even Marines in the dry air, searching the land below from up above as part of CBP's Air and Marine Operations division. From the north, out of ICE Air Operations in Mesa, Arizona, come Boeing 737s and MD-80s full of people hurtling toward the Caribbean, Central America, and South America. Like seemingly everything having to do with US immigration enforcement, air deportation has been privatized, shifting from the purview of the US Marshals Service to a network of planes chartered from corporate brokers. The contracts work like Russian dolls. Classic Air Charter has secured ICE's primary contract, but open it up and you will find that Classic Air Charter subcontracts other companies, including Swift Air and World Atlantic Airlines, for flights. The subcontractors then subcontract for the pilots, security guards, and medical personnel who make the flight possible.[10]

When all the money is sorted, a little over one hundred passengers shuffle onto a privately chartered plane in wrist, waist, and foot shackles that will be removed a few minutes before landing. If a chartered flight will not reach capacity, ICE sends people back on commercial flights. Guatemala is ICE Air's most frequent destination, followed by Honduras, El Salvador, Haiti, and the Dominican Republic. ICE Air also shuttles detainees between ICE field offices across the United States. Most deported Mexican nationals are flown as far as border cities, transferred to buses, and deposited on the other side.[11]

ICE is sending back forbidden people, and more than ever, sending back information in an effort to keep those people landlocked within the borders of their home countries. In July 2010 Department of Homeland Security (DHS) officials first announced that as part of the CHIS program, US immigration authorities planned to electronically share with the Mexican government criminal history and biometric (photographs and fingerprints) information from EID pertaining to repatriated Mexican nationals. Since the initiation of the program, DHS has expanded CHIS agreements to El Salvador, Guatemala, Honduras, Jamaica, the Dominican Republic, the Bahamas, and most recently, Cape Verde.[12] Raymond Villanueva, assistant director of international operations for Homeland Security Investigations, identified CHIS as a priority program slated for expansion to additional countries in the coming years as part of a larger focus on international information-sharing initiatives.[13]

The information that may be shared with foreign partners as part of the CHIS program consists of identifying numbers, name, alias, date of birth, city of birth, country of birth, mother's name, father's name, gender, gang flag, photographs, fingerprints, National Crime Information Center (NCIC) code(s) for the eighty-five crimes enumerated in the cooperation agreements, description of crime, and date of conviction.[14]

Although DHS announced the development of the CHIS program in 2010, it appears that the department did not begin to release CHIS notifications to foreign partners until 2014, when it expanded partnership agreements beyond Mexico. Between April 2014, when the first CHIS notifications were released, and September 2017, the last month for which I obtained data, CHIS notifications to partner countries hovered between roughly eight hundred and fourteen hundred per month. During both 2014 and 2015, notifications peaked near the fourteen hundred mark in October. For 2016 and 2017, the peak time for the release of notifications shifted to the summer.

By far the greatest proportion of CHIS notifications each year were distributed to the Mexican government, the original program partner. Although Mexico maintains the most CHIS notifications over the time period for which data is available, there is increasing

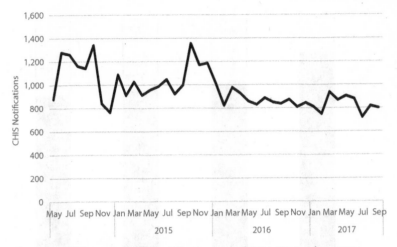

Figure 4. CHIS program total notifications, April 2014–September 2017.
Source: Data from analyzed FOIA requests.

diversity in the partner countries receiving notifications as the program progresses. Across all four years for which data is available, the Bahamas consistently received the fewest notifications, followed by Jamaica. The Dominican Republic, Honduras, Guatemala, and El Salvador progressively assumed slightly greater proportions of notifications over time.

THE BORDER IS a haunting thing. It calls people back repeatedly, and for the ones who do not come, it *follows*. Those who maintain borders are unsettled; they have a compulsion to push beyond the line drawn in the sand, to push the function of borders outward from physical border territory, to externalize border control.[15] Alan D. Bersin, commissioner of US Customs and Border Protection (CBP) during Obama's first term, articulated border externalization as a primary objective after September 11: "We began to understand that our borders begin not where our ports of entry are located, but rather, where passengers board air carriers and freight is loaded on maritime vessels bound for those ports of entry."[16] In this way,

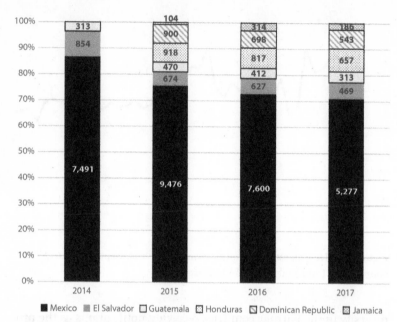

Figure 5. CHIS notifications by citizenship, 2014–2017. (Bahamas not visually represented due to low numbers: 0 notifications in 2014 and 2015; 49 notifications in 2016; 34 notifications in 2017.) Data for 2014 begins May 14, 2014; data for 2017 ends October 1, 2017. *Source:* Data from analyzed FOIA requests.

borders are an ending, a last line of defense rather than a first point of contact.[17]

US law enforcement agencies justify externalization through claims they are entitled to follow illegal activity, particularly gang activity, to its so-called geographical origins.[18] Of course, to conceptualize the movement of danger as something that originates in a foreign land and is brought by outsiders across US borders to victimize Americans is inaccurate. MS-13 and 18th Street—entities that have become the transnational bogeymen that the US government has thrown billions of dollars into chasing—are American made, and violence is exacerbated by the long-term effects of US exploitation of the Global South.

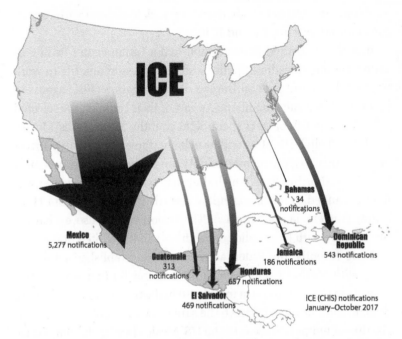

Map 4. Cartographic representation of CHIS notifications for most recent year of available data, January–October 2017. *Credit:* Nat Case, INCase, LLC.

The "war against gangs" nonetheless provides the engine for many of the US government's externalization efforts.[19] US officials have not only focused to this end on the US's southern border; they have also become entranced by Mexico's southern border. For decades, the US government has incentivized and coerced the Mexican government to strengthen controls on its border with Guatemala and Belize in order to disrupt Central American immigration routes to the United States. In 2001 the Mexican government, with assistance from the United States, kicked off Plan Sur, deploying hundreds of agents to its southern border and setting up new roadblocks and checkpoints. Additionally, through the Merida Initiative, the United States provides funding for Mexican biometrics initiatives and information systems.[20] DHS has also established academies in Mexico to train agents to work in concert with American counterparts in CBP and ICE.

In 2017 the United States established a fusion center in El Salvador to train Salvadoran police and immigration officials to work with US DHS and Federal Bureau of Investigation (FBI) agents to identify alleged gang members. As part of their training, the selected Salvadoran police officers spent eight months at the Texas-Mexico border to "help DHS, state and local law enforcement identify, arrest or deny entry to gang members."[21] At the US border, migrants meet the very authorities from which they may be fleeing. The center was later expanded to include criminal records information from Honduras, Guatemala, and Mexico. The fusion center also exchanges information with local police departments in the United States.

More recently, the Biden administration established an agreement with Mexico, Guatemala, and Honduras for increased border security in Central America in order to make the journey north more difficult for migrants. In much the same way the Clinton-era militarization of temperate areas of the US-Mexico border did not reduce migration but rather increased migrant death, attempts to militarize the southern Mexican and Central American borders have done less to stem migration than to push migrants into riskier and more remote routes.[22]

Externalization of US border control to Mexico's southern border has particular implications for African, Caribbean, and other Black migrants. As European countries have made immigrating more difficult, African migrants have made their way to South and Central America and attempted to enter the United States or Canada through Mexico.[23] Along the way, Black migrants are discriminated against and targeted by Mexican border officials, government workers, and residents.[24]

While the US government's land-based externalization efforts disproportionately target Mexican and Central American immigrants, in patrolling the maritime border the US Coast Guard has focused primarily on the interception of migrants who travel across the Caribbean.[25] Before becoming a site for the indefinite detention of prisoners from the war on terror, Guantanamo Bay was used to detain Haitian migrants intercepted at sea, preventing them from reaching US territory and triggering asylum and other protections. When Guantanamo overflowed, the Clinton administration established additional detention centers in Panama.[26]

It is not just ICE and CBP who engage in global policing. Similar to the constellation of local and federal agencies involved in racialized policing on the US-Mexico border and in internal borderland circuits throughout the United States, a variety of federal and local law enforcement agencies are involved in externalized enforcement. Since the 1970s, Drug Enforcement Administration (DEA), FBI, and DHS agents have regularly partnered with law enforcement in Mexico and Central America to target gang and drug trafficking activity.[27] Local law enforcement agencies from major US metropolitan areas have also increasingly engaged in international policing partnerships. The Los Angeles Police Department (LAPD) participates in law enforcement exchange programs in Central America to target criminal gangs. The New York Police Department (NYPD) deployed detectives overseas in the 1980s to investigate transnational organized crime families, and after September 11 to investigate terrorist suspects. The NYPD currently maintains ten overseas offices dedicated to anti-terrorism work.[28]

Digital surveillance and interoperability initiatives amplify externalization and represent a key objective of US immigration and domestic surveillance. Security companies like Raytheon and Boeing produce technology that is used by local police, federal law enforcement, and the US military against people in US cities, on the US-Mexico border, and in sites of American imperialism around the world.[29] In the process, the objectives, technology, and data of domestic policing, immigration control, homeland security, and military agencies converge.[30]

"SHE HAD A list." Luis rubs his hand over his chin and cringes at the memory. "It seemed like she had a list that was pre-prepared."

I return to Luis's LA office after weeks of driving around unfamiliar familiar places, deserts I used to know that are now unpredictable, crawling with newly deployed Border Patrol agents pushing past the one-hundred-mile border zone. A saguaro I once relied on as a marker to orient my internal compass, gone.

Luis's desert is an asylum office, and his gut-punch comes in the form of a list. He talks about a recent asylum interview gone awry, tries to make sense of it all. He has accompanied so many clients to asylum interviews over the years, and they all went roughly as expected:

> They [United States Citizenship and Immigration Services (USCIS) officers] always ask, "Have you ever participated or aided, abetted, etc., groups that hurt other people?" So that's a gang question. If the client admits that they were a gang member, it's a potential grounds of inadmissibility, because gangs are considered a group that harms other people, persecutors. It can make someone inadmissible if they admit to it. But they don't generally ask more gang questions unless gangs are in the narrative that the client tells.

But this one was different. This USCIS Officer opened a folder and pulled out a list. Then, going down the list of questions, she interrogated his client, a teenage girl from Central America named Karla, about her connection to gangs for forty-five minutes.[31] This interrogation was different, because of both its length and its content. The USCIS officer went far beyond the routine questions about Karla's possible gang involvement or her family members' and friends' possible participation in gang activity. No, this time it was expansive. The officer asked about gang members she'd seen in passing in her hometown and if she knew anything about the gang's hierarchy. How many people are in the gang? Had Karla or her family ever given money to the gang? Did she help the gang do things, even unwillingly? The officer asked about gangs in Karla's school and on her street in the United States. "It seemed more like intel-gathering," Luis says in a whisper, almost more to himself than to me.

If the USCIS officer who ground Karla down with a nearly hour-long gang interrogation discretionarily decides to categorize her as gang involved and reject her asylum claim, then Karla will most likely be loaded onto the privately chartered plane in shackles, with a digital record traveling in parallel to the authorities in her home country, advising them about her alleged gang connections. What might authorities in Mexico, Central America, and the Caribbean do with this information?

Some scholars and policy experts contend that sharing deported people's US-based criminal histories with the governments of their home countries might decrease precarity by assisting home governments in their efforts to support and reintegrate people upon their return.[32] There are indications, however, that authorities in Mexico, Central America, and the Caribbean use US-based criminal history information in less benevolent ways, namely for incapacitation, which can take several forms: incarceration or otherwise restricting a person's contact with the larger community or, in the most extreme form of incapacitation, capital punishment or death.

As the opening vignette of this chapter and a collection of journalistic and scholarly reporting make clear, upon return to their home countries, alleged criminal aliens and gang members have been hunted down, assaulted, and even killed at the hands of state police or civilian vigilantes.[33] In Haiti, "criminal deportees" have been immediately incarcerated upon return, sometimes indefinitely in prisons with harsh conditions and high death rates.[34] In sending labels that originate at the confluence of the racialized US criminal justice and immigration systems, the United States influences labeling and policing practices in other countries to potentially severe ends.

In sharing criminal history information as part of the CHIS program, US immigration authorities seek to enable deported migrants' incapacitation in their home countries, an act of *externalized incapacitation* that makes a return to the United States less likely. Externalized incapacitation is dependent on pressuring other countries to contain their own citizens and migrants passing through their territory. Coutin argues that in the process migrants' countries of origin become "places of confinement." After long periods in the United

States, people deported back to their countries of origin often remain on the cultural fringes, outsiders in the place they were born.[35] Borders thus both repel and contain. On both sides, those who manage borders gather their lists, and the interrogations begin.

Although US immigration authorities have framed deportation as a way of expelling unwanted elements from US territory, mass deportations, criminal labeling, and enhanced information sharing may have the opposite long-term effect. The global spread of punitive enforcement makes transnational migration more, not less, likely by aggravating conditions of precarity. The policing of non-White immigrants by local law enforcement in the United States results in the detention, classification, and forced return of people to their home countries, where the label of criminal alien or alleged gang member may cause someone to face restricted opportunities or violence. Consequently, deported individuals are forced to seek opportunities again through migration, often back into the United States, where the process begins anew.[36] As a result of the cycle of violent policing, migration, more violent policing, detention, deportation, violent policing, migration, and so on, people who try to move across borders become permanently beholden to borders. They are precariously placed, subject to state violence yet excluded from safety nets and protection.

I hope that the USCIS officer who interrogated Karla does not put her back into this cycle. I hope Karla gets asylum, constructs her life as she envisions, and is not subject to incapacitation or confinement. Luis, of course, also hopes so. Aside from Karla's particular case, the list, it bothers him: the unfamiliar familiarity of that asylum interview, the ambush of the gang interrogation, the intelligence-gathering nature of it. He tries to imagine where each piece of information goes and how it might affect his clients down the line, either in the United States or in their home countries: the notations scribbled down by the USCIS officer going into some database somewhere, waiting like a time bomb.

PEDRO APPLIED FOR asylum too. After US immigration agents detained him for the second time, in Texas in 2007, he spent two years in jail for illegal reentry, a charge leveled against people who enter the United States again, without authorization, after having been previously deported or denied admission. Illegal reentry was one of the many punitive additions packaged in the 1996 IIRIRA legislation that dramatically increased criminal immigration prosecutions, detention, and deportations. Pedro served a criminal sentence of two years in jail, then another four years in immigration detention. Unlike Karla, who has Luis to guide her, Pedro could not find a lawyer. He launched an asylum bid on his own; it was not successful. US immigration agents put Pedro on a plane and returned him to Guatemala, to a country that was largely foreign to him, a country that last received him with jagged glass.[37] The United States offered no reprieve; this is, after all, a country of wall building, both material and digital.

Pedro's fate is unknown to me after the point at which Georgetown Human Rights Action researchers interviewed him at the Guatemala City air force base after his deportation in 2007. If he returned to the United States again and was detained, it is likely that upon his return to Guatemala, the US government shared his information with Guatemalan authorities as part of CHIS. And there is yet another dimension to this story: the Guatemalan government may also have sent information pertaining to Pedro back to US law enforcement agencies.

In addition to sending data abroad, US law enforcement encourages foreign partners to reciprocally "share with DHS criminal history information for these same aliens who have been convicted of the same or equivalent felonies in the partner's country, and DHS will enter this information into the alien's EID record."[38] US authorities will then map the criminal history information onto a "matrix" that translates the criminal convictions from foreign countries into equivalent convictions in the US legal code.[39] The matric represents DHS's attempt at not only technological interoperability but also legal and cultural interoperability.[40]

The in-kind information from foreign partners will help ICE to "create a more comprehensive criminal history database for these aliens" and "assist DHS in making more informed decisions about aliens' custody, detention, and over-all risk to public safety and security while they remain in ICE custody or if they return to ICE custody in the future."[41] In the case of a migrant's return to the United States, ICE could use this information for the risk assessment processes covered in chapter 4 or to share with local and state law enforcement, either through the Law Enforcement Notification System (LENS) or through other gang-intelligence-sharing mechanisms.

Based on data I have obtained, Mexico and the new partner country, Cape Verde, did not actively send information to ICE during the period for which I attained data on the program (2014–2017).[42] The Bahamas and Jamaica have sent very few records to US authorities; each country sent two incoming records in 2016 and none in any other of the years for which I obtained data. Guatemala, El Salvador, the Dominican Republic, and Honduras, however, are substantively participating, dispatching thousands of records that include biographical and criminal information, including gang allegations.

The governments of El Salvador and Honduras in particular emerged early on as the leaders in sending incoming information. In 2015, the first year during which CHIS partner countries began to send incoming information to the United States, El Salvador sent 874 records. The next year El Salvador sent criminal records pertaining to 4,846 of its citizens to US authorities. In 2015 Honduras sent records pertaining to 8,601 of its citizens to the United States; in 2016, it sent 18,844 such records.

CHIS is a relatively new program, having substantively started in 2014 when ICE began to send information back with deported people. Since then, the US government has progressively expanded the amount of information exchanged as well the countries with whom it is exchanged. It is likely that DHS and ICE will continue to invest in these programs, attempting to increase the likelihood that officials in other countries will collaborate in externalized incapacitation while building dossiers on migrants should they continue to try to migrate to the United States.

THE CIRCUITS ARE nearly complete. They spread inward and are thrown outward into the south. Deserts freeze, the sea rises to take back cities, and people flee. Madmen oversee burning nations. The price of eggs and corn flour skyrockets. Time moves faster. People go hungry and then they flee, and the interrogations begin. The list of questions grows longer. The databases bulge. The police meet in a theme park conference room. Border guards set their snares. Politicians take pictures in the borderlands. The mountains are so big and the sky, it screams blue. The Wall looks bigger than I remember. The circuits flicker.

8 A Hand Searches for a Root

I CATCH MY jaw grinding the enamel from my teeth. I feel my neck
locking into my shoulders. So, I am going back out into the light.
I am going back out into the desert. In the late morning, the warm
sun collides with the cold air, shifting the proportion of each until
the warmth wins. The metallic blade of a bulldozer scythes through
saguaro flesh in Organ Pipe Cactus National Monument. Everything
nearby is absorbed in its rotation. I thought it was a felony to kill a
saguaro, but here they are, severed arms tumbling to the ground. A
distinct borderland culture is being destroyed, and I am left with a
map to a land that does not exist anymore. It causes me some sort of
geo-emotional disorientation.

It is November 2019, and the US government has picked a contractor to build The Wall, several actually. Southwest Valley Con-
structors Co. received a combined $891 million from the Pentagon
to dynamite forty-three miles of Organ Pipe and replace it with a
wall. For an additional $408 million, Southwest Valley Constructors
Co. also took the San Pedro River, the ancient lifeblood of Southern

Arizona. Fisher Sand & Gravel Co. took $268 million and the thrill of violating Cabeza Prieta National Wildlife Refuge with thirty-one miles of wall. BFBC, LLC pilfered $381.2 million to bleed the Colorado River and the edges of the Reserva de la Biosfera El Pinacate y Gran Desierto de Altar.[1]

The land is so beautiful and the demolition so shattering that together they cut and soothe in almost imperceptible succession: a split followed by an immediate salve followed by another split. Monsoons and other storm systems offer temporary reprieve, blowing sections of The Wall onto its side and eroding the soil beneath.[2] Call it La Llorona's revenge, foreseen by Gloria Anzaldúa: "To show the white man what she thought of his arrogance, *Yemaya* blew that wire fence down."[3] Nonetheless, despite the fight of the land and its people, it seems, at least for now, that political and law enforcement leaders have successfully deployed the specter of violent cross-border criminals and gang members to justify the destruction of land for border militarization.

Similar events unfurl in myriad locations around the world where territorial borders are etched across forests, flood plains, iced peaks, rivers, sand dunes, and city streets. One morning there is barbed wire freshly strung like horrifying Christmas lights through main squares, playgrounds, and cemeteries. During some witching hour the night before, soldiers set out armed with posts, steel wire, and a mandate to draw a line and reinforce it. People awake to find themselves on one side or the other, and a new life begins. Then, over its lifespan, the boundary metastasizes into a heavily guarded concrete or steel barrier and, for reasons unfathomable to me, lots of people come to respect it as legitimate. It is an old story, tiresome really: a demarcation, some people in uniforms, orders to break beautiful things. Then the deracination, inspection, categorization, and filtering, cold batons and interrogations, the pat downs with a hand sliding over an ass or down a shirt, the simultaneous abandonment and ceaseless hunting down.[4] There is little creativity in the imaginings of the powerful; the denouements are alarmingly predictable across time and space, if only with slight variations in degree.

In the US-Mexico borderlands, and many other borderlands, people risk their lives to get from one side to the other. A criticism of border walls is that they are ultimately relatively ineffectual at preventing border crossing. Over, under, around: people find a way, and death dissuades few. I see blunt effectiveness, however, as a fairly peripheral function of this piece of architecture. Rather, the power of The Wall is the cruel symbolism of its message. The US-Mexico border wall is a monolith of White supremacy and of the supremacy of the Global North, an anti-beacon warning outsiders to turn back because there is no shelter for you here. The more visible, the more imposing, the better. The physical barrier and the accompanying searches and interrogations, the violence that happens here, remind people that they are outsiders; it reinforces their identities of non-belonging.[5] The Wall also serves as a constant warning to marginal insiders that they can easily be rendered foreign if the current political modality calls for it.

Just as border wall construction is the architecture of White supremacy, this book provides a partial map of the technological infrastructure building of White supremacy, a machine horror. As the militarization of the border has expanded, so has the invisible circuitry that haunts criminalized subjects. The less visible, the less imposing, the better.

In addition to wall contractors, the US government has selected tech contractors—Palantir, Amazon, Booz Allen Hamilton, Northrop Grumman, Dev Technology Group, SRA International—to build digital surveillance systems that will reinforce already existing borders, deterritorialize traditional border control methods, construct new borderlands, and construct immigrants and US-born people of color as dangerous. In turn, border militarization contractors will engorge the campaign coffers of drum-beating electeds.

Surveillance technology facilitates the functional expansion of border.[6] Programs like the Law Enforcement Notification System

(LENS) and regionally interconnected gang databases create a circuit of geographically internal borderlands. Initiatives like the Criminal History Information Sharing (CHIS) program allow for border externalization without having to dispatch personnel to other countries. Borderland circuitry both hardens borders in the name of national security and expands the US sphere of control outside US borders, not through acquisition of new physical territory but rather through information exchange and extraterritorial surveillance.

Linked by interoperable circuitry, multiple policing jurisdictions participate in controlling the movement of people of color within US territory as well as controlling the entry of non-White people into the country. Examining multiple institutions of state violence—local police, state law enforcement, immigration enforcement, federal law enforcement, intelligence services, and military agencies—widens the framework and offers a method to examine a range of strategies of racialized spatial containment, banishment, and forced movement. These dynamics can include, for example, police clearing groups of youth of color from US city streets under anti-loitering ordinances; federal law enforcement clearing large groups of racialized immigrants from the country; and the forced displacement (enforced by local and county law enforcement) of poor people as a result of gentrification, development, and eviction. The forced movement and containment of criminalized people has long been integral to the police function, and it is now facilitated by interoperable digital surveillance technology.

It is important to recognize that although this book focuses predominantly on formal information-sharing agreements, even when US local, state, and federal law enforcement agencies do not officially engage in joint enforcement, they work toward the same ends because they are united by a framework of racialized state violence. Local police, for example, indirectly engage in immigration policing in the course of their daily work through the disproportionate policing of non-White and immigrant neighborhoods. Immigration agents reinforce the racial power structure through racialized enforcement against immigrants from certain regions. Furthermore, as we saw so clearly in the dispatching of federal agents (many of whom were Border Patrol agents) to Portland, Chicago, and Albuquerque in response to Black Lives Matter protests in the summer of 2020, immigration and homeland security agents quite literally engage in domestic policing.

Speaking specifically to the surveillance of Blackness, Simone Browne argues that spectacle and insidious discipline are both instrumental in racialized surveillance. This dynamic is visible on the border and beyond, as the spectacular visibility of The Wall, the cops, and the brutality works in concert with the invisible surveillance circuitry that spreads far and wide. The visible and the invisible feed off one another, each made stronger by the other and always searching for more targets.

WITH THE BULLDOZERS, that is it; there is no home to which to return. What is there to do next but to push the saguaro arms aside momentarily and pick up the blueprints? This book is full of maps, and they will change; they probably already have. But they tell us something deeper than the momentary empiricism they cartographically communicate. In examining the archaeology of law enforcement technology, we can deduce certain preferences. First, law enforcement, on the federal level most clearly, is moving toward centralized data systems. ICEGangs, a failure of a database, is one example of boutique databases being cast aside in favor of larger general databases like TECS and the Enforcement Integrated Database/Enforcement Case Tracking System (EID/ENFORCE), in which immigration authorities can centralize an array of information on any given person.

Information sharing and interoperability are also priorities for law enforcement at the local, state, and federal levels. Legacy data systems, like TECS, have been substantially refurbished to permit up-to-date information sharing between federal law enforcement agencies as well as with local, state, and international partners. On the local and state levels too, law enforcement agencies seek to maximize information-sharing capacity.

But these circuits, they flicker. Rather than a utopia of smoothly flowing interconnected technology, there are constant bumps. When we look inside law enforcement agencies, what we often see is not seamless coordination but rather a mix of competence and incompetence. Things often do not go to plan. For example, sometimes the CHIS notifications released from Immigration and Customs Enforcement (ICE) enter a black hole because the authorities on the other side do not have an information system that is capable of importing the information. US law enforcement agencies have difficulty getting on the same page as foreign partners who do not have parallel technological systems, legal systems, capacity, or will, despite US-funded efforts to build capacity in Central America and the Caribbean.

Additionally, despite attempts to establish a web of internal borders, there are continuous issues with CalGang connectivity to partner agencies. CalGang administrators' notes are full of the phrase "Still working on connectivity issues." During the lifespan of ICE-Gangs, as a result of interoperability glitches CalGang administrators often conducted data dumps to ICE instead of enjoying real-time information sharing. On top of it all, ICEGangs was supposed to revolutionize federal gang intelligence gathering but instead crashed and burned.

The surveillance state is a bumbling evil and a banal one at that.[7] Sifting through the archives of an atrocity in motion is not an encounter with fiery manifestos. Rather, the concerns at hand are copies that need to be made and PowerPoint presentations that need to be finished. The archives of this atrocity are filled with routine email exchanges like one I obtained, for example, between various ICE personnel that goes on for thirty-five pages, with everyone unsure about what to do with all of the information in the recently decommissioned ICEGangs Database.

Grand dreams of omnipresent surveillance are always just out of reach, yet the power of the vision explodes worlds, shatters cities; it draws the lines on the field within which we are forced to live.[8] A lot of things do not work as planned, most of the daily work is bureaucratic and seemingly bloodless, and yet somehow, it adds up to more than the sum of the parts: something big and horrible and messy that destroys so many people's lives.

The resulting precarity is stunning. Gang allegations and other criminal labels make immigrants more vulnerable to heavy policing, brutality, detention, and deportation. Immigrants affected by borderland circuitry within the United States are simultaneously subjected to policing and excluded from benefits like Deferred Action for Childhood Arrivals (DACA). Sandro Mezzadra and Brett Neilson refer to this as a process of "differential inclusion," whereby people are not completely excluded and expelled from society but rather are technically included in the body politic, yet with caveats. Nicolas De Genova similarly posits that inclusion through "illegalization" both subjugates and incorporates migrants into the labor market.[9] Immigrants are thus able to stay in the country, but only under specific, subpar conditions that benefit capitalist accumulation and slot them into subordinate racial hierarchies.[10]

US citizens too can move into a state of "irregularized" citizenship as a result of racialization or criminalization, wherein they are denied the rights to which they are entitled.[11] Racialized and criminalized native-born people thus face internal borders, differential inclusion, and increased precarity. Alleged gang members who are US citizens have their worlds cabined as they are pushed inside their homes and out of public spaces in an effort to avoid police harassment. They may lose employment opportunities as a result of background checks that uncover their names in CalGang and other databases. The threat of a decade-long gang enhancement may pressure an alleged gang member to accept a plea deal out of fear of going to trial and battling a gang allegation, even if the allegation is extremely questionable.

Another thing we can see is that key to the regime of state surveillance and violence is the diffusion of categorizations of criminality and danger. As punitive control and surveillance technology have diffused from the border to the territorial interior and exterior, criminalizing categories have also diffused to larger groups of people. The desecration of both bodies and ecosystems proceeds because for decades policymakers, political commentators, anti-immigration activists, and immigration enforcement personnel have vilified and dehumanized large swaths of people. "Neither random accidents nor natural disasters produce the death of noncitizen border-crossers in this terrain," Gilberto Rosas argues with eloquent directness. "They happen because states and governments designate certain groups to the racialized category of illegal."[12] They *choose* to make a beautiful land ugly with bulldozers and blood.

THE VILIFICATION TACTICS are cliché but effective, as cliché things often are, and while they happen with or without digital databases, the development of advanced surveillance technology adds new dimensions. Law enforcement deploys technology in such a way as to optimize the number of targets and to justify enforcement. Department of Homeland Security (DHS) and ICE have developed mass surveillance systems that consolidate secondary information to more easily ensnare people's data and bodies in a brutal system. Giving routine personal information to the Department of Motor Vehicles, a health provider, or a child's school becomes a high-risk act that eventually results in the identification of "deportable" people. A benefit of secondary information collection for law enforcement is that it is noninvasive. Unlike when an officer collects information directly from someone by questioning them, when law enforcement nonconsensually pulls an individual's information from another database, that person may be none the wiser. The less obtrusive, the less noticeable, the more intrusive, the better.

ICE uses semiautomated programs like the Risk Classification Assessment and ICE Level analysis to label as many people as possible a safety or flight risk and thus increase detentions and deportations. Since 2016 in particular, there have been steep increases in the

number of immigrants discretionarily classified as gang members or
as "criminal" based on charges, arrests, and discretionary decisions
that have not been adjudicated. These sleights of hand allowed the
Trump administration to claim that the number of immigrant gang
members and criminal aliens is steeply increasing when really the
government had changed the way gang membership and criminality
is categorized in order to maximize the optics of threat. Once a criminalized category has been legitimized, law enforcement and policymakers can expand the category to other populations, thus enabling
enhanced enforcement actions against more people.[13]

Notably, the mechanisms of spatial control and the methods of
classification that I cover in this book are based on procedures that
lack markers of due process. For example, gang allegations enable
law enforcement to harass and detain people without ever charging
them with a crime, and immigration proceedings are exempt from
basic protections that are present (albeit inadequately) in the criminal justice system, including compulsory legal defense, protection
against self-incrimination, and restrictions on hearsay and illegally
obtained evidence.[14] In the field, immigration agents are allowed to
consider race and ethnicity in deciding whether or not to stop someone, increasing opportunities for federal law enforcement to target
non-White immigrants.[15]

Many of the procedurally problematic aspects of the immigration system have their antecedents in the US government's early
attempts at racialized spatial control. For example, to achieve the
provisions of the Fugitive Slave Law of 1850, the US government
constructed a large federal bureaucracy dedicated to the detainment
and forced movement of people based on race. Years later, beginning most notably with the race-based exclusion of Chinese laborers,
this bureaucracy would provide the conceptual model for the contemporary deportation system in the United States.[16] As a result of
this genealogy, the ensnarement is not equal opportunity but rather
directed at racialized immigrants from Latin America, the Caribbean,

the Middle East, Southeast Asia, and Africa. As Kunal Parker points out, Latin American and Caribbean immigrants are being removed from the country through deportation as native-born Black and Latino people are removed from society through imprisonment.[17] There are multiple ways to disappear people.

Ruha Benjamin reminds us that race itself is a technology, "a kind if tool—one designed to stratify and sanctify social injustice as part of the architecture of everyday life."[18] While the digital technology is becoming more complex, the data collection more voluminous, and the classifications of dangerousness more frequent, the racialized categorizations themselves remain simplistic. The gang member label, for example, is a land largely without topographic variation. It presents a binary model in which one is or is not a gang member and once initiated into the racialized category, it will be nearly impossible to get out. Whatever the complex form of data analysis, the outcome is stark, archaic, and hinges on racialization: criminal/noncriminal, good/bad, insider/outsider.[19]

The Trump administration was particularly eager to eat up information, package it, and spit it back out in ways that vilify part of the populace and terrify another part, but people in power have always collected and *performed* data to support their narratives. The Obama administration targeted "felons, not families" (as if these two things are mutually exclusive) by directing ICE to prioritize the detention and deportation of "high-risk" immigrants, criminal aliens, and alleged gang members. In the process, the good/bad immigrant split was further solidified under the nefarious assumption that the criminal justice system provided a neutral assessment of danger or worth. Under the Obama administration, gang profiling and risk assessment became ingrained into the enforcement and administrative arms of the immigration system. The Trump administration then hyperaccelerated the expansive application of the gang member label and other categorizations of danger that had already been legitimized during the Obama years.

The sacrifice of people deemed dangerous or criminal offers a bipartisan middle ground that permits a retreat from true challenges to dehumanization. Instead, the atrocities can recommence with a clear conscience. It is highly likely then that the bulk of these practices will continue largely unchanged under the Biden administration and future Democratic administrations, with the exception that the horror will be less explicit. Once criminalization has been sanctioned and unleashed, it has no boundaries. ICE has an enforcement compulsion, as do all law enforcement agencies. Power eats everything, then looks for more.

Scholars have traced how Western authorities have used surveillance and the criminal categorization of surveillance subjects for the purposes of Foucauldian discipline and more recently for the purposes of regulation and banishment.[20] More than that, though, we are faced with an immigration regime that categorizes people as dangerous in order to engage in large-scale horror for its own sake: officers and doctors in detention centers reportedly committing forced hysterectomies, sexual assaults, and torture; Border Patrol agents shooting young people in the back of the head; a state that disappears children; bureaucrats who are rewarded for sending a teenage girl back into a civil war.[21] This is a regime of bodily horror that springs from disembodied data flows.[22]

Do NOT LET the catchphrases obscure the reality. While current law enforcement practices may be efficient and technology driven, technology is created and programmed by people and thus, in the hands of law enforcement, it has functioned in service of the destruction of flesh: human, plant, and animal alike.

The Risk Classification Assessment described in chapter 5, for example, has bestowed a technical face on a devastatingly corporeal detention process in which people are raped, exposed to harsh chemicals, denied medical care, and left to die.[23] ICE and DHS personnel characterize a technological tool like EID as an active agent doing all sorts of things, seemingly on its own: retrieving criminal history information, automatically populating it into the Risk Classification Assessment, using business rules to produce a detention recommendation. But *people* are behind all of it. Police on the street target, harass, brutalize, and arrest people of color to create the criminal record in the first place. ICE and Border Patrol agents stalk and arrest immigrants according to a practice of legally sanctioned racial profiling. Law enforcement officers make subjective assessments and classify people of color as gang members based on stereotypes or even fabricated evidence. The racialized data is then put into databases, where it becomes legitimate, reliable information. Once the data reaches immigration detention, ICE officers and private contractors ultimately make the assessments that confine people to horrific detention conditions. ICE has used the cleansing bath of technology to make the brutality and death appear clean and neutral, but an automated computer program does not do any of these things.

Legal scholar Margaret Hu demonstrates that in the context of immigration and national security, wherein courts often defer to government discretion, the federal judiciary is unlikely to rule in favor of constitutional challenges to categorizations in databases, particularly when it (mis)understands algorithms, automation, and risk classifications to be unbiased tools. Hu goes on to point out that the discrimination that results from new surveillance may not be characterized by the "traditional" markers that courts are used to looking for ("discrimination on the basis of a historically protected class, for instance, race, color, ethnicity, national origin, and sex"). Rather, suspicious people will be characterized by "foreignness." In addition to illustrating that judges are buying ICE's claims that its technologically assisted categorization process is unbiased, Hu indirectly makes two points. First is that rendering people literally or conceptually "foreign" is central to the current regime of state violence. Second, Hu's analysis makes clear that what is constitutional is not the same as what is just.[24] Something else, then, besides constitutional challenges and reforms, is required of us. To understand what that may be, let us pull back into a wider shot for a moment.

ON MARCH 22, 2021, JOURNALIST Cerise Castle released, via the outlet Knock LA, the first in a multipart series about gangs in the Los Angeles County Sheriff's Department (LASD). According to the series, the sheriff's deputies who are part of gangs in the department have tattoos that identify them with their specific set. They flash gang signs to one another and have engaged in violent behavior together, including beating jail inmates and killing people on the street. Even though these groups of deputies meet the STEP ACT definition of a gang, LASD spokespeople insist they are "cliques" or "subgroups." Despite LASD's rhetorical gymnastics, Cerise Castle dared to do what scholar Elana Zilberg has also done: point out that a not insignificant number of cops engage in the same horrific behavior they claim to fight, that they can be "the biggest gang of all," and that there is something rotten at the core of policing.[25]

On April 20, 2021, about a month after the series was published, Cerise Castle was detained by the LASD while covering an LASD press conference, joining the scores of journalists across the country who have had their press credentials disregarded by law enforcement. Over the past couple of years, police at protests in several cities across the nation have targeted journalists with batons, rubber bullets, tear gas, and arrest, with increasing frequency.[26] ICE has also targeted journalists for retaliation.[27] This is a bad sign.

In addition to targeting journalistic coverage of protests, state legislatures are targeting the very act of protesting. The day before Cerise Castle was detained in Los Angeles, the Florida State Legislature created a new crime, that of "mob intimidation" to characterize (leftist) protesters as violent looters and rioters. In response to the widespread and persistent protests sparked by the murder of George Floyd, the Florida law, among other things, enhances punishment for protesters who block roadways and denies bail to anyone arrested at a protest. Antiprotest legislation appears to be spreading across the United States. Several states have introduced bills that give immunity to drivers who run over protesters.[28] These are dark omens of what is to come.

At one point during the protests of the summer of 2020, people in Portland, Oregon, reported that "men in green military fatigues and generic 'police' patches" pulled up in unmarked vans, then detained and searched them. They were then taken to another location and after refusing to answer questions, released, still unsure of who had abducted them. US Customs and Border Protection (CBP) soon after clarified that the balaclava-clad men in fatigues jumping out of vans were their own agents, specifically from the Border Patrol Tactical Unit (BORTAC).[29] The United States has traditionally deemed domestic policing to be a local affair, done by municipal police and state law enforcement. Nonetheless, in the summer of 2020 a shadowy collection of federal agents, many of whom were trained as immigration, homeland security, and border control agents, acted more like a national police force, specifically an unidentified police force that appeared to detain people engaging in political activity that challenged their power. In US cities, these agents use military technology and weaponry against protesters that was initially developed for use in America's forever wars overseas.[30]

Suppression of a free press, the illegalization of protest, and abductions of people off the streets by an unidentified armed unit: these are very bad signs. In casual conversation, I hear people compare the current political moment in the United States to 1930s Germany or to the beginning of the dirty war in 1970s Argentina wherein a broad range of people considered to be "dissidents" were disappeared to detention centers, leaving the larger populous with a destabilizing sense of horror and uncertainty. While there are shades of European fascism and US-backed South American dictatorships, whatever emerges here will be a distinctly US phenomenon, with law enforcement agencies as radicalizing White supremacist incubators.[31]

Along these lines, in addition to staying vigilant about local police actions, the evolution of our immigration, border control, and homeland security agencies—specifically their adoption of new policing roles—should be watched closely in the next decade. It was no surprise to me that it was immigration and homeland security agents who pulled protesters into unmarked vans and absconded with them to clandestine interrogation sites. DHS, ICE, and CPB agents are well-versed in administering apparatuses of large-scale suffering. They have separated children from their parents, lost those children, been accused of abusing and letting children die, and reportedly allowed doctors to remove women's uteruses without consent, amid many other horrific acts.[32] This training in the inhuman is difficult to contain.

US immigration and homeland security agencies (as well as domestic policing agencies in their current form) are incompatible with a truly democratic society and a liberated people. ICE, DHS, and CBP leadership, as well as some large number of frontline officers, have become thoroughly entrenched in far right ideology. Both the ICE and Border Patrol unions endorsed Donald Trump for president, and DHS and ICE leadership campaigned for his reelection. Thousands of Border Patrol officers maintain a racist and sexist private Facebook page.[33] Furthermore, these agencies are incredibly nontransparent and unaccountable. As I expand on in the methodological appendix, immigration and homeland security agencies have experienced unchecked growth in their power and budgets while remaining exempt from transparency and oversight requirements.

Immigration agents have greater latitude than do other law enforcement officers in the extent to which they are allowed to consider race and ethnicity in deciding whether or not to stop someone. Border Patrol agents have the exceptional ability to engage in search and seizure without probable cause or a warrant. They are essentially exempt from key components of the Constitution, and according to James Tomsheck, former chief of internal affairs with US CBP, they take this to heart. In 2020, Tomsheck told The Intercept's Ryan

Devereaux: "Border Patrol brings to the position a strong paramilitary self-identity, believing they are not restrained by the same constitutional restraints placed upon all of law enforcement."[34]

As these federal agencies, as well as local and state law enforcement agencies, continue to ratchet up the political repression, watch for the gang member label to become an even more important tool. For example, in prosecuting Black Lives Matter protesters, prosecutors in certain jurisdictions have charged protesters with gang enhancements and entered them into databases as gang members associated with the "ACAB" (All Cops Are Bastards) gang.[35] Chicago's gang database lists the Black Panthers as a violent criminal street gang, a conflation of racialized "criminal deviance" and "political deviance." Police and prosecutors are using gang allegations explicitly for political persecution. We should also understand, however, that gang allegations, even when applied in contexts that are not so boldly dedicated to the suppression of free speech and political activity, are still a form of racialized political persecution that reinforces a White supremacist system. Resisting the criminalization of people through the category of gang member thus contributes to the fight against authoritarianism and the broad attack on speech.

THE PAST FEW pages may seem like a digression, but I assure you they are not. When we talk about policing, border building, and surveillance nothing less than life and death is at stake. Therefore I find it difficult, standing in the middle of the horror wrought by authoritarian violence, to believe in the capacity of reformist policies to pose a formidable challenge to White supremacy or authoritarianism or to think that surveillance powers can be harnessed "to make policing more just and equitable."[36] I do not believe that what we see in the world is the result of misguided, benign lawmakers and law enactors, which can be fixed with technocratic solutions. Rather, what the work of race scholars like Ruha Benjamin and Simone Browne teaches us is that policing and surveillance is inherently raced and therefore its practice repeatedly, inevitably, results in anti-Blackness. This is what it is supposed to do.

Remaining beholden to the "pull of the policy audience" encourages a certain conceptual narrowness.[37] As a result, some scholars focus on strengthening surveillance systems by taking on small reforms like, for example, the issue of inaccuracy. These scholars lament the flaws in automated information systems that lead to the targeting of "countless innocents," such that even "people with no criminal record, who have done no wrong and have nothing to hide may yet have much to fear."[38]

While the potential for erroneous information is distressing, a disproportionate focus on technological error capitulates to the oppressive politics endemic to the classification of people as criminal. It is not that concerns about inaccuracy are bad, but they are, as Harsha Walia writes about the related concern with establishing innocence, limiting political stances.[39] If we could create a perfectly accurate database, with no errors, then what? We are still left with the questions of whether this surveillance bureaucracy should exist, whether a violent immigration detention and deportation system should exist, whether policing should take the form it does, and whether deportation policy should be based on criminal records produced by an abominable criminal justice system. I propose we start with the big questions.

Other scholars have taken to arguing that more surveillance is needed because more information can lead police to rely less on stereotypes that link crime, age, race, gender, and other characteristics to criminality, thus more objectively differentiating "honors students" from "dropouts with long rap sheets" or a "gangbanger" from a "grandmother."[40] Yet a long rap sheet is not a neutral document but rather is built through contact with a racist criminal justice system. Nor is "gang member" a neutral categorization but rather one that is arrived at through vague, highly racialized classification criteria. Unfortunately, the liberal practice of criminalization-for-some paired with salvation-for-others has been supported not only by groups of scholars

but also by moderate reformist sectors of the immigrant rights movement that support enforcement against alleged gang members and
criminal aliens. These movement sectors seek to identify who is *really*
criminal so that, for instance, immigration detention no longer "com-
mingles immigrants with *actual* criminals in state and local jails."[41]

The problem with this perspective is that there exists no *actual*
criminal, no objective label, because criminality is a politically driven
concept constructed by people in power. Law enforcement does not
simply react to threats but rather actively defines certain populations as criminal and records this information to justify continued
social control.[42] Furthermore, there is ultimately no salvation. As
policymakers recalibrate the net to cover broader swaths of immigrants, criminalization rears back to bite even those who thought
themselves safe.

TECHNOCRATIC APPROACHES ARE incapable of opposing the behemoth of surveillance and brutality with which we find ourselves
faced. In fact, narrow reforms may actually strengthen it. The dis-
tinction between "reformist reforms" and "nonreformist abolitionist reforms" is instructive here.[43] The former do not fundamentally
challenge unequal social, political, and economic arrangements.
Rather, isolated moderate reforms constitute a public relations strategy wherein law enforcement organizations and their supporters
seek to pacify oppositional movements while leaving untouched the
larger structural arrangements that ensure the violent subjugation of
marginalized peoples. An abolitionist reform, in contrast, "advances
reform as a strategy or tactic toward transformation, rather than an
end in itself."[44] Legal scholar Amna A. Akbar argues that abolition
"pushes us to reconceive reform not as an end goal, but as a strategy
for broader transformation. In an abolitionist horizon, policing is
an obstacle to—not a tool for—achieving a just society. Thus, abolitionist thinking reorients reform projects away from improving the
police to limiting police power and the space in which it operates."[45]
Abolition also requires us to think about what transformations are

needed across the social structure in order to render law enforcement obsolete.[46]

Take my local law enforcement agency, the Los Angeles Police Department (LAPD), as an example of the repeated pitfalls of reformist reforms. After the LAPD maimed several protesters in the summer of 2020, using batons, foam and sponge bullets, and beanbag projectiles, LA city councilmember Joe Buscaino, a former police officer, boasted, "The LAPD is already the most reformed department in our nation."[47] In March 2021, only a couple of weeks after oversight reports criticized the LAPD's approach to the summer 2020 protests, the most reformed department in the nation once again used batons and projectiles against houseless people and their allies encamped at Echo Park Lake.[48] As I write the final draft of this book in the late summer of 2021, I take a break to watch a video of an LAPD officer firing a beanbag projectile into someone at point blank range during a trans rights protest.[49]

The thing is, Joe Buscaino is right, just not in the way he thinks. *This* is the legacy of reform. The pattern holds true: every few years, the general public becomes outraged about police brutality and corruption. Each time, the LAPD swears to have instituted the most robust police reform package in history. The department receives an infusion of resources for its bad behavior. Only a short time later, officers again violate more people, and a new crop (or sometimes, the same old crop) of experts steps in who are convinced that they have the right reforms, the keys that will fix all of this. It is almost as if the police are aware that they can spark chaos, brutalize people of color and the poor, and instead of receiving punishment, use these acts as a rationalization to increase their budgets and level of militarization, with the support of academic experts.[50]

While this example focuses on LAPD, the same can be said of police departments across the nation as well as federal law enforcement agencies. The LAPD, ICE, CBP, and others are not organizations to be partnered with as part of problem-solving policing initiatives; these types of initiatives cannot make what are essentially illegitimate and antidemocratic law enforcement agencies into democratic institutions. Furthermore, through collaborations between academics and law enforcement, public educational institutions fund already bloated police departments at the cost of local communities and community organizations. Hurting Black people and Indigenous people and poor people and queer people and immigrants is endemic to the work law enforcement agencies do, and so they must have their power and budgets removed.

Abolitionists have long warned about tinkering with ineffective, unambitious, and unimaginative reforms as the world around us implodes, rather than facing the reality of a problem and its solution, however overwhelming both may be. This type of painful "truth telling"—about how the past haunts the present and about what is truly required of us to transform the future—is an antidote to nihilism.[51] It is an important, hard-earned lesson, discovered through praxis and buttressed by centuries-old lineages of thoughtful intellectualism, yet it is dismissed by mainstream writers and politicians as a fashionable "slogan."[52] But all of the patronizing repudiations cannot deny that the behemoth continues to enable the mass suffering and murder of racially subjugated peoples. The people who do not suffer under the behemoth, the people who make the key decisions that run the behemoth, manage to absorb reforms and plow forward with a horrific system that remains largely unchanged in ways that matter.

Although interventions in specific surveillance tools that authorities use to criminalize and control subjugated groups can momentarily disrupt the system of state violence, they are not particularly useful unless situated within radical political opposition that rejects respectability politics. Seminal surveillance scholars Kevin Haggerty and Richard Ericson presciently observed more than twenty years ago:

> As it is multiple, unstable and lacks discernible boundaries or responsible governmental departments, the surveillant assemblage cannot be dismantled by prohibiting a particularly unpalatable technology. Nor can it be attacked by focusing criticism on a single bureaucracy or

institution. In the face of multiple connections across myriad technologies and practices, struggles against particular manifestations of surveillance, as important as they might be, are akin to efforts to keep the ocean's tide back with a broom—a frantic focus on a particular unpalatable technology or practice while the general tide of surveillance washes over us all.[53]

The interventions result in a very temporary slowing down of a system that quickly adapts, resets, and finds a new way to devour communities of color. I have no doubt that if CalGang is discontinued, for example, another database will quickly take its place. As such, attacking a specific piece of technology or singular policing tactic does not ultimately touch the core of the thing.

Thus, while the technology may be my empirical focus, the heart of the matter is the politics of subjugation, which are refracted and magnified through technology. Any real challenge requires bigger thinking and mass movements. It also requires that, as scholars, we refuse to do things like work with authorities to develop guidelines for the "proper" use of law enforcement databases, thus legitimating them. It means challenging the entire endeavor, questioning the need for surveillance tools and bringing to the surface the carnage that is wrought by even their most proper use. It means finding ways to cut off the limbs of institutions of state violence—be they local police, border control, immigration enforcement, or homeland security—by not only opposing expansions in their power but also actively working to defund and discontinue large sectors of their work and distribute resources to alternatives. It means mass noncompliance when authorities insist on plowing forward anyway. It means loving the people who protest in the streets, rather than criticizing, from a position of safety, their demands as a slogan or fad.

Relatedly, it also means challenging border building and border policing as an organizing principle. Movement from one place to another is not a crisis. It is not an act of war.[54] Rather, as Walia contends, *"a border is the crisis."*[55] Abolition in this context means not only abolishing the border as a physical thing but also abolishing the colonizing social relations, capitalist exploitation, climate destruction, and politics of empire that make the border possible.[56]

The people who live in the US-Mexico borderlands have engaged in an abolitionist project, generation after generation, by undermining the domination of the nation-state and its violent agencies in their day-to-day actions. Since the international boundary's inception, fronterizos have casually moved across it, northward or southward, to get lunch, gas, prescriptions, dental work, schooling, or a post-volleyball game beer with fellow fronterizos. They have built community without regard for the border between them. Anzaldúa knew that inhabiting the borderlands is painful but also potentially transformative. A hole cut in the border fence is a portal to other possibilities.

GO OUT INTO the borderlands at the exact moment the sun sets behind the mountains, when dust particles swirl in the low light and the ground still retains warmth from the day. It is a good, clear heat, a land electric. It is the time of day when laborers start to pack up their trucks and head toward home. Go to ground, taste the mud, reach for the heart of it, and wrench out the rot in its entirety. If you have ever dug into the land and extracted a plant with the root ball intact, then you know how to do this.

Acknowledgments

I am incredibly grateful to everyone who read and provided feedback on this project throughout its development, including Keramet Reiter, Simon Cole, Stefan Timmermans, Luis Fernandez, Susan Coutin, Mona Lynch, Geoff Ward, Anil Kalhan, Jennifer Chacón, Sora Han, Michael Gottfredson, Valerie Jenness, the anonymous reviewers of the drafts of this book, and the people I have almost certainly unintentionally forgotten. Inés Valdez's feedback provided me with an intellectual breakthrough at a key time. Thanks to Heath Cabot and Georgina Ramsay for organizing the De-exceptionalizing Displacement Symposium and to those in attendance for feedback on early drafts of this work.

Thank you to Kaaryn Gustavson, Katie Tinto, Patricia Soung, Sameer Ashar, Caitlin Bellis, Alma Leyva, Graciela Lopez, Paolo Jara-Riveros, Héctor Plascencia, Laura Flores, Mayra Yoana Jaimes Peña, Saba Waheed, Janna Shadduck-Hernandez, Josh Green, Aisha Alfa, and Eric and Kristi Thomas for being an invaluable support system and constant source of inspiration. I am grateful to Sean Kennedy of Loyola Law School for supporting and endorsing my first book.

Thanks to all the creative and kind people passing through Hill House, including Te'Amir Sweeny, Tutu Sweeny, Carrie Thammavongsa, Sasha Ali,

Henry D'Ambrosio, and most of all, Semere-Ab Etmet Yohannes for presiding over the debauchery. Te'Amir's music in particular helped me to stay focused as I sorted through page after page of horror during my research process. Rest in power, Sonny Abegaze.

A special thank you to Adam Vine, brilliant and gentle muse, partner, writer, and collaborator.

A big thank you to Matthew Strugar of the Law Office of Matthew Strugar, my intrepid Freedom of Information Act (FOIA) litigator, without whom I would not have attained many of the novel documents and data that form the basis of this book.

My gratitude to Nat Case, of INCase, LLC, for the beautiful cartographic and design work.

I owe a few belated thank you's to Nura Dualeh and Andrew Huerta for running the McNair Achievement Program at the University of Arizona, without which I would not have a PhD; Nicole Guidotti-Hernández for encouraging me to apply to the McNair Program; and Jim Shockey for mentoring me in and beyond the program.

Thank you to the Institute for Citizens and Scholars for the Mellon Emerging Faculty Leaders Award and the Hellman Foundation for the Hellman Fellowship, which supported the research for this book.

Thank you to the UC Press Board, who unequivocally supported this perhaps unusual book about land, databases, flowers, memory, horror, and rebellion. Madison Wetzell, editorial assistant, thank you for making this production process run. And thank you so much, Maura Roessner; you understood and fought for the work from the beginning and for that, you are the best.

Portions of the following chapter are used in chapter 1:

Muñiz, Ana. "Steel Bloom: Lineages and Landmarks of Borderland Violence," in *Between Catastrophe and Revolution: Essays in Honor of Mike Davis*, edited by Daniel Bertrand Monk and Michael Sorkin. New York: OR Books, 2021, published in association with Terreform.

Portions of the following article are used in chapter 2:

Muñiz, Ana. "Secondary Ensnarement: Surveillance Systems in the Service of Punitive Immigration Enforcement." *Punishment & Society* 22(4) (2020):461–482.

Portions of the following article are used in chapters 6 and 7:

Muñiz, Ana. "Bordering Circuitry: Border Externalization and Internalization in the Age of Immigration Surveillance." *UCLA Law Review* 66 (2019):1638–1681.

Methodological Appendix

I DEMAND SOME DOCUMENTS

BURNED BRIDGES AND HIDDEN PAPERS

I burned bridges. For years I conducted ethnography with law enforcement and prosecutors to examine racialized policing practices. When I wrote my first book, I did not think twice about portraying the stark reality of what I observed: the explicitly and implicitly racist practices of law enforcement and the entitlement of the upper-class, largely white, communities that reproduced racial terror alongside them. However, that kind of honesty also meant I would be unable to conduct research with law enforcement approval again. The fires were necessary, so I lit the match and it was done.

Scholars take divergent approaches to access, truth, and representation. Researchers who are dependent on authorities for access (to a police department, a prison, or an immigration detention center, for example) sometimes massage representations of law enforcement in their writing. They report general results while tempering their analysis of law enforcement or omitting the more critical findings. I tend to favor a scorched earth approach, which results in gaining access once and never again. Consequently, I realize that my career will have to be one in which I constantly reinvent my methodological strategies. Out of necessity, I have recently turned to following paper trails more than words given to me in interviews or observations gleaned in the field. Due to a reliance on documents, this book is limited in the extent to which it can comment on how federal law enforcement personnel use databases and surveillance systems in the field in day-to-day activities. Although access is difficult, more ethnographic research is called for, particularly inquiry focused on how various entities—law enforcement officers and civilian tech personnel, government employees and employees of private companies contracted by the government—work together on racialized surveillance.

While a number of ethnographers have observed local law enforcement officers' use of technology, immigration and homeland security authorities are far less penetrable. Consequently, surveillance scholars Emma Knight and Alex Gekker argue for document analysis as a viable alternative to the "de-facto impossible requirement of observing the deployment of the software or accessing those using it."[1]

The findings presented in this book are derived from an institutional ethnographic method, which includes more limited nonparticipant observation, semistructured, open-ended interviews, and field interviews, alongside an extensive archival analysis of thousands of primary documents. First, between August 2016 and May 2018, I conducted semistructured, open-ended interviews with nineteen legal advocates who practice in the Southern California region at the intersections of criminal, juvenile, and immigrant defense work, specifically with clients accused of gang membership or affiliation. I also conducted ethnographic observation of legal advocates in the course of their work, during which I engaged in informal field interviews. I took shorthand notes in notebooks in the field and typed extended field notes immediately afterward. Interviews were digitally audio recorded and transcribed verbatim.

The ethnographic observation, semistructured interviews, and field interviews served as a jumping off point to further explore the research topic through an extensive analysis of primary documents. Moving from observations on the ground to the textual organization of surveillance, I conducted an analysis of organizational documents. I mapped the law enforcement workflows that are organized through coordinating texts, including manuals, directives, strategic plans, and budget documents.[2] Classification systems as a work practice enable the standardization and coordination of work across time and geographic sites. Thus, the organizational administrative level establishes categorization schemes, institutional priorities, and protocols "that require distinctions to be made on the ground and shape how that categorization unfolds and for what purposes it is pressed into service."[3] My mapping practice goes beyond tracing technological developments to mapping their underlying power dynamics. Technological tools are developed by humans for specific purposes and are therefore imbued with human biases and political struggles.

I initially intended to tackle a much narrower research project, seeking to answer the question: How do immigration authorities categorize immigrants as gang members and use gang databases for immigration enforcement purposes? However, it quickly became apparent that answering a question about Immigration and Customs Enforcement's (ICE's) and Department of Homeland Security's (DHS's) gang profiling and enforcement practices required a broader knowledge of immigration and nonimmigration databases on the federal, state, and local levels. I now realize this is the case because immigration authorities prefer to track gang membership in general federal databases rather than discrete gang databases and because cross-jurisdictional information sharing is so key to gang profiling. I subsequently decided to map the life courses of several key interconnected information systems.

I decided to map the databases that participants in my interview and ethnographic research identified as importation: the CalGang and ICE-Gangs Databases, TECS, and the Enforcement Case Tracking System (ENFORCE). I conducted systematic searches of the *Federal Register*, looking for information systems that held or processed records pertaining to immigrants. The *Federal Register* is the official outlet through which the US government publishes public notices and proposed rule changes. The Enforcement Integrated Database (EID) kept appearing in my searches, and upon further investigation I deduced that ENFORCE is a package of applications that connect to EID. I located an identifier that allowed me to track EID back to the Deportable Alien Control System (DACS). Later on, I traced the ways in which EID connected to TECS, and TECS connected to ICEGangs, and ICEGangs was built to mirror CalGang, and so on, to form a maddeningly jumbled ball of information exchange.

The documents I analyzed are divisible into three general levels. The first level represents macro-level plans drafted by government officials that provide insight into institutional logics: executive orders, presidential proclamations, memorandums, and strategic plans.

The second level contains documents produced further into the implementation process that reveal more specific protocols governing the manner in which technologies are implemented: System of Records Notices, Privacy Impact Assessments, budgets, technical manuals, and training materials. A System of Records is defined as "a group of any records under the control of an agency from which information is retrieved by the name of the individual or by some identifying number, symbol, or other identifying particular assigned to the individual."[4] The Privacy Act of 1974 requires that federal agencies give public notice of records systems via the *Federal Register* in the form of System of Records Notices and Privacy Impact Assessments. The DHS's privacy officer has authority under the Homeland Security Act of 2002 to require that federal agencies produce Privacy Impact Assessments to describe their methods for collecting and storing personally identifiable information.[5]

System of Records Notices and Privacy Impact Assessments include an overview of the proposed system modifications, such as descriptions of the information to be collected and of the ways in which the government plans to use the information.[6] The public can comment on the proposed modifications through the regulations.gov website and via paper or electronic mail. However, the notices are not well publicized, and public comment is relatively rare. The US government's obligation to notify the public of its intention to gather and store the public's information is satisfied primarily through the publication of System of Records Notices and Privacy Impact Assessments. For example, a TECS Privacy Impact Assessment states: "CBP [Customs and Border Protection] provides notice through the publication of this PIA [Privacy Impact Assessment], and TECS source system PIAs, SORNs [System of Records Notices], and implementing regulations associated with individual programs and subsystems that information collected may be shared with other programs and government agencies."[7] This disclaimer means that Customs and Border Protection does not need to attain your explicit informed consent in order to collect or share your biometric or biographic information. Rather, the Privacy Impact Assessment or System of Records Notice serves as the informed consent, even though most people have no idea these documents exist.

The third level of documents I accessed pertains to DHS Office of Inspector General audits and reports and federal agencies' implementation memos that offer a window into the application of information systems for enforcement. The documents ranged anywhere from four to several hundred pages in length.

Additionally, in order to acquire novel data about information systems and information sharing programs, I successfully filed four Freedom of Information Act (FOIA) lawsuits between 2016 and 2020 to compel the release of additional documents and descriptive statistics pertaining to the databases on which I chose to focus. One lawsuit enabled me to access information on the ICEGangs Database, namely the following information maintained by ICE between January 1, 2008, and April 1, 2016: materials used to train ICE agents and support personnel on the definition of a street gang and gang membership criteria; the number of people that have been added to and removed from the ICEGangs Database broken down by sixty-five demographic and descriptive categories; the percentage of current entries who are confirmed gang members and the percentage who are alleged gang members; the percentage of current database entries who have been convicted of a crime; the budget amount spent on developing the ICEGangs database, the annual budget for the operation and maintenance of the ICEGangs database, and the amount and sources of any federal funding used for ICEGangs; and all memorandums of understanding between ICE and other federal, state, or local law enforcement entities who are afforded access to records in ICEGang or afford ICE access to their own gang databases.

A second FOIA lawsuit uncovered information about the Law Enforcement Notification System (LENS) and Criminal History Information Sharing (CHIS) program. I received statistical data on the number of individuals whose information was shared as part of LENS between January 1, 2015, and October 1, 2017, broken down by forty-nine demographic and descriptive categories. I also received statistical data on the number of repatriated individuals whose criminal history information was shared with foreign countries under the CHIS program between January 1, 2010, and October 1, 2017, broken down by citizenship and notification date. Seth Alan Williams, a PhD student and graduate research assistant in the Department of Criminology, Law & Society at the University of California, Irvine, cleaned and analyzed the statistical data.

Third, I requested data from United States Citizenship and Immigration Services (USCIS) pertaining to individuals denied status adjustments, denied deferred action, removed, or deemed removable from the United States due to accusations of gang involvement or affiliation between January 1, 2012, and June 1, 2017. During mediation for the subsequent FOIA lawsuit, counsel for USCIS claimed that the agency did not maintain information in a separate database on gang-labeled people who had been denied benefits or reported to ICE for enforcement purposes. As a result, they would have had to comb through individual immigration files for the information. Furthermore, USCIS claimed that much of this information was not yet digitized, and therefore the search would have necessitated pulling and reviewing paper files. After negotiations between my legal representation and USCIS, the agency produced the guidelines and training materials according to which USCIS officers investigate and assess applications for deferred action, specifically regarding gang involvement by applicants.

The fourth FOIA lawsuit produced statistical data on individuals for whom ICE or DHS received criminal history information from foreign partners under the CHIS program between January 1, 2010, and October 1, 2017, broken down by year, country of birth, gang flag, and National Crime Information Center (NCIC) Code(s) for the eighty-five crimes enumerated in the cooperation agreements.

Additionally, I submitted and received data in response to California Public Records Act (PRA) requests to the California Department of Justice concerning memorandums of understanding established from January 1, 1998, to January 1, 2019, between an administrator of the CalGang Database (including but not limited to the California Department of Justice, the CalGang Executive Board, and the California Gang Node Advisory Committee) and an outside agency; CalGang Executive Board and the California Gang Node Advisory Committee meeting notes; and CalGang purge data.

I also reviewed relevant case law and policies, specifically Obama- and Trump-era executive orders, presidential proclamations, and memorandums; and Department of Justice memorandums and rulings pertaining to immigration enforcement, immigration administration, border control, federal criminal prosecution, databases, and information systems.

I employed an abductive analytical process to develop my argument.[8] With the documents and qualitative data, I conducted an initial round of open coding by hand to inductively elicit general coding categories. I used the topics that emerged from the first round of coding to proceed with a second round of more directed coding, once again by hand. Specifically, I looked for indications that there were changes to information systems concerning the following components: (1) recording of criminal history information, (2) broader forms of criminal classification, (3) automation, (4) standardization, (5) interoperability, (6) risk assessment, (7) information sharing, and (8) privacy regulation. I conducted several more rounds of coding to search for additional dimensions that may have been overlooked. I sorted data excerpts and drafted memos through an iterative analytical process in which I integrated themes drawn inductively from the data set with theory from relevant literature.

REQUESTS UNDER THE PUBLIC RECORDS ACT
AND FREEDOM OF INFORMATION ACT

Enacted in 1966, the FOIA "establishes a presumption that records in the possession of agencies and departments of the executive branch of the U.S. Government are accessible to the people." As such, individuals are legally entitled to request the release of records held by government agencies. The FOIA established guidelines for determining whether a given record is disclosed, withheld, or released with redactions.[9]

Relatedly, the Privacy Act of 1974 regulates the maintenance and disclosure of records by the federal government. Under the act, "most individuals" can seek access to their own federal records, and in the case that they discover inaccurate information, can request amendment to their records.[10] However, the Privacy Act prohibits disclosure of personally identifiable information to someone other than the subject of the record. Executive Order No. 13768, Enhancing Public Safety in the Interior of the United States, clarified in 2017 that the right to request amendment of records is limited to US citizens and lawful permanent residents.[11] Being unable to access or contest one's personal information in immigration databases carries lifelong consequences, as the standard retention time frame for immigration related-data is seventy-five to one hundred years.[12]

Thus, the FOIA and the Privacy Act of 1974 regulate the maintenance and accessibility of two types of information: records with personally identifiable information and records that contain information on government agencies. For this book, I did not request personally identifiable information. Rather, I accessed de-identified data or aggregated information that does not include personal identifiers and is often used for research purposes. The ICEGangs data sets accessed for this book are one example; they are quantitative data sets organized in Excel spreadsheets and provide demographic information on the people whose information is maintained in the ICEGangs database, but do not specifically identify any one individual. Additionally, documents that describe the ICEGangs budget, development process, and procedures for use have personally identifiable information redacted.

Nonetheless, even without personally identifiable information, government agencies still attempt to withhold entire records or substantial portions of records by claiming that their release would compromise investigations or intelligence operations. The US government maintains that substantial portions of surveillance systems are exempt from disclosure because release of information "could enable the individual who is the subject of a record to impede the investigation, to tamper with witnesses, destroy or conceal evidence, and flee to avoid detection or apprehension."[13] As I have demonstrated throughout this book, the classification of surveillance systems as containing investigative and intelligence information can be misleading. Investigative information suggests information that is used to solve a crime. Intelligence information enables the preemption of future illegal activities. The information maintained in databases reviewed here pushes the boundaries of what could be defined as investigative or intelligence information because an individual does not have to be suspected of violations to have their information entered into most of the surveillance systems discussed in this book.

My recent attempts to access primary documents have been more fraught with resistance than were my previous attempts to access law enforcement agencies to conduct ethnographic observation and interviews. Law enforcement agencies seem to view public information as their own private property. As a result, I have spent the last several years litigating public records requests at the local, state, and federal levels to access novel data.

In my experience, law enforcement officers take great offense at public records requests. I once watched an assistant police chief growl, "I thought we trusted one another!" to a group of attorneys who filed a public records request after repeated attempts to gain the information through informal requests to the police department and repeatedly unfulfilled promises by the department to produce the information. Law enforcement responses to requests for information are reflective of what legal scholar Frank Rudy Cooper describes as "cop fragility," the overblown anger and defensiveness with which police respond to even the slightest criticism or challenge. Cooper argues that as Black Lives Matter movements amplify awareness of police violence, law enforcement agencies respond by portraying themselves as victims and contend that non–law enforcement entities have no right to judge them or hold police accountable for their actions.[14] Thus, state-sponsored forces with military grade weapons and qualified immunity claim the mantle of oppression. Cooper further notes that in addition to reflecting the characteristics of white fragility, cop fragility is riddled with masculine insecurities.

Just as I have seen law enforcement officers be outraged about public records requests, I have also watched academics concede. After I once suggested that a collaborative research body of which I was a member file suit to forcibly compel the release of records from police departments, several academics in the room quickly tried to stamp out the fire: "No, no, no, we *never* file a public records request. It would break the relationship we have worked so hard to build with police departments."[15] It is common for criminologists to collaborate with law enforcement as part of research partnerships. In these arrangements, they rely on the police department to provide them with data; in return, the researchers provide the department with evidence-based suggestions that improve their operations or simply legitimate the way the department already functions.

Academic refusals to challenge cop fragility by accepting law enforcement's stonewalling of information only further enable entitlement, to terrifying ends, some of which I discuss in the conclusion (i.e., increasingly bold authoritarianism, violence, and suppression of free speech and other basic democratic values). What seems to have been lost in many academic collaborations is the commitment to hold law enforcement organizations accountable as government agencies with a mandate of responsiveness and transparency. Accessing data from a public agency is not a controversial action. The data does not belong to the police but to the public. It is *our* data. If a government organization refuses to release public data, it is not protecting its own property, but rather privatizing and pilfering public property.

ASKING FOR AND DEMANDING INFORMATION

The first step to accessing public information is crafting a formidable PRA or FOIA request. One must file a PRA request for information from a local or state agency and an FOIA for information from a federal agency. I have included a sample FOIA and a sample California PRA request at the end of this appendix. Some government agencies now prefer that requesters fill in standardized online forms rather than submit a request in letter form. In that case, I simply copy and paste the relevant sections from the request into the form. It is also a good idea to have an attorney familiar with public records help prepare the request (more on that later).

As for the request itself, it is first important to specify the documents you seek; provide a paragraph or two of background and identify a specific date range. Agencies are likely to reject requests that do not include a date range or in which the date range is too broad on the grounds that the scope of requested information is unmanageable. Additionally, describe in as much detail as possible the records you seek. For example, in researching the CHIS program, I accessed a Privacy Impact Assessment outlining all of the information collected and shared as part of the program. In my request, which is included at the end of this appendix, I list verbatim the information outlined in the Privacy Impact Assessment and select the date range from January 1 of the year CHIS was first instituted (2010) up until the month of my request (October 1, 2017).

Second, I make explicit that I am not requesting personally identifiable information and am open to redactions unless, of course, I am requesting something like police misconduct records, for which the personally identifying information of the officer in question is both key and statutorily public. Agencies will quickly reject a request that can be construed as seeking the names, birthdates, addresses, and other sensitive information of people in their databases. For example, when I initially requested information on a specific Border Patrol raid, I did not include a line indicating that I was not seeking personally identifiable information, and the agency rejected my request, stating that I would need to obtain signatures from the hundreds of people swept up in the raid in order to access the information. When I appealed, I included the line about redactions and also cited case law to argue that the exemption cited by the Border Patrol was not relevant. I was then able to access the de-identified information.

I request a waiver of all costs as an individual who seeks the information for public benefit and who is situated within an academic institution, journalistic organization, or nonprofit group. I also note that in the case the waiver is denied, I am willing to pay fees up to $250 but require notification of any additional cost. In the example request provided, I picked $250, but you can name any amount with which you feel comfortable. In previous requests, I have stated that I will only pay fees up to $25.

The section in my requests labeled "Request for Release of All Responsive Records" is an attempt to preempt noncomprehensive searches. Unfortunately, public records requests are ultimately dependent on the law enforcement agency to maintain and disclose all relevant records. Law enforcement agencies may legally purge and destroy several categories of records after five years. Consequently, some of the records you seek may no longer exist. Purging schedules are less of an issue in immigration-related data systems, where the standard data retention time frame is seventy-five to one hundred years. Alternately, agencies may not keep their records well-organized and therefore may take an extended amount of time to locate the records and deliver them without any identifiable organizational scheme. As a result, you will have to sort through thousands of documents and connect information on one specific case that is spread across myriad documents.

Ultimately, it is impossible to be completely certain that the agency has produced all of the relevant documents. There are, however, a few ways to check for obvious acts of withholding. For example, a city attorney's office rejected my PRA request based on the claim that they had no information on a specific case. I located a news article in which a representative from the city attorney's office stated that the office had submitted a brief in the case. I wrote a response to the initial denial of the request, referring to the article as evidence that the office did possess documents relevant to the case.

Another function of the "Request for Release of All Responsive Records" section is to preempt overredaction. While redactions are necessary, agencies may implement them overenthusiastically. For example, Amtrak responded to one reporter's records request with a document in which everything was redacted with stark black bars except the words "no snack car."[16] A public records attorney can assess when it makes sense to press for less redaction.

Finally, in the closing I indicate that I expect that the agency will write to me within the legally required time period (twenty working days for FOIA requests and ten for California PRA requests), confirming the receipt of my request and outlining a reasonable timeline for the delivery of the requested documents to my possession. PRA regulations will differ by state, so you will need to research your state's specific regulations.

The FOIA has established an adjudicative process for those denied access to records, namely filing a FOIA lawsuit to legally compel the government to release the requested records. State statutes also provide bases on which to sue agencies for nonresponsiveness to or rejection of PRAs. On the local and state levels, I have had success with attorneys writing letters to agencies urging them to respond to my records request and informing them of intent to file suit if they do not. Sometimes a strongly worded warning is enough.

The federal level is quite different. The routine by which I access FOIA information nearly always proceeds as follows. First, I submit the request to the agency that maintains the information I seek. When the agency does not respond by the statutorily required date, I inquire via email several times. After several weeks of nonresponsiveness by the government agency, I engage an attorney to file suit to compel the immediate release of the requested information. Only at this point is the request engaged. Usually, a federal judge orders the agency in question to establish a timeline for the release of documents to my legal representation.

It is important to note that FOIA *requires federal agencies to provide the fullest possible disclosure* of information to the public. The history of the act reflects that it is a disclosure law. It *presumes that requested records will be disclosed*, and the agency must make its case for any withholding in terms of the act's exemptions to the rule of disclosure.[17]

The statute is presumptive in favor of the disclosure of records, and the burden is on the government to adequately prove that disclosure is unwarranted or harmful.

In the FOIA context, filing suit is important, because it moves your request to a more competent office. When an initial FOIA request is submitted, it is processed by a bureaucrat at the FOIA office. Once a suit is filed, it moves to an attorney who is required to engage the request at the order of a judge. I initially pay about $600 to cover the fees to file a FOIA lawsuit, all of which is returned to me upon completion of the case if the government agency is found to be at fault; if it has failed to respond to requests and release documents, it is at fault. Under supervision of a judge, my attorney and the government attorney establish a timeline for the release of documents as well as negotiate the information to be released and the level of redaction.

I am able to repeatedly submit requests and file suit because I have adequate resources, access to a willing attorney, and the institutional literacy gained from a doctoral education and over a decade of research experience. Accessing information from public agencies is a basic democratic right, and it should be easier. Much more de-identified information should be automatically released to ensure transparency and accountability, and individuals should be able to confidentially access their own unredacted files.

Unfortunately, many law enforcement and government agencies try their best to restrict access to public records. For example, in June 2020 the Trump administration designated ICE as a "Security Agency," thus restricting publicly accessible information on the agency and its employees. Substantively, the Security Agency classification puts ICE in a league with high-level intelligence agencies, a predictable development consistent with the move toward broad surveillance functions traced throughout this book. Unsurprisingly, the justification for the reclassification is based on the claims to victimization that are central to cop fragility, specifically, "the increase in threats, intimidation, and doxing directed at ICE personnel in recent years," for which no evidence is presented.[18] Agencies will no doubt continue to pursue similarly restrictive methods.

The pervasiveness of private contractors in the collection, maintenance, and analysis of surveillance data further complicates data accessibility. Private companies may be able to circumvent privacy provisions that allow release of public information. Political scientist Matthew Longo argues that privately maintained data can no longer be said to be under the unilateral control of the US government.[19] For all of these reasons, I suggest accessing information through other more informal means as well. Ask ethnographic and interview participants about documents they are able to share, and maintain a secure, encrypted form of communication in case someone wants to engage in protected communication.

SAMPLE FOIA

RE: Request under the Freedom of Information Act (FOIA)

Dear FOIA Officer:

I am writing to request information under the Freedom of Information Act ("FOIA"), 5 U.S.C. § 552 et seq. for records pertaining to individuals whose information has been processed through the Criminal History Information Sharing Program. I request disclosure of records* that were prepared, received, transmitted, collected and/or maintained relating or referring to the following information. *Please note that I am not interested in receiving any personally identifying information.*

I. Background

1. The Privacy Impact Assessment Update for the Enforcement Integrated Database (EID) Criminal History Information Sharing (CHIS) Program, DHS/ICE/PIA-015(h), dated

* The term "records" as used herein includes but is not limited to all records or communications preserved in electronic or written form, including but not limited to correspondence, documents, data, videotapes, audio tapes, faxes, files, e-mails, guidance, guidelines, evaluations, instructions, analyses, memoranda, agreements, notes, orders, policies, procedures, protocols, reports, rules, technical manuals, technical specifications, training manuals, or studies, including records kept in written form, or electronic format on computers and/or other electronic storage devices, electronic communications, and/or video tapes.

January 15, 2016, states, "Since 2010, U.S. Immigration and Customs Enforcement (ICE) has shared certain criminal history information with foreign countries concerning nationals of those countries who are being repatriated from the United States and who were convicted of certain felonies in the United States" (see page 1). The document explains that the following information will be shared with foreign partners from the Enforcement Integrated Database (EID): "A-Number, Subject ID, name, alias, date of birth, city of birth, country of birth, mother's name, father's name, gender, gang flag, photographs, fingerprints, NCIC Code(s) from the 85 crimes enumerated in the cooperation agreements, description of crime, and date of conviction" (see page 5).

II. Records Requested

All records containing, describing, pertaining to, or referring to:

1. The number of repatriated individuals for whom U.S. Immigration and Customs Enforcement (ICE) has shared certain criminal history information with foreign countries under the Criminal History Information Sharing program between January 1, 2010 and October 1, 2017 broken down by year; country of birth; gang flag; and National Crime Information Center (NCIC) Code(s) from the 85 crimes enumerated in the cooperation agreements.

III. Waiver of All Costs

I request the preceding information for the purposes of academic research housed at the University of California, Irvine, a research public university. I request a waiver of all costs pursuant to 5 U.S.C. § 552(a)(4)(A)(iii) ("Documents shall be furnished without any charge ... if disclosure of the information is in the public interest because it is likely to contribute significantly to public understanding of the operations or activities of the government and is not primarily in the commercial interest of the Requester."). The public interest/benefit fee waiver provisions of the FOIA are to be "liberally construed" and are "consistently associated with requests from journalists, scholars, and non-profit interest groups who it was intended to benefit." See Judicial Watch, Inc. v. Rossotti, 326 F.3d 1309, 1312 (D.C. Cir. 2003) ("Congress amended FOIA to ensure that it be 'liberally construed in favor of fee waivers for noncommercial requesters.'"); see also 6 C.F.R. § 5.11(k).

Further, Congress has provided that a "minimal showing" is all that is necessary for an agency to grant a FOIA fee waiver.

> [T]he legislative history . . . demonstrates that Congress intended independent researchers, journalists, and public interest watchdog groups to have inexpensive access to government records in order to provide the type of public disclosure believed essential to our society. Moreover, in the 1986 amendments to FOIA, Congress ensured that when such requesters demonstrated information in a way that contributes to public understanding of the operations of government agencies, no fee attaches to their request. Institute for Wildlife Protection v. U.S. Fish & Wildlife Serv., 290 F. Supp. 2d 1226, 1232 (D. Or. 2003).

For all of these reasons, disclosure of the requested records is required by the FOIA and a total fee waiver is justified. If the fee waiver request is denied, while reserving my right to appeal the denial, I will pay fees up to $250.00. If you estimate that the fees will exceed this limit, please inform me.

IV. Request for Release of All Responsive Records

I believe that all of the records requested are subject to disclosure, and I request prompt processing and release of the requested information. I also request a complete list of documents covered by the request. I expect that all records will be provided in complete form. To the extent that any requested records are marked classified, please redact only the necessary portions of those records and immediately provide me with the remaining portions. If any records are withheld, please state the exemption claimed and provide a list of the records being withheld. If you deny this request in whole or in part, please provide a written explanation for that denial, including reference to the specific statutory provisions upon which you rely, and notify me of appeal procedures available under the law.

V. Conclusion

I expect a written response to this FOIA Request by the close of the statutory time period, which is within 20 working days of your receipt of this letter, and to a reasonably speedy delivery of the requested documents. See 5 U.S.C. § 552(a)(6)(A)(ii). Without waiving any other appeal rights, I reserve the right to appeal a constructive denial of this Request as well as decisions to withhold any information, to deny a waiver of fees, or to deny a limitation of processing fees. I also reserve the right to challenge the adequacy of the search for responsive documents and any redactions in the materials produced in response to this request.

Thank you in advance for your prompt response to this Request. Please provide responsive documents as soon as they are identified.

SAMPLE CALIFORNIA PRA

RE: Request under the California Public Records Act

I am writing to request information under the California Public Records Act (Government Code Section 6250 et seq.), for records pertaining to the CalGang Database (i.e. CalGang system). I hereby request disclosure of certain records in your possession relating to the CalGang Database obtained between January 1, 1998 and January 1, 2019. I request disclosure of records* that were prepared, received, transmitted, collected and/or maintained relating or referring to the following information. Please note that I am not interested in receiving any personally identifying information and would not oppose redactions meant to protect such information.

---

* The term "records" as used herein includes but is not limited to all records or communications preserved in electronic or written form, including but not limited to correspondence, documents, data, videotapes, audio tapes, faxes, files, e-mails, guidance, guidelines, evaluations, instructions, analyses, memoranda, agreements, notes, orders, policies, procedures, protocols, reports, rules, technical manuals, technical specifications, training manuals, or studies, including records kept in written form, or electronic format on computers and/or other electronic storage devices, electronic communications, and/or video tapes.

I. Records Requested

I request all records containing, describing, pertaining to, or referring to any Memorandum of Understanding, established between January 1, 1998 and January 1, 2019, between an administrator of the CalGang Database (including but not limited to the California Department of Justice, the CalGang Executive Board, and the California Gang Node Advisory Committee) and another agency, including but not limited to: California Department of Corrections; California Department of Corrections and Rehabilitation; Western States Information Network; Regional Information Sharing Systems; United States Immigration and Customs Enforcement; United States Federal Bureau of Investigation; Arizona Department of Public Safety; United States Bureau of Alcohol, Tobacco, Firearms and Explosives; Internal Revenue Service Alcohol, Tobacco, and Firearms Division; United States Department of Homeland Security; United States Customs and Border Protection; law enforcement agencies in Washington State, New Mexico, Texas, Maryland, Washington DC, Virginia, Nevada, and California; Los Angeles Sheriff's Department; and state divisions of Homeland Security.

II. Waiver of All Costs

I request the preceding information for the purposes of academic research housed at the University of California, Irvine, a public university. Therefore, I request a waiver of all costs. If the fee waiver request is denied, while reserving my right to appeal the denial, I will pay fees up to $50.00. If you estimate that the fees will exceed this limit, please inform me.

III. Request for Release of All Responsive Records

I believe that all of the records requested are subject to disclosure, and request prompt processing and release of the requested information. I also request a complete list of documents covered by the request. I expect that all records will be provided in complete form. To the extent that any requested records are marked classified, please redact only the necessary portions of those records and immediately provide me with the remaining portions. If any records are withheld, please state the exemption claimed and provide a list of the records being withheld. If you deny this request in whole or in part, please provide a written explanation for that denial, including reference to the specific statutory provisions upon which you rely, and notify me of appeal procedures available under the law.

IV. Conclusion

I look forward to a written response to this Request by the close of the statutory time period, which is within 10 working days of your receipt of this letter. Without waiving any other appeal rights, I reserve the right to appeal a constructive denial of this Request as well as decisions to withhold any information, to deny a waiver of fees, or to deny a limitation of processing fees. I also reserve the right to challenge the adequacy of the search for responsive documents and any redactions in the materials produced in response to this request.

Thank you in advance for your prompt response to this Request. Please provide responsive documents as soon as they are identified.

Acronyms

ADT	alternatives to detention
CBP	United States Customs and Border Protection
CHIS	Criminal History Information Sharing program
DACA	Deferred Action for Childhood Arrivals program
DACS	Deportable Alien Control System
DHS	United States Department of Homeland Security
EID	Enforcement Integrated Database
ENFORCE	Enforcement Case Tracking System
FOIA	Freedom of information Act
ICE	United States Immigration and Customs Enforcement
ICM	Investigative Case Management system
INA	Immigration and Nationality Act
INS	Immigration and Naturalization Service
LAPD	Los Angeles Police Department
LENS	Law Enforcement Notification System
NCIC	National Crime Information Center Database
OSUP	order of supervision
PRA	Public Records Act
TECS	Treasury Enforcement Communications System
USCIS	United States Citizenship and Immigration Services

Notes

CHAPTER 1. THE LAND GETS TANGLED IN WALLS AND CIRCUITRY

1. Anzaldúa, *Borderlands/La Frontera*, 3.

2. Longo, *Politics of Borders*, 68; Salter, "Theory of the /," 734); and Anzaldúa, *Borderlands/La Frontera*, 2 characterize borders as scars, sutures, and open wounds, respectively.

3. Chacón, "Overcriminalizing Immigration," 633.

4. Carby, *Imperial Intimacies*, 12.

5. Wonders and Jones, "Doing and Undoing Borders," 137.

6. United States Customs and Border Protection, *Other Border Wall RFP*, 8.

7. Lytle Hernandez, *Migra!*, 130.

8. Longo, *Politics of Borders*, 51–52; and Macías-Rojas, *From Deportation to Prison*, 140.

9. Macías-Rojas, *From Deportation to Prison*, 140 writes that when she spoke with local government officials in border cities, they complained that the landing mats were "ugly" and had convinced Border Patrol to replace them with a more "aesthetically pleasing" border barrier.

10. Longo, *Politics of Borders*, 52.

11. Ibid.; and Dowling and Inda, *Governing Immigration through Crime*, 13–14.

12. Macías-Rojas, *From Deportation to Prison*, 140.

13. United States Immigration and Customs Enforcement, *Targeting Operations Subscription Data Service Request*, 1.

14. Lyon, *Surveillance after September 11*, 5; Gilliom and Monahan, *SuperVision*, 2; Browne, *Dark Matters*, 16; and Selod, *Forever Suspect*, 24. There is a fascinating body of research that explores the subjectivities and counterstrategies of surveilled populations. I do not address this topic in this book. For research in this vein, see, for example, Mann, Nolan, and Wellman, "Sousveillance"; Browne, *Dark Matters*; Newell, Gomez, and Guajardo, "Censors, Cameras, and the New 'Normal' in Clandestine Migration"; Singh, "Decoding Dress"; and Topak, "Humanitarian and Human Rights Surveillance." While I am interested in countersurveillance techniques, I explore these in my own time and enact them through social movement work, the details of which I choose not to reveal here.

15. Browne, *Dark Matters*, 76–82; and Parenti, *Soft Cage*, 29–32.

16. Selod improves upon older, race-neutral definitions of surveillance by conceptualizing "racialized surveillance" as "the monitoring of select bodies by relying on racial clues." Selod, *Forever Suspect*, 24. Similarly, Browne positions "racializing surveillance" as the "practices, policies, and performances" that "reify boundaries, borders, and bodies along racial lines." See Browne, *Dark Matters*, 16.

17. Browne, *Dark Matters*, 17.

18. Lyon, *Surveillance after September 11*, 5; and Marx, *Windows into the Soul*, 20.

19. Anil Kalhan introduced "migration border" to describe this decoupling of border control practices from the territorial border and the emergence of a set of virtual boundary points at which authorities screen migrants for admission or expulsion. See Kalhan, "Immigration Surveillance," 9. Similarly, Ayelet Shachar refers to the "shifting border of immigration regulation" ("Shifting Border of Immigration Regulation,"167).

20. Lyon, "Border is Everywhere," 66; and Balibar, *Politics and the Other Scene*, 78.

21. Balibar argues that entire countries and continents can become borderland space. See Balibar, "Europe as Borderland." See also Amoore, "Biometric Borders"; Bigo, "Security, Exception, Ban and Surveillance"; Braverman, "Civilized Borders"; Aas, "Analysing a World in Motion"; Côté-Boucher, "Diffuse Border"; and Kalhan, "Immigration Surveillance."

22. United States Customs and Border Protection, "Air and Marine Operations Operating Locations."

23. Bersin, "Lines and Flows," 394.

24. Georgetown University Law Center, *Between the Border and the Street*, 1–2.

25. Wonders identifies such developments as examples of the border being "performed" on certain bodies away from an actual geographic border. See Wonders, "Flows, Semi-Permeable Borders and New Channels of Inequality," 66.

26. Shachar, "Shifting Border of Immigration Regulation," 818.

27. Friedman, *Unwarranted*, 28.

28. Salter, "Theory of the /," 750.

29. I realize that my focus on state agents overlooks other forms of "border work" done by nonstate entities that are diffused throughout society, but this is the scope I have necessarily delineated to focus my project. See the work of Chris Rumford for theorizing on border work by nonstate entities and the co-optation of private entities (i.e., airlines, hotels, other business owners) into border work (Rumford, "Citizens and Borderwork in Europe," "Theorizing Borders," and "Towards a Multiperspectival Study of Borders").

30. For a detailed discussion of methods, see the appendix.

31. Borderland circuitry is akin to Elana Zilberg's "securityscapes" and Suvendrini Perera's "borderscapes," which both capture the patterns of circulation and violence that result from the efforts of governments to control the mobility of migrants. However, borderland circuity specifically captures the deployment of surveillance technology to achieve control. See Zilberg, *Spaces of Detention*, 3; and Perera, "Burning Our Boats," 4–6.

32. Some of the information-sharing programs that I cover also extend into other geographic areas on which I do not focus in this book. For example, gang databases and information-sharing initiatives between ICE and state/local law enforcement are popular in the mid-Atlantic United States (New York, New Jersey, Maryland, Washington, D.C., and Virginia) and affect immigrants from parts of Africa and Southeast Asia. However, for the purposes of scope, I choose to focus on the geographic areas in which several information-sharing programs overlap and concentrate surveillance in the US, namely the American West and Southwest, and internationally in Mexico, Central America, and the Caribbean.

33. Parker, *Making Foreigners*, ix (emphasis added).

34. For example, Arkansas attempted to deport all free Black people from its borders just before the Civil War, and the Missouri constitution

prohibited the entry of free "blacks and mulattoes" from that state. In slave states, free Black people were functionally "aliens," forced to register and maintain documented proof of status. See Kanstroom, *Deportation Nation*, 75–76, 92–93.

35. Kanstroom, *Deportation Nation*, 76; and Parker, *Making Foreigners*, 61. Similarly, Tsuda refers to "racial foreignization." See Tsuda, "'I'm American, Not Japanese!,'" 419.

36. Parker, *Making Foreigners*, 41; and Volpp, "Indigenous as Alien," 293–294.

37. Luiselli, *Tell Me How It Ends*, 17.

38. Kanstroom, *Deportation Nation*, 207.

39. Ibid., 18.

40. Johnson, "Forgotten 'Repatriation,'" 2.

41. Kade Crockford, director of the ACLU's Technology for Liberty Project, has referred to this use of technology to legitimize discriminatory law enforcement practices as "tech-washing." See Burrington, "What Amazon Taught the Cops."

42. Linnemann and McClanahan, "From 'Filth' and 'Insanity,'" 302.

43. Singh, *Race and America's Long War*, 146.

44. Shachar, "Shifting Border of Immigration Regulation," 811.

45. Anzaldúa, *Borderlands/La Frontera*, 194–195.

46. Moreover, this type of hybridity is carried in the body, always, wherever one travels. Similarly, Amoore describes a "biometric border" that people carry in their bodies. See Amoore, "Biometric Borders," 338.

47. Salter, "Theory of the /," 750.

48. Stumpf, "Crimmigration Crisis," 382; Chacón, "Unsecured Borders," 1846–1847; and Sklansky, "Crime, Immigration, and Ad Hoc Instrumentalism," 177. In 1986, the INS removed 1,978 noncitizens for criminal violations (both criminal justice system convictions and criminal immigration violations), which constituted 3 percent of all removals. By 2015, 139,950 removals (42 percent) were criminal removals. See United States Department of Homeland Security, *Yearbook of Immigration Statistics, 2015*, 113.

49. Miller, "Citizenship and Severity," 633.

50. Stumpf, "Crimmigration Crisis," 383–384; Miller, "Citizenship and Severity," 632; and Warner, "The Social Construction of the Criminal Alien," 57.

51. Miller, "Citizenship and Severity," 649.

52. Moreover, the definition of criminal alien varies between federal agencies. For example, while the United States General Accounting Office

considers criminal aliens to be noncitizens who reside in the United States, legally or illegally, and have been convicted of any crime, the Immigration and Nationality Act defines the category more narrowly to include "noncitizens—whether present with or without authorization—who have committed criminal offenses that render them excludable or deportable under the INA." See United States General Accounting Office, *Information on Criminal Aliens Incarcerated in Federal and State Prisons and Local Jails*, 6; and Chacón, "Whose Community Shield?," 319.

53. Executive Office of the President, *President Donald J. Trump's State of the Union Address*; Executive Office of the President, "Executive Order 13773," 10691; and Smith, "Trump Announces 'Surge' of Federal Officers into Democratic-Run Cities."

54. Chacón, "Whose Community Shield?" 320.

55. Carby, *Imperial Intimacies*, 65.

56. Singh, *Race and America's Long War*, 43.

57. Bigo, "Globalized (In)security," 18.

58. See, for example, Monica Martinez's historical tracing of the racist vigilante roots of the Texas Rangers, Border Patrol, and other carceral agencies (*Injustice Never Leaves You*). See also Ward's discussion of "white supremacist policing," which includes "racist ideologies, violence, and other political actions of law enforcement authorities, and underpolicing of White supremacist threats by legal authorities" ("Living Histories of White Supremacist Policing," 168).

CHAPTER 2. YOU CROSS A BORDER AND THE FEDS BUILD A DATABASE

1. Parrish, "U.S. Border Patrol and an Israeli Military Contractor"; and Newell, Gomez, and Guajardo, "Censors, Cameras, and the New 'Normal' in Clandestine Migration," 25.

2. Vega, "Empathy, Morality, and Criminality," 2545.

3. Building on the work of Daniel Kanstroom and Kunal Parker, I situate the American system of immigration control within a broader context of racial control and forced movement. Kanstroom, for example, argues that deportation specifically should be conceptualized as "the application of majoritarian power—through legal structures and with the use of force—against a particular group of people, largely identifiable by race or nationality, to compel their removal from one place to another" (*Deportation Nation*, 7). Various systems of racial control in the United States

have been built from and continue to support one another. See also Kanstroom, *Deportation Nation*, 74, 77–80, 92–93; and Parker, *Making Foreigners*, 123.

4. Parrish, "U.S. Border Patrol and an Israeli Military Contractor." In *Empire of Borders*, Todd Miller notes that in traveling to interview border authorities around the world, at every location, personnel had visited the US-Mexico border to receive training from the US government in border control; Boeing was also slated to install towers, radar, and motion sensors in Arizona, but the US government canceled the contract in 2011 "due to concerns about the price, timeline, and 'effectiveness' of the technology." See Miller, *More Than a Wall*, 36.

5. Parrish, "U.S. Border Patrol and an Israeli Military Contractor."

6. United States Customs and Border Protection, "Trusted Traveler Programs."

7. Unite States Customs and Border Protection, "About CBP."

8. CBP's mission reflects what Nancy Wonders characterizes as "border reconstruction projects," efforts to keep borders open for capital, cheap labor, or the wealthy, and closed to racialized migrants. See Wonders, "Globalization, Border Reconstruction Projects, and Transnational Crime," 36.

9. De Genova similarly refers to "the amorphous temporalities of indefinite (possibly perpetual) waiting" ("Detention, Deportation, and Waiting," 7). Border studies scholars Mezzadra and Neilson conceptualize immigration detention centers not so much as mechanisms to exclude immigrants but more as a way to regulate the time and speed of their integration into labor markets. As a result, detention creates borders that are more temporal than spatial, or "zones of temporal suspension." See Mezzadra and Neilson, *Border as Method*, 132, 136, 154.

10. Ainsley, "U.S. Officials Made List of Reporters, Lawyers, Activists to Question at Border."

11. Meissner et al., *Immigration Enforcement in the United States*, 70.

12. United States Department of Homeland Security, *Privacy Impact Assessment for the TECS System: CBP Primary and Secondary Processing*, 4–5.

13. United States Department of Homeland Security, *Privacy Impact Assessment for CBP License Plate Reader Technology*, 2.

14. See the density meters developed for CBP by Campbell/Harris Security Equipment Company. (CSECO, "Choose the Density Meter CBP Agents Helped Design").

15. Kalhan, "Immigration Surveillance," 42.

16. United States Department of Homeland Security, *Privacy Impact Assessment for the TECS System: CBP Primary and Secondary Processing*, 4.

17. United States Department of the Treasury, "Treasury Enforcement Communications System (TECS) System of Records," 53029.

18. United States Department of Homeland Security, "Advance Passenger Information System (APIS)—Privacy Impact Assessment," 17858–17861; and United States Department of Homeland Security, "U.S. Customs and Border Protection 011 TECS System of Records Notice," 77780.

19. Kalhan, "Immigration Surveillance," 42; United States Department of Homeland Security, *Privacy Impact Assessment for the TECS System: Platform*, 9; and United States Department of Homeland Security, *Privacy Impact Assessment Update for the CBP Portal (e3) to EID/IDENT*, 10.

20. United States Department of Homeland Security, "Office of the Secretary [DHS-2006-0060]," 64543.

21. United States Department of Homeland Security, *Privacy Impact Assessment for the TECS System: CBP Primary and Secondary Processing*, 16–17.

22. United States Department of Homeland Security, "Office of the Secretary [DHS-2006-0060]," 64543, 43651. Margaret Hu notes that big data technologies allow screening and classification to occur simultaneously as opposed to past practice, wherein paper-based screening preceded classification. See Hu, "Algorithmic Jim Crow," 660.

23. Wonders, "Globalization, Border Reconstruction Projects, and Transnational Crime," 34. See generally Torpey, "Coming and Going" for discussions of identity documents and legitimate movement.

24. United States Department of Homeland Security, *Privacy Impact Assessment for the TECS System: Platform*, 11, 28.

25. Knight and Gekker, "Mapping Interfacial Regimes of Control," 232.

26. Palfrey and Gasser, *Interop*, 5.

27. Lyon, *Surveillance after September 11*, 88–91.

28. Meissner et al., *Immigration Enforcement in the United States*, 5.

29. Benefits granting work and determination of eligibility are inherently twinned with enforcement work.

30. Dowling and Inda, *Governing Immigration through Crime*, 12; Palitro and Heyman, "Theorizing Cross-Border Mobility," 317; Lyon, *Identifying Citizens*, 77; Coutin, "Rights of Noncitizens in the United States," 300–301; and Coutin, "Falling Outside," 570.

31. United States Department of Homeland Security, *Privacy Impact Assessment for the TECS System: CBP Primary and Secondary Processing*, 23; and United States Department of Homeland Security, "U.S. Customs and Border Protection 011 TECS System of Records Notice," 77778.

32. US Customs and Border Protection, "CBP through the Years."

33. Herzog and Sohn, "Co-mingling of Bordering Dynamics," 184.

34. Ibid.

35. United States Department of Homeland Security, "U.S. Customs and Border Protection 011 TECS System of Records Notice," 77778.

36. United States Department of Homeland Security. *Privacy Impact Assessment Update for the CBP Portal (e3) to EID/IDENT*, 8.

37. United States Department of Homeland Security, *Privacy Impact Assessment Update for the CBP Portal (e3) to EID/IDENT*, 2; United States Department of Homeland Security, *Privacy Impact Assessment for the Enforcement Integrated Database (EID)*, 2; United States Department of Homeland Security. *Privacy Impact Assessment Update for the Enforcement Integrated Database (EID) Risk Classification Assessment (RCA 1.0), ENFORCE Alien Removal Module (EARM 5.0), and Crime Entry Screen (CES 2.0)*, 2.

38. Office of Inspector General, *Detention and Removal of Illegal Aliens*, 19; and Office of Inspector General, *Review of U.S. Immigration and Customs Enforcement's Detainee Tracking Process*, 1–3. For a more detailed history of DACS and the transition to ENFORCE and EID, see Muñiz, "Secondary Ensnarement."

39. Office of Inspector General, *Review of U.S. Immigration and Customs Enforcement's Detainee Tracking Process*, 3–5; Office of Inspector General, *Detention and Removal of Illegal Aliens*, 19–21; and Office of Inspector General, *Immigration and Naturalization Service's Removal of Aliens Issued Final Orders*, 2.

40. Office of Inspector General, *Immigration and Customs Enforcement's Tracking and Transfers of Detainees*, 3–4.

41. Office of Inspector General, *Supervision of Aliens Commensurate with Risk*, 2.

42. United States Department of Homeland Security, *Privacy Impact Assessment for the Enforcement Integrated Database (EID)*, 2; and United States Department of Homeland Security, *Privacy Impact Assessment Update for the Enforcement Integrated Database (EID) Risk Classification Assessment (RCA 1.0), ENFORCE Alien Removal Module (EARM 5.0), and Crime Entry Screen (CES 2.0)*, 2. EID is also accessed through

another set of applications called the EID Arrest Guide for Law Enforcement (EAGLE) to process arrests, including biometric information, in the field. For purposes of scope, I do not cover EAGLE in this book. For more information on EAGLE see United States Department of Homeland Security, *Privacy Impact Assessment Update for the Enforcement Integrated Database (EID)—EAGLE*; National Immigration Project, *Who's Behind ICE?*, 12; and SRA International, Inc., *RFQ#HSCEMD-13-Q-00013*, 3–7.

43. United States Department of Justice, "Deportable Alien Control System (DACS) System of Records," 52699.

44. United States Department of Homeland Security, "Immigration and Enforcement Operational Records (ENFORCE) System of Records," 75(39) Fed. Reg. 9238.

45. It is unclear if this is restricted to immigrants in proceedings or refers to a broader population of "deportable" immigrants, including those not in proceedings.

46. Brayne, *Predict and Surveil*, 51–52, 62, 139.

47. United States Department of Homeland Security, *Privacy Impact Assessment for the Enforcement Integrated Database (EID)*, 7–9, 21; and United States Department of Homeland Security, "Immigration and Enforcement Operational Records (ENFORCE) System of Records," 75 Fed. Reg. 23276 (May 3, 2010).

48. Brayne, *Predict and Surveil*, 77.

49. United States Department of Homeland Security, *Privacy Impact Assessment Update for the Enforcement Integrated Database (EID)* (2010), 2–3; and United States Immigration and Customs Enforcement, *Risk Classification Assessment ICE Leadership Scope Brief*, 28–30.

50. Noferi and Koulish, "Immigration Detention Risk Assessment," 67; and Reiter and Coutin, "Crossing Borders and Criminalizing Identity," 577.

51. Lageson, *Digital Punishment*, 55.

52. United States Department of Homeland Security, *Privacy Impact Assessment for the Enforcement Integrated Database (EID)*, 9–11, 18.

53. For an in-depth exploration of big data policing see Ferguson, *Rise of Big Data Policing*; for big data surveillance see Brayne, "Big Data Surveillance." An earlier concept, d*ataveillance*, defined as "the systematic use of personal data systems in the investigation or monitoring of the actions or communications of one or more persons," captures the nascent emergence of big data surveillance. See Clarke, "Information Technology and Dataveillance," 499.

54. Harcourt, *Exposed*, 19.

55. Knight and Gekker, "Mapping Interfacial Regimes of Control," 234. Brayne demonstrates how LAPD leadership were easily dazzled by new technology hawked by private developers (*Predict and Surveil*, 39–40).

56. Fang and Biddle, "Google AI Tech Will Be Used for Virtual Border Wall."

57. Miller, *More Than a Wall*, 1, 5.

58. Ibid., 3–4.

59. Ibid., 54–55.

60. Borders, Trade, and Immigration (BTI) Institute, *Program Year 5 Annual Report 01 July 2019–30 June 2020*, 90.

61. United States Department of Homeland Security, *Privacy Impact Assessment for ICE Investigative Case Management*, 4.

62. For a list of contractors involved with the TECS modernization process, see National Immigration Project, *Who's Behind ICE?*, 29, 31, 34–35.

63. Knight and Gekker, "Mapping Interfacial Regimes of Control," 237.

64. United States Department of Homeland Security, *Privacy Impact Assessment for ICE Investigative Case Management*, 1.

65. Knight and Gekker, "Mapping Interfacial Regimes of Control," 236, 240.

66. Anzaldúa, *Borderlands/La Frontera*, 2.

67. Pacheco, *Battles in the Desert*, 117.

68. Gallón, "When Neighbors Played Volleyball over the U.S.-Mexico Border Fence."

CHAPTER 3. CALIFORNIA COPS BECOME THE TIP OF THE SPEAR

1. Harcourt, *Exposed*, 93; and Davis, *City of Quartz*, 224, 242–243.

2. Tieu, "Picturing the Asian Gang Member," 44.

3. Most of the information in CalGang is entered by local law enforcement agencies, including police at secondary schools, colleges, and universities, as well as prison and juvenile detention staff. However, there have also been entries made in CalGang by employees of public service agencies, transit authority, social services, and hospitals. See Garcia-Leys and Brown, *Analysis of the Attorney General's Annual Report*, 21.

4. These two bodies administered CalGang until 2018, when California Assembly Bill 90 transferred oversight to the California Department of Justice.

5. CalGang Executive Board, *CalGang Executive Board Meeting Minutes.*

6. SRA International, Inc., *Technical Proposal in Response to RFQ#HSCEMD-10-Q-00035*, 14–17.

7. Hardy, "SRA to Buy Orion."

8. Van Hofwegen, "Unjust and Ineffective," 682.

9. Pittman, "Constructing a Compromise," 1515.

10. Los Angeles County Sheriff's Department, *CalGang Criminal Intelligence System Audit Report*, 7. The STEP Act defines street gangs as groups that meet the following criteria: "1) a formal or informal group of three or more individuals, 2) with a primary activity of committing one or more crimes, 3) who have a common name or identifying symbol, and 4) whose members individually or collectively engage in a pattern of criminal activity." See Van Hofwegen, "Unjust and Ineffective," 682.

11. California State Auditor, *CalGang Criminal Intelligence System*, 15.

12. Van Gennip et al., "Community Detection Using Spectral Clustering on Sparse Geosocial Data," 69.

13. Brayne, *Predict and Surveil*, 76–77.

14. Gang intelligence data is integral to predictive policing efforts, a topic on which I focused more extensively in my first book. Predictive policing "refers to analytic techniques used by law enforcement to forecast potential criminal activity," as defined by Brayne (*Predict and Surveil*, 35–37, 69–70, 74). Using a variety of data and analytic techniques, police attempt to decipher patterns and predict the people most likely to commit crimes or the places most likely to host crimes. Private industry and academic institutions have been at the forefront of technological development, providing law enforcement with the proprietary algorithms, network analysis tools, and other surveillance machinery. Brayne notes that the LAPD may be moving from predictive policing to precision policing that more surgically targets individual repeat offenders. However, it is unclear as yet if precision policing is simply predictive policing by another name. The NAACP Legal Defense Fund argues that *precision policing* is a term used to disguise unconstitutional stop-and-frisk-like practices that the NYPD deploys as part of "military-style gang takedowns that target low-income communities of color across New York City." See NAACP Legal Defense Fund, "Abuse of Police Discretion."

15. Winston, "You May Be in California's Gang Database and Not Even Know It."

16. California State Auditor, *CalGang Criminal Intelligence System*, 12.

17. Woods, "Systemic Racial Bias and RICO's Application to Criminal Street and Prison Gangs," 307.

18. Winston, "Prosecutors Are Using Gang Laws to Criminalize Protest."

19. Lam, "Asian American Youth Violence as Genocide," 255. See also Lam, *Youth Gangs, Racism, and Schooling*.

20. Lam, "Racism, Schooling, and the Streets," 10; and Tieu, "Picturing the Asian Gang Member," 63–68.

21. Maharaj, "Rights Suit Involving Police Photos Is Settled," N.P; and Tieu, "Picturing the Asian Gang Member," 50; also see Tieu, "Picturing the Asian Gang Member," 51–54 for a similar case in Union City, California.

22. See generally Novich and Hunt, "'Get Off Me.'"

23. Garcia-Leys, Thompson, and Richardson, *Mislabeled*, 1; and California State Auditor, *CalGang Criminal Intelligence System*, 16.

24. SRA International, *White Paper GangNet Software*, 2. Other private companies contracted by the US government to assist with training and maintenance related to ICEGangs include Knowledge Consulting Group, Inc., Booz Allen Hamilton, Advanced Technologies and Laboratories International, Inc., and IBM Cognos Analytics.

25. *Memorandum of Understanding between the California Department of Justice, Bureau of Investigation (DOJ) and The Las Vegas Metropolitan Police Department*.

26. *Interconnection Services & Security Agreement . . . between California Department of Justice and Spokane Police Department*; *Interconnection Services & Security Agreement . . . between California Department of Justice and Washington-Baltimore HIDTA*; and *Interconnection Services & Security Agreement . . . between California Department of Justice and Arizona Department of Public Safety* (2011). Under the Washington-Baltimore High Intensity Drug Trafficking Area Program, the White House Office of National Drug Control Policy provides funding to federal, state, local, and tribal agencies in Maryland, Washington, D.C., Virginia, and West Virginia to coordinate drug enforcement efforts. See Washington-Baltimore High Intensity Drug Trafficking Areas, "Who We Are."

27. SRA International, *RFQ#HSCEMD-13-Q-00013, . . . Intelligence Analyst and Programmer Support*, 3–5; SRA International, *Technical Proposal in Response to RFQ#HSCEMD-10-Q-00035*, 18; CalGang Executive Board, *CalGang Executive Board Meeting Minutes*, September 9, 2010; and CalGang Executive Board, *CalGang Executive Board Meeting Minutes*, September 6, 2012.

28. CalGang Executive Board, *CalGang Executive Board Meeting Minutes*, September 27, 2007.

29. CalGang Executive Board, *CalGang Executive Board Meeting Minutes*, September 11, 2008.

30. *Memorandum of Understanding between the United States Department of Justice, Bureau of Alcohol, Tobacco, Firearms, and Explosives and California Department of Justice, Bureau of Investigation Regarding the Sharing of Information Relating to Criminal Street Gangs*; and CalGang Executive Board, *CalGang Executive Board Meeting Minutes*, January 26, 2006, and January 17, 2008.

31. *Memorandum of Understanding between the Federal Bureau of Investigation and California Department of Justice, Bureau of Investigation Regarding the Sharing of Information Relating to Criminal Street Gangs*; CalGang Executive Board, *CalGang Executive Board Meeting Minutes*, September 27, 2007.

32. Chacón, "A Diversion of Attention?" 1594; and Zilberg, *Space of Detention*, 93.

33. United States Department of Justice, *Attorney General Sessions Gives Remarks to Federal Law Enforcement*.

34. SRA Internatonal, Introduction to ICEGangs PowerPoint presentation; United States Department of Homeland Security, *Fact Sheet: ICEGangs*; *Memorandum of Understanding between the Department of Homeland Security, Immigration and Customs Enforcement and California Department of Justice, Criminal Intelligence Bureau Regarding the Sharing of Information Relating to Criminal Street Gangs*; SRA International, *Technical Proposal in Response to RFQ#HSCEMD-10-Q-00035*, 12.

35. Peter T. Edge, *Discontinued Use of the ICEGangs Database, US Immigration and Customs Enforcement Memorandum*.

36. SRA International ORION Center for Immigrations [sic] and Customs Enforcement, *ICE Investigations and Intelligence Systems Training*. Simultaneously, SRA developed ICE's ENFORCE applications, which would replace DACS.

37. Julie L. Myers, *US Immigration and Customs Enforcement ICE Police System (IPS), Directive*, 2–3.

38. Ibid. The Immigration and Nationality Act does not define gangs or delineate immigration consequences for gang membership or affiliation.

39. Office of Information Governance and Privacy, Immigration and Customs Enforcement, *Privacy Threshold Analysis*, 3. ICEGangs maintained the following information on subjects: name, photo, age, race,

gender, physical descriptors, scars/marks/tattoos, identifying numbers (including A-number, FBI number, inmate number, TECS record ID number, TECS case number, ENFORCE number, FINS number, SEVIS number, CIS identification number, SSN, passport number, driver's license number, and state IS number), gang membership status, gang, weapons, weapon model number, weapon serial number, employers, vehicle license plate number, VIN, locations frequented, and phone number.

40. "From: [REDACTED], To: HIS Division 2 Tasking, Subject: FW: 83455: Discontinued Use of the ICEGangs Database FOLDERID 83455," internal email obtained by author, June 20, 2016.

41. SRA International, *Technical Proposal in Response to RFQ#HSCEMD-10-Q-00035*, 17.

42. Marston, "Guilt by Alt-Association," 931–932. It should be noted that criminologists have long lent legitimacy to the idea that self-admission is an unproblematic and reliable indicator of gang involvement. See Barrows and Huff, "Gangs and Public Policy," 675–704.

43. United States Customs and Border Protection, "CBP Attaches [*sic*]."

44. Miller, *Empire of Borders*, 25–26, 35; and US Immigration and Customs Enforcement, "International Operations."

45. CalGang Executive Board, *CalGang Executive Board Meeting Minutes*, December 17, 2008.

46. Garcia-Leys and Brown, *Analysis of the Attorney General's Annual Report on CalGang for 2018*, 3.

47. Edge, *Discontinued Use of the ICEGangs Database*.

48. Ibid.

49. Edge, *Discontinued Use of the ICEGangs Database*; and Office of Information Governance and Privacy, Immigration and Customs Enforcement, *Privacy Threshold Analysis*, 2.

50. Ibid., 7.

51. United States Immigration and Customs Enforcement, *Fiscal Year 2018 ICE Enforcement and Removal Operations Report*, 11–12.

52. California State Senate Media Archive, *Senate Public Safety Committee Hearing*.

53. The notification requirement is nonretroactive, meaning that law enforcement is only required to notify newly designated minors and not required to notify minors who are already listed in CalGang. Senate Bill 458 also provides alleged gang members, associates, and affiliates the right to contest their designation. However, people under age eighteen represented only about 2 percent of the total CalGang universe at the time.

54. CA Stat § Gangs: Statewide Database 797-186.34 (2013–2014); and CA Stat § Criminal Gangs 752-186.34 (2015–2016).

55. CA Stat § Criminal Gangs 695-186.36 (2017–2018).

56. Puente and Winton, "LAPD's Data-Driven Culture."

57. Rector and Poston, "Officer Alleges LAPD Had Quotas."

58. Chabria, Rector, and Chang, "California Bars Police from Using LAPD Records in Gang Database."

59. ICE has increasingly directed resources to gang enforcement in Virginia and Maryland and has established partnerships with local police and schools to identify alleged gang members, particularly after several MS-13–related murders in 2019. See Matthew Barakat, "Police Link Random Slayings in Northern Virginia to MS-13," AP News, October 13, 2020.

60. "Palantir at The Los Angeles Police Department"; and Brayne, *Predict and Surveil*, 45, 53.

CHAPTER 4. A LAWYER WATCHES A WRECK UNFOLD

1. All names of attorneys are pseudonyms.

2. See generally, Green et al., "Modeling Contagion through Social Networks"; Rivera-Castro et al., "Mathematical Modelling, Analysis and Simulation of the Spread of Gangs"; and Sooknanan, Comissiong, and Bhatt, "Life and Death in a Gang." Yxta Maya Murray brilliantly deconstructs the problems with epidemiological conceptualizations of violence, namely the depoliticization and undercomprehension of violence. See Murray, "Pedagogy of Violence."

3. Goodman, "'It's Just Black, White, or Hispanic'"; Lopez-Aguado, *Stick Together and Come Back Home*; and Noferi and Koulish, "Immigration Detention Risk Assessment."

4. Hing, "ICE Admits Gang Operations Are Designed to Lock Up Immigrants."

5. Stern, "Bad Liars."

6. Del Bosque, "The Case That Made an Ex-ICE Attorney Realize the Government Was Relying on False 'Evidence' against Migrants."

7. Napolitano, *Exercising Prosecutorial Discretion*.

8. An applicant meets the basic DACA eligibility requirements if they were under the age of thirty-one as of June 15, 2012; came to the United States before their sixteenth birthday; have continuously resided in the United States from June 15, 2007, up to the present time; were physically present in the United States on June 15, 2012, and at the time of their

DACA application; had no lawful status on June 15, 2012; are currently in school, have graduated, or have obtained a certificate of completion from high school, have obtained a general education development (GED) certificate, or are an honorably discharged veteran of the Coast Guard or Armed Forces of the United States; and have not been convicted of a felony, significant misdemeanor, or three or more other misdemeanors and do not otherwise pose a threat to national security or public safety. See USCIS.gov.

9. Johnson, *Policies for the Apprehension, Detention and Removal of Undocumented Immigrants*, 3.

10. United States Citizenship and Immigration Services, *Consideration of Deferred Action for Childhood Arrivals*, 4.

11. Miller, *More Than a Wall*, 46.

12. United States Citizenship and Immigration Services, *DACA Refresher Training—Evaluating Issues of Criminality, Public Safety, and National Security*, 13, 22, 53, 66–67, 82.

13. Ibid., 83.

14. United States Citizenship and Immigration Services, *Revised Guidance for the Referral of Cases*, 3–4.

15. Zilberg, "Fools Banished from the Kingdom," 759.

16. López and Krogstad, *Key Facts about Unauthorized Immigrants Enrolled in DACA*; and Galli, "A Rite of Reverse Passage," 12.

17. United States Immigration and Customs Enforcement, National Gang Unit, *Operation Community Shield*.

18. Artola, "In Search of Uniformity," 864; and Chacón, "Diversion of Attention?," 1605.

19. Chacón, "Diversion of Attention?," 1604.

20. See generally Epp et al., *Pulled Over*; United States Department of Justice, Civil Rights Division, *Investigation of the Baltimore City Police Department*.

21. See generally Lynch, *Hard Bargains*; and Van Cleve, *Crook County*.

22. García Hernández, "Immigration Detention as Punishment," 1382–1389; and Reiter and Coutin, "Crossing Borders and Criminalizing Identity," 594.

23. Chacón, "Diversion of Attention?," 1566.

24. Ibid., 1570.

25. Morgan-Trostle and Zheng, *State of Black Immigrants*, 19–21.

26. United States Citizenship and Immigration Services, *DACA Refresher Training*, 75.

27. Kalhan, "Immigration Surveillance," 62–63.

28. See Valdez, "Reconceiving Immigration Politics."

29. Levine and Cooke, "Mexican 'DREAMer' Nabbed."

30. Lind, "ICE Has Access to DACA Recipients' Personal Information.,"

31. Nyers, *Irregular Citizenship, Immigration, and Deportation*, 207.

32. Carranza, "Homeland Security Chief Tours Wall Construction."

33. Miller, *More Than a Wall*, 60, 61.

34. Prendergast, "Contract for Stretch of Arizona Border Wall"; and Prendergast, "Ancient Watering Hole at Risk from Border Wall Construction."

35. Hesson, "Trump's Pick for ICE Director"; Kim, "Trump Warns against Admitting Unaccompanied Migrant Children"; and Rodríguez, *Letter to The Honorable Charles E. Grassley.*

36. Shaw, "At Helm of DHS."

CHAPTER 5. ICE RIGS AN ALGORITHM

1. "Class Petition for Writ of Habeas Corpus and Class Complaint for Declaratory and Injunctive Relief," 7, Velesaca v. Wolf et al. (S.D.N.Y. 2020, Case No. 1:20-cv-01803).

2. Schriro, *Immigration Detention Overview and Recommendations*, 17.

3. Morton, *Civil Immigration Enforcement*, 1.

4. Noferi and Koulish, "Immigration Detention Risk Assessment," 45.

5. Lageson, *Digital Punishment*; Ferguson, *Rise of Big Data Policing*; Brayne, *Predict and Surveil*; and Eubanks, *Automating Inequality*.

6. Morton, *Civil Immigration Enforcement*, 1–2.

7. ICE Levels were initially developed for the Secure Communities program, in which the fingerprints of people booked into local jails were automatically shared with federal immigration authorities during routine criminal records database checks. Secure Communities interoperability relies on other information systems, which are too extensive to go into here. See Morton, *Civil Immigration Enforcement*, 1–2.

8 United States Department of Homeland Security, *Privacy Impact Assessment Update for the Alien Criminal Response Information Management System (ACRIMe) & Enforcement Integrated Database (EID)*, 2.

9. Ibid., 5.

10. Foer, "How Trump Radicalized ICE." Inés Valdez, Mat Coleman, and Amna Akbar's concept of "paralegality" in the immigration system is helpful here. The authors define paralegality as "a number of sometimes clashing, sometimes complementary, practices that include legislation

and court cases (the legal), and also executive-level directives, administrative decisions, front-line actions by immigration enforcement officers and non-federal law enforcement officers, political wrangling at the state level, and pronouncements by the powerful union of Immigration and Customs Enforcement (ICE)." Rather than characterizing written directives as the true seat of immigrant control that frontline enforcement decisions either adhere to or deviate from, the authors situate written law, procedure, and discretionary frontline action as collectively constituting "actually existing" immigration control. Far from being a top-down affair, "immigration lawmakers and courts are frequently playing catch-up with the frontline officers charged with the task of immigration control" ("Missing in Action," 559).

11. Brayne, *Predict and Surveil*, 104. With the election of Donald Trump, the enforcement approaches and ideologies of the president, ICE leadership, and most officers more directly aligned, unleashing frontline officers to engage in brutal zero tolerance enforcement. See Foer, "How Trump Radicalized ICE."

12. United States Department of Homeland Security, *Privacy Impact Assessment Update for the Alien Criminal Response Information Management System (ACRIMe) & Enforcement Integrated Database (EID)*, 5, 7; and United States Department of Homeland Security, *Privacy Impact Assessment Update for the Enforcement Integrated Database (EID) Risk Classification Assessment (RCA 1.0), ENFORCE Alien Removal Module (EARM 5.0), and Crime Entry Screen (CES 2.0)*, 2–3.

13. United States Department of Homeland Security, *Privacy Impact Assessment Update for the Alien Criminal Response Information Management System (ACRIMe) & Enforcement Integrated Database (EID)*, 6.

14. Ibid.

15. Lyon, "Technology vs 'Terrorism,'" 673.

16. Citron, "Technological Due Process," 1263-1267.

17. Citron, "Technological Due Process," 1297; Strahilevitz, "Reputation Nation," 1667; Lyon, *Surveillance after Snowden*, 80; Eubanks, *Automating Inequality*, 190; and Brayne, *Predict and Surveil*, 18.

18. Lyon, *Surveillance as Social Sorting*, 13.

19. United States Immigration and Customs Enforcement, *Risk Classification Assessment ICE Leadership Scope Brief*, 4.

20. United States Department of Homeland Security, *Privacy Impact Assessment Update for the Enforcement Integrated Database (EID) Risk*

Classification Assessment (RCA 1.0), ENFORCE Alien Removal Module (EARM 5.0), and Crime Entry Screen (CES 2.0), 2–3; United States Department of Homeland Security, *Privacy Impact Assessment Update for the Alien Criminal Response Information Management System (ACRIMe) & Enforcement Integrated Database (EID)*, 5; and United States Immigration and Customs Enforcement, *Risk Classification Assessment ICE Leadership Scope Brief*, 11.

21. United States Department of Homeland Security, *Privacy Impact Assessment Update for the Enforcement Integrated Database (EID) Risk Classification Assessment (RCA 1.0), ENFORCE Alien Removal Module (EARM 5.0), and Crime Entry Screen (CES 2.0)*, 11.

22. United States Department of Homeland Security, *Privacy Impact Assessment Update for the Alien Criminal Response Information Management System (ACRIMe) & Enforcement Integrated Database (EID)*, 7.

23. United States Department of Homeland Security, *Privacy Impact Assessment Update for the Enforcement Integrated Database (EID) Criminal History Information Sharing (CHIS) Program*, 3.

24. United States Department of Homeland Security, *Privacy Impact Assessment Update for the Alien Criminal Response Information Management System (ACRIMe) & Enforcement Integrated Database*, 2–3.

25. "Class Petition for Writ of Habeas Corpus and Class Complaint for Declaratory and Injunctive Relief," 14, Velesaca v. Wolf et al. (S.D.N.Y. 2020, Case No. 1:20-cv-01803).

26. Bosworth, "Affect and Authority in Immigration Detention," 547.

27. Borger, "US Ice Officers 'Used Torture to Make Africans Sign Own Deportation Orders'"; and Kriel, "ICE Guards 'Systematically' Sexually Assaulted Detainees."

28. Foer, "How Trump Radicalized ICE."

29. United States Immigration and Customs Enforcement, *Risk Classification Assessment ICE Leadership Scope Brief*, 9.

30. United States Department of Homeland Security, *Privacy Impact Assessment Update for the Enforcement Integrated Database (EID) Risk Classification Assessment (RCA 1.0), ENFORCE Alien Removal Module (EARM 5.0), and Crime Entry Screen (CES 2.0)*; and Office of Inspector General, *U.S. Immigration and Customs Enforcement's Alternatives to Detention (Revised)*, 4–5.

31. United States Department of Homeland Security, *Privacy Impact Assessment Update for the Enforcement Integrated Database (EID) Risk*

Classification Assessment (RCA 1.0), ENFORCE Alien Removal Module (EARM 5.0), and Crime Entry Screen (CES 2.0), 4.

32. Office of Inspector General, *U.S. Immigration and Customs Enforcement's Alternatives to Detention (Revised)*, 11.

33. United States Department of Homeland Security, *Privacy Impact Assessment Update for the Enforcement Integrated Database (EID) Risk Classification Assessment (RCA 1.0), ENFORCE Alien Removal Module (EARM 5.0), and Crime Entry Screen (CES 2.0)*, 5–6.

34. Ibid.

35. Ibid.

36. Ibid., 4–5; and Noferi and Koulish, "Immigration Detention Risk Assessment," 45.

37. United States Department of Homeland Security, *Privacy Impact Assessment Update for the Enforcement Integrated Database (EID) Risk Classification Assessment (RCA 1.0), ENFORCE Alien Removal Module (EARM 5.0), and Crime Entry Screen (CES 2.0)*, 11.

38. Ibid., 11, 13.

39. Zadvydas v. Davis, 533 U.S. 678 (2001); Clark v. Martinez, 543 U.S. 371 (2005); and Rodriguez v. Robbins, 715 F. 3d 1127 (2013). See generally Pantoja, Menjívar, and Magaña, "Spring Marches of 2006"; and Nicholls, *DREAMers*.

40. Brayne, *Predict and Surveil*, 36. As more and more law enforcement agencies adopt data-driven practices, outstanding agencies may eventually conform out of isomorphic pressure.

41. Office of Inspector General, *U.S. Immigration and Customs Enforcement's Alternatives to Detention (Revised)*, 18.

42. Ibid., 2.

43. Ibid., 11.

44. Ibid., 11–12.

45. Breisblatt, "Government Detains LGBT Immigrants at Higher Rates."

46. Ibid.; and Walia, *Border & Rule*, 81.

47. Noferi and Koulish, "Immigration Detention Risk Assessment," 86–87.

48. Ibid.

49. Starr, "Evidence-Based Sentencing and the Scientific Rationalization of Discrimination," 803. See also Harcourt, "Risk as a Proxy for Race" (scientific language); and Noferi and Koulish, "Immigration Detention Risk Assessment," 87 ("detention will continue").

50. Werth, "Theorizing the Performative Effects of Penal Risk Technologies," 3; and Koulish, "Sovereign Bias, Crimmigration, and Risk," 10.

51. Office of Inspector General, *U.S. Immigration and Customs Enforcement's Alternatives to Detention (Revised)*, 15.

52. Kalhan, "Immigration Policing and Federalism through the Lens of Technology, Surveillance, and Privacy," 1135–1136.

53. Ibid., 1135; Noferi and Koulish, "Immigration Detention Risk Assessment," 87; and Citron, "Technological Due Process," 1271.

54. Brayne, *Predict and Surveil*, 99–100.

55. "Deposition of Judith Almodovar," 151, November 18, 2020, Velesaca v. Wolf et al. (S.D.N.Y. 2020, Case No. 1:20-cv-01803).

56. Gary Mead, "To: All ERO Employees; Subject: Risk Classification Assessment," email, n.d.

57. United States Immigration and Customs Enforcement, *Risk Classification Assessment ICE Leadership Scope Brief*, 4.

58. Ibid., 9, 26.

59. Brayne, *Predict and Surveil*, 98.

60. United States Department of Homeland Security, *Privacy Impact Assessment Update for the Enforcement Integrated Database (EID) Risk Classification Assessment (RCA 1.0), ENFORCE Alien Removal Module (EARM 5.0), and Crime Entry Screen (CES 2.0)*, 11; United States Department of Homeland Security, *Privacy Impact Assessment Update for the Alien Criminal Response Information Management System (ACRIMe) & Enforcement Integrated Database (EID)*, 7; and Noferi and Koulish, "Immigration Detention Risk Assessment," 86–87.

61. Economists estimate that anywhere between 9 percent and nearly 40 percent of jobs in industrialized countries are vulnerable to replacement by automation in the next twenty years. See Arntz, Gregory, and Zierahn, "Revisiting the Risk of Automation," 158.

62. As Brayne notes, automation does not replace discretion but rather moves discretion to other parts of the enforcement process: often earlier, less visible parts. See Brayne, *Predict and Surveil*, 19.

63. Speri, "Detained, Then Violated; Borger, "US ICE Officers 'Used Torture to Make Africans Sign Own Deportation Orders'"; Kriel, "ICE Guards 'Systematically' Sexually Assaulted Detainees"; Olivares and Washington, "'He Just Empties You All Out'"; and Stamm et al., *Detained and Denied*.

64. Lyon, *Identifying Citizens*, 13.

65. United States Immigration and Customs Enforcement, *Fiscal Year 2018 ICE Enforcement and Removal Operations Report*, 2.

66. Ibid.

67. United States Immigration and Customs Enforcement, *Fiscal Year 2017 ICE Enforcement and Removal Operations Report*, 3 (emphasis added).

68. Rosenberg and Levinson, "Trump's Catch-and-Detain Policy Snares Many"; and "Class Petition for Writ of Habeas Corpus and Class Complaint for Declaratory and Injunctive Relief," 2, Velesaca v. Wolf et al. (S.D.N.Y. 2020, Case No. 1:20-cv-01803). The fact that ICE personnel continued to use the risk classification assessment process even though the outcome was predestined can also be seen as reflective of a phenomenon uncovered in law and society research, wherein organizations point to antidiscrimination polices and grievance procedures as proof of compliance with antidiscrimination laws, regardless of how well they actually achieve the goal of nondiscrimination. See, for example Edelman et al., "When Organizations Rule."

69. Rivera, "Acting Homeland Security Secretary Hops on ATV"; and Greene and Block, "Bush Visits Arizona-Mexico Border to Tout Changes."

70. Brean, "Unprecedented Saguaro 'Side Blooms' Could Be a Bad Sign"; and Davis, "Cruz-ing Again," A1, A2.

71. Hesson, "Trump's Pick for ICE Director"; and Dreier, "I've Been Reporting on MS-13 for a Year."

CHAPTER 6. WE MAKE OUR OWN MAPS

1. California Department of Justice, *California Department of Justice's Review of Immigration Detention in California*, 33; and Dreisbach, "Despite Findings of 'Negligent' Care, ICE to Expand Troubled Calif. Detention Center."

2. United States Department of Homeland Security, *Privacy Impact Assessment Update for the Enforcement Integrated Database (EID) Law Enforcement Notification System (LENS)*, 1–2; and United States Department of Homeland Security, *Privacy Impact Assessment Update for the Enforcement Integrated Database (EID) Prosecutions Module (PM), Electronic Removal Management Portal (eRMP), Operations Management Module (OM²), Law Enforcement Notification System (LENS), and Compliance Assistance Reporting Terminal (CART)*, 7.

3. Detention based on categorizations of danger is covered extensively in chapter 5. Prioritized deportation for criminality and alleged gang membership is covered in chapters 3 and 4. For examples of solitary confinement and police brutality directed at alleged gang members,

see Associated Press, "California Prisons to End Solitary Confinement of Gang Members"; and Tieu, "Picturing the Asian Gang Member," 43.

4. Valdez, "Immigration Enforcement, Technology, and the Banishment of Politics."

5. The LAPD has developed outreach programs to incorporate immigrant communities and claims to adhere to departmental mandates that limit the LAPD's practice of immigration policing and cooperation with ICE. However, the LAPD has been criticized for alerting ICE to immigrants in LAPD custody. See, for example, the case of Xochitl Hernandez. See also Armenta, "Between Public Service and Social Control" for an examination of similar tensions within the Metropolitan Nashville Police Department.

6. Homeland Security Advisory Council, *Task Force on Secure Communities Findings and Recommendations*, 7–10.

7. Lai and Lasch, "Crimmigration Resistance," 547.

8. Kobach, "Quintessential Force Multiplier," 181.

9. Cox and Miles, "Policing Immigration," 93.

10. United States Department of Homeland Security, "Immigration and Enforcement Operational Records (ENFORCE) System of Records," 80 Fed. Reg. 24269 (April 30, 2015).

11. Luquetta, Manning, and Miller, "Predictive Policing Case Studies in Los Angeles and Chicago," 61; for more on chronic offender identification and targeting see Brayne, *Predict and Surveil*, 75.

12. Executive Office of the President, "Executive Order 13768," 8801.

13. Mai-Duc, "Federal Judge Bars Trump Administration from Tying Immigration Enforcement to Anti-Gang Money."

14. United States Department of Homeland Security, *Privacy Impact Assessment Update for the Enforcement Integrated Database (EID) Law Enforcement Notification System (LENS)*, 2. In a study of the LAPD, Brayne finds this same language related to chronic offender bulletins. Officers told Brayne that the bulletins are for "situational awareness" and do not provide probable cause to stop someone. See Brayne, *Predict and Surveil*, 75–76.

15. United States Congress, House Committee on Oversight and Government Reform, *Criminal Aliens Released by the Department of Homeland Security*, 5.

16. National Center for Campus Public Safety, *Weekly Snapshot*.

17. For those who prefer to think in terms of calendar years, from March 2015 (when the data begins) to December 2015, ICE released 524 LENS

notifications; between January 2016 and December 2016, 2,664 notifications; and between January 2017 and September 2017, 4,910 notifications.

18. Flynn, "¿Dónde Está La Frontera?," 26.

19. De León, *Land of Open Graves*, 6–7.

20. Walia, *Border & Rule*, 107, 110.

21. Miller, *More Than a Wall*, 19.

22. Recall that ICE sends LENS notifications to both the city into which an immigrant is released from ICE custody and if different, the city in which the immigrant settles. In about 90 percent of all cases, the receiving city is different from the release city, indicating that immigrants released from detention are leaving to other locales followed by LENS notification to local law enforcement.

23. Chacón, "Whose Community Shield?," 326; and Lynch, "Backpacking the Border," 116.

24. Macías-Rojas, *From Deportation to Prison*, 55–57.

25. Lam, "Asian American Youth Violence as Genocide, 255; Lam, "Racism, Schooling, and the Streets," 10; Tieu, "Picturing the Asian Gang Member," 63–68; and Novich and Hunt (2016), "'Get Off Me.'"

26. Walia, *Border & Rule*, 31; Selod, *Forever Suspect*, 65; and Morley et al. *"There Is a Target on Us,"* 20.

27. See generally Armenta, "Between Public Service and Social Control"; Chacón, "Unsecured Borders"; Lynch, "Backpacking the Border"; Provine and Doty, "Criminalization of Immigrants as a Racial Project"; Van Cleve, *Crook County*; and Zilberg, *Space of Detention*.

28. Stop LAPD Spying Coalition, *Fuck the Police, Trust the People*, 3.

29. Raustiala, *Does the Constitution Follow the Flag?*, 184; Menjívar, "Immigration Law Beyond Borders," 357 (intraterritorial enforcement); and Kalhan, "Fourth Amendment and Privacy Implications of Interior Immigration Enforcement," 1165 ("physical border itself").

30. Kanstroom, *Deportation Nation*, 6.

31. McDowell and Wonders refer to raids, checkpoints, and racist harassment by law enforcement as constituting "enforcement rituals." See McDowell and Wonders, "Keeping Migrants in Their Place," 57; and De Genova, *Working the Boundaries*, 246.

32. Selod, *Forever Suspect*, 63.

33. Leyva et al., "Part 3: Pol[ICE] in My Head," 2.

34. See, for example, United States Customs and Border Protection, "Western Hemisphere Travel Initiative (WHTI) Frequently Asked Questions."

35. Treviso et al., "Beyond the Wall," F2, F18.

36. Rosas, "Managed Violences of the Borderlands," 404–405.

37. For more on racial terror committed by both law enforcement and civilian vigilantes, see Ward, "Living Histories of White Supremacist Policing," 172.

38. Foer, "How Trump Radicalized ICE"; and Blitzer, "Veteran ICE Agent, Disillusioned with the Trump Era, Speaks Out."

39. Hamilton, Winton, and Queally, "'Border Patrol Detains 22-Year-Old Cal State L.A. Student Activist."

40. Raustiala, *Does the Constitution Follow the Flag?*, 155.

CHAPTER 7. A BORDER BLEEDS OUT

1. Georgetown University Law Center, *Between the Border and the Street*, 1–2.

2. Coutin, "Confined Within," 206.

3. Zilberg, "Fools Banished from the Kingdom," 772, 776; Zilberg, "Gangster in Guerilla Face," 41; and Coutin, "Exiled by Law" 353, 363, 367.

4. Georgetown University Law Center, *Between the Border and the Street*, 2–3; and Zilberg, "Gangster in Guerilla Face," 39–40. Despite the global presence of MS-13, scholars and experts have doubts that subsets in different locations act in concert under a unifying organizational structure. See Barak, León, and Maguire, "Conceptual and Empirical Obstacles in Defining MS-13."

5. Carter emphasizes that the term *mara* does not simply describe a gang but rather refers to the "intersection of state and non-state criminal activity, and the social worlds established there." The concept of *mara* captures street violence *and state corruption* in the shadow of a destabilized state. See Carter, "Carceral Kinship," 32.

6. Zilberg, "Gangster in Guerilla Face," 49.

7. Carter, "Carceral Kinship," 32; and Zilberg, "Gangster in Guerilla Face," 49.

8. United States Congress, House Committee on Foreign Affairs, Subcommittee on the Western Hemisphere, *Deportees in Latin America and the Caribbean*, 14–15, 38, 66; Temple, "Merry-Go-Round of Youth Gangs," 193–194; United States Congress, House Committee on Foreign Affairs, Subcommittee on the Western Hemisphere, *Violence in Central America*, 11–22; Pinkham, "Assessing the Collateral International Consequences of

the U.S.' Removal Policy," 228; and Taylor and Aleinikoff, "Deportation of Criminal Aliens," N.P.

9. United States Congress, House Committee on Foreign Affairs, Subcommittee on the Western Hemisphere, *Deportees in Latin America and the Caribbean*, 15–16; United States Congress, House Committee on Foreign Affairs, Subcommittee on the Western Hemisphere, *Violence in Central America*, 9–10.

10. Prior to the Classic Air Charter Contract, CSI Aviation was ICE Air's main data broker. See University of Washington Center for Human Rights, *Hidden in Plain Sight*.

11. United States Immigration and Customs Enforcement, *ICE Air Operations Fact Sheet*; and Burnett, "ICE Air."

12. United States Department of Homeland Security, *Privacy Impact Assessment Update for the Enforcement Integrated Database (EID)* (2010); and United States Department of Homeland Security, *Privacy Impact Assessment Update for the Enforcement Integrated Database (EID)* (2014).

13. United States Congress, House Committee on Foreign Affairs, Subcommittee on the Western Hemisphere, *Combatting Transnational Criminal Threats in the Western Hemisphere*, 75.

14. United States Department of Homeland Security, *Privacy Impact Assessment Update for the Enforcement Integrated Database (EID) Criminal History Information Sharing (CHIS) Program*. DHS/ICE/PIA-015(h), 3-4.

15. Menjívar, "Immigration Law Beyond Borders," 355.

16. Bersin, "Lines and Flows," 392.

17. Kalhan, "Immigration Surveillance," 60.

18. Raustiala, *Does the Constitution Follow the Flag?*, 159.

19. For a discussion of deterritorialized "securocratic wars of public safety," see Feldman, "Securocratic Wars of Public Safety," 330–350.

20. Miller, *Empire of Borders*, 28, 37–38.

21. Del Bosque, "Immigration Officials Use Secretive Gang Databases to Deny Migrant Asylum Claims."

22. *Guardian* staff and agencies in Washington, "Biden Strikes International Deal."

23. Morley et al., *"There is a Target on Us"*, 10.

24. Ibid., 10, 36.

25. Menjívar, "Immigration Law Beyond Borders," 358; Ryan, "Extraterritorial Immigration Control," 3, 24–26; and Provine and Doty, "Criminalization of Immigrants as a Racial Project."

26. Shachar, "Shifting Border of Immigration Regulation," 188; and Miller, *Empire of Borders*, 112.

27. Raustiala, *Does the Constitution Follow the Flag?*, 161–162.

28. See Central American Law Enforcement Exchange (CALEE), "Stories"; CBS Los Angeles, "LAPD Trains Central American Police Officers on Anti-Gang Tactics"; Raustiala, *Does the Constitution Follow the Flag?*, 163; and Graham, *Cities under Siege*, xvi.

29. Partlow and Miroff, "U.S. Gathers Data on Migrants Deep in Mexico"; United States Congress, House Committee on Foreign Affairs, Subcommittee on the Western Hemisphere, *Combatting Transnational Criminal Threats in the Western Hemisphere*, 64–65; Longo, *Politics of Borders*, 87, 113; Andreas, "Redrawing the Line," 90; and Graham, *Cities under Siege*, xxii.

30. Graham, *Cities under Siege*, 90.

31. All names of migrants are pseudonyms.

32. Pinkham, "Assessing the Collateral International Consequences," 228, 241.

33. Zilberg, "Fools Banished from the Kingdom," 772, 776; Zilberg, "Gangster in Guerilla Face," 41; Coutin, "Exiled by Law" 353, 363, 367; and Georgetown University Law Center, *Between the Border and the Street*, 1–2.

34. Pinkham, "Assessing the Collateral International Consequences," 229–231, 236–237.

35. Coutin, "Confined Within," 201.

36. Zilberg, "Gangster in Guerilla Face," 37, 41, 44; and Coutin, "Exiled by Law," 353, 363, 367.

37. Georgetown University Law Center, *Between the Border and the Street*, 1–2.

38. United States Department of Homeland Security, *Privacy Impact Assessment Update for the Enforcement Integrated Database (EID)* (2014), 5.

39. Ibid., 4–5.

40. See Palfrey and Gasser for a discussion of four modes of interoperability: technological, data, human, and institutional. Institutional interoperability involves ensuring that societal systems, including legal systems, are compatible enough to make the information exchanged substantively meaningful (*Interop*, 6).

41. United States Department of Homeland Security, *Privacy Impact Assessment Update for the Enforcement Integrated Database (EID)* (2014), 5.

42. Cape Verde is not a partner country to which ICE and DHS send outgoing information.

CHAPTER 8. A HAND SEARCHES FOR A ROOT

1. Prendergast, "Contract for Stretch of Arizona Border Wall Raises Concerns."

2. Trevizo, "A Privately Funded Border Wall Was Already at Risk"; Prendergast, "Monsoon Storm Floods Border Wall Project"; and Miroff, "Trump's Border Wall, Vulnerable to Flash Floods."

3. Anzaldúa, Borderlands/La Frontera, 3.

4. This simultaneous abandonment and violation in some ways exemplifies Giorgio Agamben's concept of "bare life," in which colonial powers exercise unmitigated violence alongside a complete withdrawal of other supports to the population. See generally Agamben, Homo Sacer.

5. Longo, Politics of Borders, xiv.

6. Ibid., 57.

7. In Eichmann in Jerusalem: A Report on the Banality of Evil, Hannah Arendt writes about the banality of evil in the context of Holocaust perpetrators who abdicated responsibility for their actions, instead claiming to have only followed orders, adhered to the law, or done their jobs.

8. See Bowker and Star: "True universality is necessarily always out of reach. At the same time, the vision of global data gathering and sharing is enormously powerful, and it needs to be understood on its own terms" (Sorting Things Out, 108).

9. Mezzadra and Neilson, Border as Method, 159; and De Genova, "Migrant 'Illegality' and Deportability in Everyday Life," 439.

10. Walia, Border and Rule, 2–4.

11. Nyers, Irregular Citizenship, Immigration, and Deportation, 16, 54–55.

12. Rosas, "Necro-subjection," 304.

13. Nancy Wonders refers to this separation of insiders and outsider through vilification as a "rhetorical border" that is "designed to criminalize and/or stigmatize border crossers." See Wonders, "Globalization, Border Reconstruction Projects, and Transnational Crime," 37.

14. Artola, "In Search of Uniformity," 864; and Chacón, "Diversion of Attention?," 1605.

15. Sullivan, "On Thin ICE," 113.

16. Kanstroom, Deportation Nation, 74, 77–80; and Parker, Making Foreigners, 123.

17. Parker, Making Foreigners, 218.

18. Benjamin, Race after Technology, 17.

19. Aas applies Calhoun's concept of "categorical identity" to describe the erasure of narrative, context, and nuance in identity construction via digital databases. See Aas, "From Narrative to Database"; and Calhoun, *Critical Social Theory*).

20. See, for example, Aas, "Bordered Penality"; and Bigo, "Globalized (In)security."

21. Borger, "US ICE Officers 'Used Torture to Make Africans Sign Own Deportation Orders"; Kriel, "ICE Guards 'Systematically' Sexually Assaulted Detainees"; Alderstein, "Not-Guilty Verdict Absolves Border Patrol of Cross-Border Killing"; Olivares and Washington, "'He Just Empties You All Out'"; and Ainsley and Soboroff, "Lawyers Say They Can't Find the Parents of 545 Migrant Children."

22. Rivera-Garza identifies the contemporary nation-state government as dedicated primarily to the invocation of spectacular horror ("Grieving"); Haggerty and Ericson discuss disembodiment and data flows as part of a surveillant assemblage ("Surveillant Assemblage").

23. Da Silva, "Over 250,000 Sign Petition to Stop ICE Using Powerful Disinfectant"; American Immigration Lawyers Association, "Deaths in Adult Detention Centers" Speri, "Detained, Then Violated"; and Stamm, et al., *Detained and Denied*.

24. Hu, "Algorithmic Jim Crow," 645, 695, 669.

25. Zilberg, "Gangster in Guerilla Face," 45. Zilberg is speaking of gang-like behavior in the LAPD's Community Resources Against Street Hoodlums (CRASH) program in the Rampart Division.

26. Cerise Castle, Twitter, April 20, 2021, https://twitter.com/cerisecastle/status/1384621148718080003?lang=en; Society of Professional Journalists, Greater Los Angeles chapter, Twitter, April 20, 2021, https://twitter.com/SPJLA/status/1384582278332878852; Castle, "Protected Class"; and Los Angeles County Sheriff's Department, *Sheriff Alex Villanueva Addresses Policy on Deputy Cliques and Subgroups with Department Members*.

27. Klippenstein, "How ICE Became a 'Propaganda Machine' for Trump."

28. Allen, "Florida Adopts Nation's Toughest Restrictions on Protests"; and Murphy, "New Legislation Would Protect Drivers Who Hit Protesters."

29. Shepherd and Berman, "'It Was Like Being Preyed Upon."

30. Graham, *Cities Under Siege*, 20.

31. German, *Hidden in Plain Sight*.

32. Devereaux, "Unchecked Union"; Olivares and Washington, "'He Just Empties You All Out'"; Ainsley and Soboroff, "Lawyers Say They Can't

Find the Parents of 545 Migrant Children"; Moore, Schmidt, and Jameel, "Inside the Cell Where a Sick 16-Year-Old Boy Died in Border Patrol Care"; and Gonzales, "Sexual Assault of Detained Migrant Children Reported in the Thousands since 2015."

33. Bergengruen, "In Last-Minute Swing through Key States, DHS and ICE Are Making the Case for Donald Trump's Re-Election"; and del Bosque, "Group of Agents Rose through the Ranks to Lead the Border Patrol."

34. Sullivan, "On Thin ICE," 113; and 6Davidson and Kim, "Additional Powers of Search and Seizure at and Near the Border," 1-4.

35. Winston, "Prosecutors Are Using Gang Laws to Criminalize Protest"; and Biscobing, "'Prime for Abuse.'"

36. Brayne, *Predict and Surveil*, 156.

37. See Sarat and Silbey, "Pull of the Policy Audience."

38. Friedman, *Unwarranted*, 28 ("countless innocents"); and Lyon, *Surveillance after Snowden*, 75–76 ("have much to fear").

39. Walia, *Border & Rule*, 83.

40. Strahilevitz, "Reputation Nation," 1667 ("dropouts with long rap sheets"); and Ferguson, *Rise of Big Data Policing*, 84 ("grandmother").

41. Rizzo, *Catch and Detain*, 4 (emphasis added).

42. Lyon, *Surveillance after Snowden*, 38.

43. Akbar, "Abolitionist Horizon for (Police) Reform," 1826–1827; and Roberts, "Abolition Constitutionalism," 114.

44. Akbar, "Abolitionist Horizon for (Police) Reform," 1788.

45. Ibid., 1838.

46. McDowell and Fernandez, "Disband, Disempower, and Disarm," 377; and Davis, *Abolition Democracy*, 75.

47. Michael Sellars, "LAPD—'Diverse, Inclusive, Evolved'"; Rector, Karlamangla, and Winton, "LAPD's Use of Batons, Other Weapons Appears to Violate Rules."

48. Rector, "'It Stood Out to Me as Egregious.'"

49. Mackey, "As Transphobes Rally Again at Los Angeles Spa, Police Attack Counterprotesters."

50. Police-academic collaborations are part of what Stephen Graham identifies as the "authoritarian turn in criminology" (*Cities under Siege*, 86).

51. See Ward for a discussion of truth telling as the first step in a transformative justice approach to combatting White supremacist policing ("Living Histories of White Supremacist Policing," 177).

52. Foer, "How Trump Radicalized ICE." Considering Foer's simplistic portrayal and dismissal of abolition, his solution is unimpressive: to return immigration enforcement to the way it functioned five to fifteen years ago!

53. Haggerty and Ericson, "Surveillant Assemblage," 609.

54. In *Cities under Siege*, Graham argues that "acts of immigration are now often being deemed little more than acts of warfare" (xx).

55. Emphasis added. See "Harsha Walia & Ayesha A. Siddiqi On the Real Migrant Crisis."

56. Mezzadra and Neilson, *Border as Method*, 267.

METHODOLOGICAL APPENDIX

1. Knight and Gekker, "Mapping Interfacial Regimes of Control," 232.

2. See generally Smith, *Institutional Ethnography*; and Smith, *Writing the Social*.

3. Bowker and Star, *Sorting Things Out*; and Goodman, "'It's Just Black, White, or Hispanic,'" 738.

4. United States Department of Homeland Security, "Office of the Secretary [DHS-2006-0060]," 64544.

5. National Archives, The Privacy Act of 1974; and Clarke, "Privacy Impact Assessment."

6. A DHS Privacy Impact Assessment template is available at www.dhs.gov/sites/default/files/publications/privacy_pia_template%202017.pdf.

7. United States Department of Homeland Security, *Privacy Impact Assessment for the TECS System: Platform*, 22.

8. Timmermans and Tavory, "Theory Construction in Qualitative Research."

9. Committee on Government Reform, *Citizen's Guide on Using the Freedom of Information Act*, 3.

10. Ibid.

11. Executive Office of the President, "Executive Order 13768," 8802.

12. United States Department of Homeland Security, *Privacy Impact Assessment for the Enforcement Integrated Database (EID)*, 16.

13. Ibid., 24–25.

14. Cooper, "Cop Fragility and Blue Lives Matter," 647. See also Jones and Norwood, "Aggressive Encounters & White Fragility," 2054–2055.

15. It is worth noting that journalists routinely file FOIA and PRA lawsuits.

16. See JPat Brown, "MuckRock's FOIA Redaction Hall of Shame."

17. Committee on Government Reform, *Citizen's Guide on Using the Freedom of Information Act*, 3 (emphasis added).

18. Klippenstein, "ICE Just Became Even Less Transparent."

19. Longo, *Politics of Borders*, 192–193.

Bibliography

Aas, Katja Franko. "Analysing a World in Motion: Global Flows Meet 'Criminology of the Other.'" *Theoretical Criminology* 11(2) (2007):283–303.

———. "Bordered Penality: Precarious Membership and Abnormal Justice." *Punishment & Society* 16(5) (2014):520–541.

———. "From Narrative to Database: Technological Change and Penal Culture." *Punishment & Society* 6(4) (2004):379–393.

Agamben, Giorgio. *Homo Sacer: Sovereign Power and Bare Life.* Palo Alto, CA: Stanford University Press, 1995.

Ainsley, Julia. "U.S. Officials Made List of Reporters, Lawyers, Activists to Question at Border." NBC News, March 6, 2019. www.nbcnews.com /politics/immigration/u-s-officials-made-list-reporters-lawyers -activists-question-border-n980301.

Ainsley, Julia, and Jacob Soboroff. "Lawyers Say They Can't Find the Parents of 545 Migrant Children Separated by Trump Administration." NBC News, October 20, 2020. www.nbcnews.com/politics /immigration/lawyers-say-they-can-t-find-parents-545-migrant -children-n1244066.

Akbar, Amna A. "An Abolitionist Horizon for (Police) Reform." *California Law Review* 108(6) (2020):1781–1846.

Alderstein, Ana. "A Not-Guilty Verdict Absolves Border Patrol of Cross-Border Killing." National Public Radio, November 25, 2018. www.npr.org/2018/11/25/670668243/a-not-guilty-verdict-absolves-border-patrol-of-cross-border-killing.

Allen, Greg. "Florida Adopts Nation's Toughest Restrictions On Protests." National Public Radio, April 19, 2021. www.npr.org/2021/04/19/988791175/florida-adopts-nations-toughest-restrictions-on-protests.

American Immigration Lawyers Association. "Deaths in Adult Detention Centers." October 8, 2021. www.aila.org/infonet/deaths-at-adult-detention-centers.

Amoore, Louise. "Biometric Borders: Governing Mobilities in the War on Terror." *Political Geography* 25 (2006):336–351.

Andreas, Peter. "Redrawing the Line: Borders and Security in the Twenty-first Century." *International Security* 28(2) (2003):78–111.

Anzaldúa, Gloria. *Borderlands/La Frontera: The New Mestiza.* San Francisco: Aunt Lute Books, 1987.

Arendt, Hannah. *Eichmann in Jerusalem: A Report on the Banality of Evil.* London: Penguin Classics, 1963.

Armenta, Amada. "Between Public Service and Social Control: Policing Dilemmas in the Era of Immigration Enforcement." *Social Problems* 63(1) (2016):111–126.

Arntz, Melanie, Gregory, Terry, and Ulrich Zierahn. "Revisiting the Risk of Automation." *Economics Letters* 159 (2017):157–160.

Artola, Lilibet. "In Search of Uniformity: Applying the Federal Rules of Evidence in Immigration Removal Proceedings." *Rutgers Law Review* 64 (2012):863–893.

Associated Press. "California Prisons to End Solitary Confinement of Gang Members after Pelican Bay Prisoners Sue." *Mercury News,* September 1, 2015.

Balibar, Étienne. "Europe as Borderland." *Environment and Planning D: Society and Space* 27 (2009):190–215.

———. *Politics and the Other Scene.* London: Verso, 2002.

Barak, Maya P., Kenneth Sebastian León, and Edward R. Maguire. "Conceptual and Empirical Obstacles in Defining MS-13." *Criminology & Public Policy* 19 (2020):563–589.

Barakat, Matthew. "Police Link Random Slayings in Northern Virginia to MS-13." AP News, October 13, 2020. https://abcnews.go.com/US

/wireStory/police-link-random-slayings-northern-virginia-ms-13
-73589009.

Barrows, Julie, and C. Ronald Huff. "Gangs and Public Policy: Constructing and Deconstructing Gang Databases." *Criminology and Public
Policy* 8(4) (2009):675–704.

Benjamin, Ruha. *Race after Technology: Abolitionist Tools for the New
Jim Code*. Medford, MA: Polity Press, 2019.

Bergengruen, Vera. "In Last-Minute Swing Through Key States, DHS and
ICE Are Making the Case for Donald Trump's Re-Election," *Time*,
October 29, 2020.

Bersin, Alan. "Lines and Flows: The Beginning and End of Borders."
Brooklyn Journal of International Law 37(2) (2012):389–406.

Bigo, Didier. "Globalized (In)security: The Field and the Ban-Opticon."
Pp. 10–48 in *Terror, Insecurity and Liberty: Illiberal Practices of
Liberal Regimes After 9/11*, edited by D. Bigo and A. Tsoukala. Abing-
don, UK: Routledge, 2008.

———. "Security, Exception, Ban and Surveillance." In *Theorizing
Surveillance: The Panopticon and Beyond*, edited by D. Lyon, 46–68.
Portland, OR: Willan Publishing, 2006.

Biscobing, Dave. "'Prime for Abuse': Lack of Oversight Lets Phoenix
Police Add Protesters to Gang Database." ABC15 Arizona, May 24,
2021. www.abc15.com/news/local-news/investigations/protest-arrests
/prime-for-abuse-lack-of-oversight-lets-phoenix-police-add-protesters
-to-gang-database.

Blitzer, Jonathan. "A Veteran ICE Agent, Disillusioned with the Trump
Era, Speaks Out." *New Yorker*, July 24, 2017.

Borders, Trade, and Immigration (BTI) Institute, a Department of
Homeland Security Center of Excellence Led by the University of
Houston. *Program Year 5 Annual Report 01 July 2019–30 June 2020*.
https://uh.edu/bti/about/bti-annual_report_py5.pdf.

Borger, Julian. "US Ice Officers 'Used Torture to Make Africans Sign Own
Deportation Orders.'" *Guardian*, October 22, 2020.

Bosworth, Mary. "Affect and Authority in Immigration Detention."
Punishment & Society 21(5) (2019):542–559.

Bowker, Geoffrey C., and Susan Leigh Star. 2002. *Sorting Things Out:
Classification and Its Consequences*. Cambridge, MA: MIT Press,
2002.

Braverman, Irus. "Civilized Borders: A Study of Israel's New Crossing
Administration." *Antipode* 43(2) (2010):264–295.

Brayne, Sarah. "Big Data Surveillance: The Case of Policing." *American Sociological Review* 82(5) (2017):977–1008.

———. *Predict and Surveil: Data, Discretion, and the Future of Policing.* Oxford: Oxford University Press, 2020.

Brean, Henry. "Unprecedented Saguaro 'Side Blooms' Could Be a Bad Sign." *Arizona Daily Star*, May 22, 2021.

Breisblatt, Joshua. "Government Detains LGBT Immigrants at Higher Rates." *Immigration Impact*, October 28, 2016.

Brown, JPat. "MuckRock's FOIA Redaction Hall of Shame." March 14, 2016. www.muckrock.com/news/archives/2016/mar/14/muckrocks -redaction-hall-shame/.

Browne, Simone. *Dark Matters: On the Surveillance of Blackness.* Durham, NC: Duke University Press, 2015.

Burnett, John. "ICE Air: The Airline You Never Want to Fly." National Public Radio, September 26, 2018. www.npr.org/2018/09/26 /651710659/ice-air-the-airline-you-never-want-to-fly.

Burrington, Ingrid. "What Amazon Taught the Cops: Predictive Policing Is Just Another Form of Supply-Chain Efficiency." *Nation*, May 27, 2015.

Bush, George W. "President Bush Signs Secure Fence Act." George W. Bush White House Archives, 2006. https://georgewbush-whitehouse .archives.gov/news/releases/2006/10/20061026.html.

CalGang Executive Board. *CalGang Executive Board Meeting Minutes.* Various dates from January 26, 2006, to September 6, 2012.

Calhoun, Craig. *Critical Social Theory: Culture, History, and the Challenge of Difference.* Oxford: Blackwell, 1995.

California Department of Justice. *The California Department of Justice's Review of Immigration Detention in California.* Sacramento, CA: Office of the Attorney General, 2021.

California State Senate Media Archive. Senate Public Safety Committee Hearing, Sacramento, CA, June 21, 2016.

California State Auditor. 2016. *The CalGang Criminal Intelligence System.* Sacramento, CA.

Campbell/Harris Security Equipment Company (CSECO). "Choose the Density Meter CBP Agents Helped Design." May 25, 2020. www.cseco .com/ChoosetheDensityMeterCBPAgentsHelpedDesign.

Carby, Hazel V. *Imperial Intimacies: A Tale of Two Islands.* London: Verso, 2019.

Carranza, Rafael. "Homeland Security Chief Tours Wall Construction, Gauges Pandemic Response at Arizona Border." *Arizona Republic,* May 12, 2020.

Carter, Jon Horne. "Carceral Kinship: Future Families of the Late Leviathan." *Journal of Historical Sociology* 32 (2019):26–37.

Castle, Cerise. 2021. "The Protected Class." Knock LA, March 22, 2021. https://knock-la.com/lasd-gangs-little-devils-wayside-whities -cavemen-vikings/.

CBS Los Angeles. "LAPD Trains Central American Police Officers On Anti-Gang Tactics." August 15, 2011. https://losangeles.cbslocal.com /2011/08/15/lapd-trains-central-american-police-officers-on-anti -gang-tactics/.

Central American Law Enforcement Exchange (CALEE). "Stories." https://archives.fbi.gov/archives/news/stories/2009/november/calee _111009.

Chabria, Anita, Kevin Rector, and Cindy Chang. "California Bars Police from Using LAPD Records in Gang Database: Critics Want It Axed. *Los Angeles Times,* July 14, 2020.

Chacón, Jennifer M. 2010. "A Diversion of Attention? Immigration Courts and the Adjudication of Fourth and Fifth Amendment Rights." *Duke Law Journal* 59:1563–1633.

———. "Overcriminalizing Immigration." *Journal of Criminal Law & Criminology* 102(3) (2012):613–652.

———. "Unsecured Borders: Immigration Restrictions, Crime Control and National Security." *Connecticut Law Review* 39(5) (2007): 1827–1891.

———. "Whose Community Shield? Examining the Removal of the 'Criminal Street Gang Member.'" *University of Chicago Legal Forum* (2007):317–357.

Citron, Danielle Keats. "Technological Due Process." *Washington University Law Review* 85(6) (2008):1248–1313.

Clarke, Roger. "Information Technology and Dataveillance." *Communications of the ACM* 31(5) (1988): 498–512.

———. "Privacy Impact Assessment: Its Origins and Development." *Computer Law & Security Review* 25(2) (2009):123–135.

Committee on Government Reform. *A Citizen's Guide on Using the Freedom of Information Act and the Privacy Act of 1974 to Request Government Records.* Washington, DC: House of Representatives, 2005.

Cooper, Frank Rudy. "Cop Fragility and Blue Lives Matter." *University of Illinois Law Review* (2020):621–661.

Côté-Boucher, Karine. "The Diffuse Border: Intelligence-Sharing, Control and Confinement along Canada's Smart Border." *Surveillance & Society* 5(2) (2008):142–165.

Coutin, Susan Bibler. "Confined Within: National Territories as Zones of Confinement." *Political Geography* 29 (2010):200–208.

———. "Exiled by Law: Deportation and the Inviability of Life." In *The Deportation Regime: Sovereignty, Space, and the Freedom of Movement*, edited by Nicholas De Genova and Nathalie Peutz, 351–370. Durham, NC: Duke University Press, 2010.

———. "Falling Outside: Excavating the History of Central American Asylum Seekers." *Law & Social Inquiry* 26 (2011):569–596.

———. "The Rights of Noncitizens in the United States." *Annual Review of Law and Social Science* 7 (2011):289–308.

Cox, Adam B., and Thomas J. Miles. "Policing Immigration." *University of Chicago Law Review* 80 (2013):87–136.

Da Silva, Chantal. "Over 250,000 Sign Petition to Stop ICE Using Powerful Disinfectant as Detainees Allegedly Suffer Serious Side Effects." *Newsweek*, June 3, 2020.

Davidson, David L., and Gina Kim. "Additional Powers of Search and Seizure at and Near the Border." *Border Policy Research Institute Publications* 33 (2009):1–4.

Davis, Angela. *Abolition Democracy: Beyond Empire, Prisons, and Torture.* New York: Seven Stories Press, 2005.

Davis, Mike. *City of Quartz: Excavating the Future in Los Angeles.* New York: Verso, 2006.

Davis, Tony. "Cruz-ing Again: New Project Putting Water Back into River." *Arizona Daily Star*, June 23, 2019.

De Genova, Nicholas. "Detention, Deportation, and Waiting: Toward a Theory of Migrant Detainability." Global Detention Project Working Paper No. 18, December 1, 2016.

———. "Migrant 'Illegality' and Deportability in Everyday Life." *Annual Review of Anthropology* 31 (2002):419–447.

———. *Working the Boundaries: Race, Space, and "Illegality" in Mexican Chicago.* Durham, NC: Duke University Press, 2005.

De León, Jason. *The Land of Open Graves: Living and Dying on the Migrant Trail.* Berkeley: University of California Press, 2015.

del Bosque, Melissa. "The Case That Made an Ex-ICE Attorney Realize the Government Was Relying on False 'Evidence' against Migrants." ProPublica, August 13, 2019. www.propublica.org/article/laura-pena -gang-database-the-case-that-made-an-ex-ice-attorney-realize-the -government-was-relying-on-false-evidence-against-migrants.

———. "A Group of Agents Rose Through the Ranks to Lead the Border Patrol: They're Leaving It in Crisis." ProPublica, February 10, 2020. www.propublica.org/article/a-group-of-agents-rose-through-the -ranks-to-lead-the-border-patrol-theyre-leaving-it-in-crisis.

———. "Immigration Officials Use Secretive Gang Databases to Deny Migrant Asylum Claims." ProPublica, July 8, 2019. www.propublica .org/article/immigration-officials-use-secretive-gang-databases-to -deny-migrant-asylum-claims.

Devereaux, Ryan. "An Unchecked Union." The Intercept, December 27, 2020. https://theintercept.com/2020/12/27/border-patrol-trump -biden-politics/.

Dowling, Julie A., and Jonathan Xavier Inda. *Governing Immigration through Crime: A Reader.* Stanford, CA: Stanford University Press, 2013.

Dreier, Hannah. "I've Been Reporting on MS-13 for a Year: Here Are the 5 Things Trump Gets Most Wrong." ProPublica, June 25, 2018. www .propublica.org/article/ms-13-immigration-facts-what-trump -administration-gets-wrong.

Dreisbach, Tom. "Despite Findings of 'Negligent' Care, ICE to Expand Troubled Calif. Detention Center." National Public Radio, January 15, 2020. www.npr.org/2020/01/15/794660949/despite-findings-of -negligent-care-ice-to-expand-troubled-calif-detention-center#:~:text =Twitter-,Despite%20Findings%20Of%20'Negligent'%20Care%2C %20ICE%20To%20Expand%20Troubled,Detention%20Center&text =Chris%20Carlson%2FAP-,The%20Adelanto%20ICE%20Processing %20Center%20in%20Adelanto%2C%20Calif.%2C%20can,contract %20with%20the%20federal%20government.

Edelman, Lauren B., Linda H. Kreiger, Scott R, Eliason, Catherine R. Albiston, and Virginia Mellema. "When Organizations Rule: Judicial Deference to Institutionalized Employment Structures. *American Journal of Sociology* (117) (2011):888–954.

Edge, Peter T. *Discontinued Use of the ICEGangs Database, US Immigration and Customs Enforcement Memorandum.* October 19, 2016.

Epp, Charles R., Donald P. Haider-Markel, and Steven Maynard-Moody. *Pulled Over: How Police Stops Define Race and Citizenship.* Chicago: University of Chicago Press, 2014.

Eubanks, Virginia. *Automating Inequality: How High-Tech Tools Profile, Police, and Punish the Poor.* New York: St. Martin's Press, 2018.

Executive Office of the President. "Executive Order 13768: Enhancing Public Safety in the Interior of the United States." 82 Fed. Reg. 8799–8803 (January 30, 2017).

———. "Executive Order 13773: Enforcing Federal Law with Respect to Transnational Criminal Organizations and Preventing International Trafficking." 82 Fed. Reg. 10691–10693 (February 14, 2017).

———. *President Donald J. Trump's State of the Union Address.* Washington, DC: The White House, January 30, 2018.

Fang, Lee, and Sam Biddle. "Google AI Tech Will Be Used for Virtual Border Wall, CBP Contract Shows." The Intercept, October 21, 2020. https://theintercept.com/2020/10/21/google-cbp-border-contract-anduril/.

Feldman, Allen. "Securocratic Wars of Public Safety: Globalized Policing as Scopic Regime." *Interventions* 6(3) (2006):330–350.

Ferguson, Andrew G. *The Rise of Big Data Policing: Surveillance, Race, and the Future of Law Enforcement.* New York: New York University Press, 2017.

Flynn, Michael. "¿Dónde Está La Frontera?" *Bulletin of the Atomic Scientists* 58(4) (2002):24–35.

Foer, Franklin. "How Trump Radicalized ICE." *Atlantic*, September 2018. www.theatlantic.com/magazine/archive/2018/09/trump-ice/565772/.

Friedman, Barry. *Unwarranted: Policing without Permission.* New York: Farrar, Straus and Giroux, 2017.

Galli, Chiara. "A Rite of Reverse Passage: The Construction of Youth Migration in the US Asylum Process." *Ethnic and Racial Studies* 41(9) (2018):1651–1671.

Gallón, Angélica. "When Neighbors Played Volleyball over the U.S.-Mexico Border Fence." Univision News, April 6, 2017. www.univision.com/univision-news/culture/when-neighbors-played-volleyball-over-the-u-s-mexico-border-fence.

Garcia Hernández, César Cuauhtémoc. "Immigration Detention as Punishment." *UCLA Law Review* 61 (2014):1346–1548.

Garcia-Leys, Sean, and Nicole Brown. *Analysis of the Attorney General's Annual Report on CalGang for 2018.* Los Angeles, CA: Urban Peace Institute, 2019.

Garcia-Leys, Sean, Meigan Thompson, and Christyn Richardson. *Mislabeled: Allegations of Gang Membership and Their Immigration Consequences.* Irvine: University of California Irvine School of Law, 2016.

Georgetown University Law Center, Human Rights Institute. *Between the Border and the Street: A Comparative Look at Gang Reduction Policies and Migration in the United States and Guatemala.* Washington, DC, 2007.

German, Michael. *Hidden in Plain Sight: Racism, White Supremacy, and Far-Right Militancy in Law Enforcement.* New York: Brennan Center for Justice, 2020.

Gilliom, John, and Torin Monahan. *SuperVision: An Introduction to the Surveillance Society.* Chicago: University of Chicago Press, 2013.

Gonzales, Richard. "Sexual Assault of Detained Migrant Children Reported in the Thousands since 2015." National Public Radio, February 26, 2019. www.npr.org/2019/02/26/698397631/sexual-assault-of-detained-migrant-children-reported-in-the-thousands-since-2015.

Goodman, Philip. "'It's Just Black, White, or Hispanic': An Observational Study of Racializing Moves in California's Segregated Prison Reception Centers." *Law & Society Review* 42(4) (2008):735–770.

Graham, Stephen. *Cities under Siege: The New Military Urbanism.* New York: Verso, 2011.

Green, Ben, Thibaut Horel, and Andrew V. Papachristos. "Modeling Contagion through Social Networks to Explain and Predict Gunshot Violence in Chicago, 2006 to 2014." *JAMA Internal Medicine* 177(3) (2017):326–333.

Greene, David, and Melissa Block. "Bush Visits Arizona-Mexico Border to Tout Changes." National Public Radio, May 18, 2006. www.npr.org/templates/story/story.php?storyId=5415852.

Guardian staff and agencies in Washington. "Biden Strikes International Deal in Bid to Stop Migrants Reaching US Border." *Guardian,* April 12, 2021. www.theguardian.com/us-news/2021/apr/12/biden-migration-security-deal-mexico-guatemala-honduras.

Haggerty, Kevin D., and Richard V. Ericson. "The Surveillant Assemblage." *British Journal of Sociology* 51(4) (2000):605–622.

Hamilton, Matt, Richard Winton, and James Queally. 2017. "Border Patrol Detains 22-Year-Old Cal State L.A. Student Activist; Her Lawyer Says It Is Retaliation." *Los Angeles Times,* May 18.

Harcourt, Bernard E. *Exposed: Desire and Disobedience in the Digital Age.* Cambridge, MA: Harvard University Press, 2015.

———. "Risk as a Proxy for Race: The Dangers of Risk Assessment." *Federal Sentencing Reporter* 27(4) (2015):237–243.

Hardy, Michael. "SRA to Buy Orion." *Federal Computer Week*, January 8, 2004.

"Harsha Walia & Ayesha A. Siddiqi on the Real Migrant Crisis." High Snobeity, n.d. www.highsnobiety.com/p/harsha-walia-interview-ayesha-siddiqi-honors-week/.

Herzog, Lawrence, and Christophe Sohn. "The Co-mingling of Bordering Dynamics in the San Diego–Tijuana Cross-Border Metropolis." *Territory, Politics, Governance* 7(2) (2019):177–199.

Hesson, Ted. "Trump's Pick for ICE Director: I Can Tell Which Migrant Children Will Become Gang Members by Looking into Their Eyes." Politico, May 16, 2019. www.politico.com/story/2019/05/16/mark-morgan-eyes-ice-director-1449570.

Hing, Julianne. "ICE Admits Gang Operations Are Designed to Lock Up Immigrants." *Nation*, November 20, 2017.

Homeland Security Advisory Council. *Task Force on Secure Communities Findings and Recommendations.* Washington, DC: United States Department of Homeland Security, 2011.

Hu, Margaret. "Algorithmic Jim Crow." *Fordham Law Review* 86(2) (2017):633–696.

Interconnection Services & Security Agreement for Interagency Information Sharing on the Law Enforcement Network between California Department of Justice and Arizona Department of Public Safety. July 26, 2011.

Interconnection Services & Security Agreement for Interagency Information Sharing on the Law Enforcement Network between California Department of Justice and Spokane Police Department. July 26, 2011.

Interconnection Services & Security Agreement for Interagency Information Sharing on the Law Enforcement Network between California Department of Justice and Washington-Baltimore HIDTA. December 5, 2011.

Johnson, Jeh Charles. *Policies for the Apprehension, Detention and Removal of Undocumented Immigrants.* Washington, DC: United States Department of Homeland Security, 2014.

Johnson, Kevin R. "The Forgotten 'Repatriation' of Persons of Mexican Ancestry and Lessons for the 'War on Terror.'" *Pace Law Review* 26(1) (2005):1–26.

Jones, Trina, and Kimberly Jade Norwood. "Aggressive Encounters & White Fragility: Deconstructing the Trope of the Angry Black Woman." *Iowa Law Review* 102(5) (2017):2017–2070.

Kalhan, Anil. "The Fourth Amendment and Privacy Implications of Interior Immigration Enforcement." *UC Davis Law Review* 41(3) (2007):1137–1218.

———. "Immigration Policing and Federalism through the Lens of Technology, Surveillance, and Privacy." *Ohio State Law Journal* 74 (2013):1105–1165.

———. "Immigration Surveillance." *Maryland Law Review* 74(1) (2014):1–86.

Kanstroom, Daniel. *Deportation Nation: Outsiders in American History.* Cambridge, MA: Harvard University Press, 2007.

Kim, Seung Min. "Trump Warns against Admitting Unaccompanied Migrant Children: 'They're Not Innocent.'" *Washington Post*, May 23, 2018.

Klippenstein, Ken. "How ICE Became a 'Propaganda Machine' for Trump." *Nation*, October 6, 2020.

———. "ICE Just Became Even Less Transparent." *Nation*, July 2, 2020.

Knight, Emma, and Alex Gekker. "Mapping Interfacial Regimes of Control: Palantir's ICM in America's Post-9/11 Security Technology Infrastructures." *Surveillance & Society* 18(2) (2020):231–243.

Kobach, Kris W. "The Quintessential Force Multiplier: The Inherent Authority of Local Police to Make Immigration Arrests." *Albany Law Review* 69(1) (2006):179–236.

Koulish, Robert. "Sovereign Bias, Crimmigration, and Risk." In *Immigration Detention, Risk and Human Rights*, edited by M. João Guia, R. Koulish, and V. Mitsilegas, 1–10. New York: Springer, 2016.

Kriel, Lomi. "ICE Guards 'Systematically' Sexually Assaulted Detainees in an El Paso Detention Center, Lawyers Say." ProPublica, August 14, 2020. www.propublica.org/article/ice-guards-systematically-sexually -assault-detainees-in-an-el-paso-detention-center-lawyers-say.

Lageson, Sarah. *Digital Punishment: Privacy, Stigma, and the Harms of Data-Driven Criminal Justice.* Oxford: Oxford University Press, 2020.

Lai, Annie, and Christopher N. Lasch. "Crimmigration Resistance and the Case of Sanctuary City Defunding." *Santa Clara Law Review* 57(3) (2017):539–613.

Lam, Kevin D. "Asian American Youth Violence as Genocide: A Critical Appraisal and Its Pedagogical Significance." *Equity & Excellence in Education* 52(2–3) (2019):255–270.

——. "Racism, Schooling, and the Streets: A Critical Analysis of Vietnamese American Youth Gang Formation in Southern California." *Journal of Southeast Asian American Education and Advancement* 7(1) (2012):1–16.

——. *Youth Gangs, Racism, and Schooling: Vietnamese American Youth in a Postcolonial Context.* London: Palgrave Macmillan, 2015.

Levine, Dan, and Kristina Cooke. "Mexican 'DREAMer' Nabbed in Immigrant Crackdown." Reuters, February 14, 2017. www.reuters.com/article/us-usa-trump-immigration-arrest-exclusiv/mexican-dreamer-nabbed-in-immigrant-crackdown-idUSKBN15T307.

Leyva, Alma, Imelda S. Plascencia, Mayra Yoana Jaimes Pena, and Saba Waheed. "Part 3: Pol[ICE] in My Head." In *Undocumented and Uninsured: A Five-Part Report on Immigrant Youth and the Struggle to Access Health Care in California.* Los Angeles: Dream Resource Center at the UCLA Labor Center, n.d.

Lind, Dara. "ICE Has Access to DACA Recipients' Personal Information Despite Promises Suggesting Otherwise, Internal Emails Show." ProPublica, April 21, 2020. www.propublica.org/article/ice-has-access-to-daca-recipients-personal-information-despite-promises-suggesting-otherwise-internal-emails-show#:~:text=Series%3A%20Zero%20Tolerance-,ICE%20Has%20Access%20to%20DACA%20Recipients'%20Personal%20Information%20Despite,Suggesting%20Otherwise%2C%20Internal%20Emails%20Show&text=But%20internal%20emails%20show%20that,decided%20not%20to%20tell%20Congress.

Linnemann, Travis, and Bill McClanahan. "From 'Filth' and 'Insanity' to 'Peaceful Moral Watchdogs': Police, News Media, and the Gang Label." *Crime Media Culture* 13(3) (2017):295–313.

Longo, Matthew. *The Politics of Borders: Sovereignty, Security, and the Citizen after 9/11.* Cambridge: Cambridge University Press, 2017.

López, Gustavo, and Jens Manuel Krogstad. *Key Facts about Unauthorized Immigrants Enrolled in DACA.* Pew Research Center, 2017.

Lopez-Aguado, Patrick. *Stick Together and Come Back Home: Racial Sorting and the Spillover of Carceral Identity.* Oakland: University of California Press, 2018.

Los Angeles County Sheriff's Department. *CalGang Criminal Intelligence System Audit Report.* Project No. 2016-13-A. Los Angeles: Audit and Accountability Bureau, 2017.

———. *Sheriff Alex Villanueva Addresses Policy on Deputy Cliques and Subgroups with Department Members.* Video, n.d. https://lasd.org /deputy-clicks-and-subgroups/.

Luiselli, Valeria. *Tell Me How It Ends: An Essay in Forty Questions.* Minneapolis, MN: Coffee House Press, 2017.

Luquetta, Oriana, Clarissa Manning, and Matthew Miller. "Predictive Policing Case Studies in Los Angeles and Chicago." Presentation at the RAND Corporation Los Angeles Policy Symposium, UCLA Luskin School of Public Affairs, Applied Policy Project, 2016.

Lynch, Mona. "Backpacking the Border: The Intersection of Drug and Immigration Prosecutions in a High-Volume US Court." *British Journal of Criminology* 57 (2017):112–131.

———. *Hard Bargains: The Coercive Power of Drug Laws in Federal Court.* New York: Russell Sage Foundation, 2016.

Lyon, David. "The Border Is Everywhere: ID Cards, Surveillance and the Other." In *Global Surveillance and Policing: Borders, Security, Identity,* edited by E. Zureik and M. B. Salter, 66–82. Portland, OR: Willan Publishing, 2005.

———. *Identifying Citizens: ID Cards as Surveillance.* Malden, MA: Polity, 2009.

———. "Introduction, & Surveillance as Social Sorting: Computer Codes and Mobile Bodies." In *Surveillance as Social Sorting: Privacy, Risk, and Digital Discrimination,* edited by D. Lyon, 1–30. New York: Routledge Press, 2003.

———. *Surveillance after September 11.* Cambridge, UK: Polity, 2003.

———. *Surveillance after Snowden.* Malden, MA: Polity Press, 2015.

———. "Technology vs 'Terrorism': Circuits of City Surveillance since September 11th." *International Journal of Urban and Regional Research* 27(3) (2003):666–678.

Lytle Hernandez, Kelly. *Migra! A History of the U.S. Border Patrol.* Berkeley: University of California Press, 2010.

Macías-Rojas, Patrisia. *From Deportation to Prison: The Politics of Immigration Enforcement in Post-Civil Rights America.* New York: New York University Press, 2016.

Mackey, Robert. "As Transphobes Rally again at Los Angeles Spa, Police Attack Counterprotesters." The Intercept, July 18, 2021. https:// theintercept.com/2021/07/18/transphobes-rally-los-angeles-spa-police -attack-counterprotesters/.

Maharaj, Davan. "Rights Suit Involving Police Photos Is Settled." *Los Angeles Times*, December 12, 1995.

Mai-Duc, Christine. "Federal Judge Bars Trump Administration from Tying Immigration Enforcement to Anti-Gang Money." *Los Angeles Times*, February 15, 2019.

Mann, Steve, Jason Nolan, and Barry Wellman. "Sousveillance: Inventing and Using Wearable Computing Devices for Data Collection in Surveillance Environments." *Surveillance & Society* 1(3) (2003):331–355.

Marston, Rebecca J. "Guilt by Alt-Association: A Review of Enhanced Punishment for Suspected Gang Members." *University of Michigan Journal of Law Reform* 52 (2019):923–935.

Martinez, Monica Muñoz. *The Injustice Never Leaves You: Anti-Mexican Violence in Texas*. Cambridge, MA: Harvard University Press, 2018.

Marx, Gary T. *Windows into the Soul: Surveillance and Society in and Age of High Technology*. Chicago: University of Chicago Press, 2016.

McDowell, Meghan G., and Luis A. Fernandez. "'Disband, Disempower, and Disarm': Amplifying the Theory and Practice of Police Abolition." *Critical Criminology* 26 (2018):373–391.

McDowell, Meghan G., and Nancy A. Wonders. "Keeping Migrants in Their Place: Technologies of Control and Racialized Public Space in Arizona." *Social Justice* 36(2) (2009–2010):54–72.

Meissner, Doris, Donald M. Kerwin, Muzaffar Chishti, and Claire Bergeron. *Immigration Enforcement in the United States: The Rise of a Formidable Machinery*. Washington, DC: Migration Policy Institute, 2013.

Memorandum of Understanding between the California Department of Justice, Bureau of Investigation (DOJ) and The Las Vegas Metropolitan Police Department. September 21, 2004.

Memorandum of Understanding between the Department of Homeland Security, Immigration and Customs Enforcement and California Department of Justice, Criminal Intelligence Bureau Regarding the Sharing of Information Relating to Criminal Street Gangs. January 3, 2006.

Memorandum of Understanding between the Federal Bureau of Investigation and California Department of Justice, Bureau of Investigation Regarding the Sharing of Information Relating to Criminal Street Gangs. November 16, 2006.

Memorandum of Understanding between the United States Department of Justice, Bureau of Alcohol, Tobacco, Firearms, and Explosives and

California Department of Justice, Bureau of Investigation Regarding the Sharing of Information Relating to Criminal Street Gangs. February 6, 2006.

Menjívar, Cecilia. "Immigration Law Beyond Borders: Externalizing and Internalizing Border Controls in an Era of Securitization." *Annual Review of Law and Social Science* 10 (2014):353–69.

Mezzadra, Saandro, and Brett Nielson. *Border as Method, Or, the Multiplication of Labor.* Durham, NC: Duke University Press, 2013.

Miller, Teresa A. "Citizenship and Severity: Recent Immigration Reforms and the New Penology." *Georgetown Immigration Law Journal* 17 (2003): 611–666.

Miller, Todd. *Empire of Borders: The Expansion of the US Borders around the World.* New York: Verso, 2019.

———. *More Than a Wall: Corporate Profiteering and the Militarization of US Borders.* Amsterdam, Netherlands: Transnational Institute, 2019.

Miroff, Nick. "Trump's Border Wall, Vulnerable to Flash Floods, Needs Large Storm Gates Left Open for Months." *Washington Post*, January 30, 2020.

Moore, Robert, Susan Schmidt, and Maryam Jameel. "Inside the Cell Where a Sick 16-Year-Old Boy Died in Border Patrol Care." ProPublica, December 5, 2019.

Morgan-Trostle, Juliana, and Kexin Zheng. *The State of Black Immigrants: Part II, Black Immigrants in the Mass Criminalization System.* New York: Black Alliance for Just Immigration and New York University Law School Immigrant Rights Clinic, 2020.

Morley, S. Priya, Goss, Molly, Abdulkareem, Yusuf, Gurmu, Tsion, and Katherine La Puente. *"There Is a Target on Us": The Impact of Mexico's Anti-Black Racism on African Migrants at Mexico's Southern Border.* Brooklyn, NY: Black Alliance for Just Immigration, 2021.

Morton, John. *Civil Immigration Enforcement: Priorities for the Apprehension, Detention, and Removal of Aliens.* Washington, DC: United States Department of Homeland Security, 2010.

Muñiz, Ana. "Secondary Ensnarement: Surveillance Systems in the Service of Punitive Immigration Enforcement." *Punishment & Society* 22(4) (2020): 461–482.

Murphy, Sean. "New Legislation Would Protect Drivers Who Hit Protesters." ABC News, February 20, 2021. https://abcnews.go.com/US/wireStory/legislation-protect-drivers-hit-protestors-76016885.

Murray, Yxta Maya. "The Pedagogy of Violence." *California Interdisciplinary Law Journal* 20(3) (2011):537–584.

Myers, Julie L. *US Immigration and Customs Enforcement ICE Police System (IPS), Directive: ICE Gang Member Identification Criteria.* August 4, 2006.

NAACP Legal Defense Fund. "Abuse of Police Discretion." 2018. www.naacpldf.org/case-issue/nypds-gang-policing-tactics/.

Napolitano, Janet. *Exercising Prosecutorial Discretion with Respect to Individuals Who Came to the United States as Children.* Washington, DC: United States Department of Homeland Security, 2021.

National Archives. The Privacy Act of 1974. 2019. www.archives.gov/about/laws/privacy-act-1974.html.

National Center for Campus Public Safety. *Weekly Snapshot*, August 31, 2016. www.nccpsafety.org/news/weekly-snapshot-archives/2016/08.

National Immigration Project of the National Lawyers Guild, Immigrant Defense Project, Mijente. *Who's Behind ICE? The Tech and Data Companies Fueling Deportations.* 2018. www.nationalimmigrationproject.org/PDFs/community/2018_23Oct_whos-behind-ice.pdf.

Newell, Bryce Clayton, Ricardo Gomez, and Verónica E. Guajardo. "Censors, Cameras, and the New 'Normal' in Clandestine Migration: How Undocumented Migrants Experience Surveillance at the U.S.-Mexico Border." *Surveillance & Society* 15(1) (2017):21–41.

Nicholls, Walter J. *The DREAMers: How the Undocumented Youth Movement Transformed the Immigrant Rights Debate.* Stanford, CA: Stanford University Press, 2013.

Noferi, Mark, and Robert Koulish. "The Immigration Detention Risk Assessment." *Georgetown Immigration Law Journal* 29 (2014):45–94.

Novich, Madeleine, and Geoffrey Hunt. "'Get Off Me': Perceptions of Disrespectful Police Behaviour among Ethnic Minority Youth Gang Members." *Drugs: Education, Prevention and Policy* 24(3) (2017):248–255.

Nyers, Peter. *Irregular Citizenship, Immigration, and Deportation.* New York: Routledge, 2018.

Office of Information Governance and Privacy, Immigration and Customs Enforcement. *Privacy Threshold Analysis (PTA) for Dispositioning an ICE System.* September 22, 2016.

Office of Inspector General. *Detention and Removal of Illegal Aliens.* OIG-06-33. Washington, DC: United States Department of Homeland Security, 2006.

———. *Immigration and Customs Enforcement's Tracking and Transfers of Detainees*. Washington, DC: US Department of Homeland Security, 2009.

———. *The Immigration and Naturalization Service's Removal of Aliens Issued Final Orders*. Report Number I-2003-004. Washington, DC: United States Department of Justice, 2003.

———. *Review of U.S. Immigration and Customs Enforcement's Detainee Tracking Process*. OIG-07-08. Washington, DC: Unites States Department of Homeland Security, 2006.

———. *Supervision of Aliens Commensurate with Risk*. Washington, DC: United States Department of Homeland Security, 2011.

———. *U.S. Immigration and Customs Enforcement's Alternatives to Detention (Revised)*. Washington, DC: United States Department of Homeland Security, 2015.

Olivares, José, and John Washington. "'He Just Empties You All Out': Whistleblower Reports High Number of Hysterectomies at ICE Detention Facility." The Intercept, September 15, 2020.

Pacheco, José Emilio. *Battles in the Desert & Other Stories*. New York: New Directions Books, 1987.

"Palantir at The Los Angeles Police Department." N.d. www.palantir.com /pt_media/palantir-at-the-los-angeles-police-department/ (no longer available).

Palfrey, John, and Urs Gasser. *Interop: The Promise and Perils of Highly Interconnected Systems*. New York: Basic Books, 2012.

Pallitro, Robert, and Josiah Heyman. "Theorizing Cross-Border Mobility: Surveillance, Security and Identity." *Surveillance & Society* 5(3) (2008):315–333.

Pantoja, Adrian D., Cecilia Menjívar, and Lisa Magaña. "The Spring Marches of 2006: Latinos, Immigration, and Political Mobilization in the 21st Century." *American Behavioral Scientist* 52(4) (2008):499–506.

Parenti, Christian. *The Soft Cage: Surveillance in America from Slavery to the War on Terror*. New York: Basic Books, 2004.

Parker, Kunal M. *Making Foreigners: Immigration and Citizenship Law in America, 1600–2000*. New York: Cambridge University Press, 2015.

Parrish, Will. "The U.S. Border Patrol and an Israeli Military Contractor Are Putting a Native American Reservation under 'Persistent Surveillance.'" The Intercept, August 25, 2019.

Partlow, Joshua, and Nick Miroff. "U.S. Gathers Data on Migrants Deep in Mexico, a Sensitive Program Trump's Rhetoric Could Put at Risk." *Washington Post*, April 6, 2018.

Perera, Suvendrini. "Burning Our Boats." *Journal of the Association for the Study of Australian Literature* 15(3) (2016):1–11.

Pinkham, Tara. "Assessing the Collateral International Consequences of the U.S.' Removal Policy." *Buffalo Human Rights Law Review* 12 (2006):223–246.

Pittman, Lauren M. "Constructing a Compromise: The Current State of Gang Database Legislation and How to Effectuate Nationwide Reform." *Iowa Law Review* 106 (2021):1513–1554.

Prendergast, Curt. "Ancient Watering Hole at Risk from Border Wall Construction." *Arizona Daily Star*, September 8, 2019.

———. "Contract for Stretch of Arizona Border Wall Raises Concerns of Improper Influence." *Arizona Daily Star*, December 7, 2019.

———. "Monsoon Storm Floods Border Wall Project across Arizona's San Pedro River." *Arizona Daily Star*, August 6, 2020.

Provine, Doris M., and Roxanne L. Doty. "The Criminalization of Immigrants as a Racial Project." *Journal of Contemporary Criminal Justice* 27(3) (2011):261–277.

Puente, Mark, and Richard Winton. "LAPD's Data-Driven Culture under Scrutiny amid Scandal over Fake Gang Identifications." *Los Angeles Times*, January 21, 2020.

Raustiala, Kal. *Does the Constitution Follow the Flag? The Evolution of Territoriality in American Law.* New York: Oxford University Press, 2009.

Rector, Kevin. "'It Stood Out to Me as Egregious': Protestors, Others Allege LAPD Violence at Echo Park Sweep." *Los Angeles Times*, March 30, 2021.

Rector, Kevin, Soumya Karlamangla, and Richard Winton. "LAPD's Use of Batons, Other Weapons Appears to Violate Rules, Significantly Injuring Protesters, Times Review Finds." *Los Angeles Times*, June 11, 2020.

Rector, Kevin, and Ben Poston. "Officer Alleges LAPD Has Quotas, Silenced Whistleblowers in Gang-Labeling Scandal." *Los Angeles Times*, August 27, 2020.

Reiter, Keramet, and Susan Coutin. "Crossing Borders and Criminalizing Identity: The Disintegrated Subjects of Administrative Sanctions." *Law & Society Review* 51(3) (2017):567–601.

Rivera, Salvador. "Acting Homeland Security Secretary Hops on ATV and Tours Border Barrier." KRQE, October 28, 2020. www.borderreport

.com/hot-topics/the-border-wall/acting-homeland-security-secretary
-hops-on-atv-and-tours-border-barrier/#:~:text=Acting%20Homeland
%20Security%20Secretary%20hops%20on%20ATV%20and%20
tours%20border%20barrier,-The%20Border%20Wall&text=SAN
%20DIEGO%20(Border%20Report)%20%E2%80%94,between%20
San%20Diego%20and%20Tijuana.

Rivera Garza, Cristina. *Grieving: Dispatches from a Wounded Country.*
New York: The Feminist Press at CUNY, 2020.

Rivera-Castro, Miguel, Pradyuta Padmanabhan, Carmen Caiseda, Padma-
nabhan Seshaiyer, and Carlos Boria-Guanill. "Mathematical Modelling,
Analysis and Simulation of the Spread of Gangs Interacting Youth and
Adult Populations. *Letters in Biomathematics* 6(2) (2019):1–19.

Rizzo, Carolina. Catch and Detain: The Detention Bed Quota and the
United States' Overreliance on Detention as a Tool for the Enforce-
ment of Immigration Laws. *Congressional Hispanic Caucus Institute
White Paper*, April 2014. https://chci.org/wp-content/uploads/2017/11
/201442123234769694-2014LawGraduateSummitWhitePaper-Carolina
Rizzo.pdf.

Roberts, Dorothy E. "Abolition Constitutionalism." *Harvard Law Review*
133(1) (2019): 1–122.

Rodríguez, León. *Letter to The Honorable Charles E. Grassley.* Washington, DC: US Citizenship and Immigration Services, 2015.

Rosas, Gilberto. "The Managed Violences of the Borderlands: Treacher-
ous Geographies, Policeability, and the Politics of Race." *Latino
Studies* 4 (2006):401–418.

———. "Necro-subjection: On Borders, Asylum, and Making Dead to Let
Live." *Theory & Event* 22(2) (2019):303–324.

Rosenberg, Mica, and Reade Levinson. "Trump's Catch-and-Detain
Policy Snares Many Who Have Long Called U.S. Home." Reuters
Investigates, June 20, 2018. www.reuters.com/investigates/special
-report/usa-immigration-court/.

Rumford, Chris. "Citizens and Borderwork in Europe." *Space and Polity*
12(1) (2008):1–12.

———. "Theorizing Borders." *European Journal of Social Theory* 9(2)
(2006):155–169.

———. "Towards a Multiperspectival Study of Borders." *Geopolitics* 17(4)
(2012):887–902.

Ryan, Bernard. "Extraterritorial Immigration Control: What Role for
Legal Guarantees?" In *Extraterritorial Immigration Control: Legal*

Challenges, edited by B. Ryan and V. Mitsilegas, 1–37. Leiden, Netherlands: Brill, 2010.

Salter, Mark B. "Theory of the /: The Suture and Critical Border Studies." *Geopolitics* 17(4) (2012):734–755.

Sarat, Austin, and Susan Silbey. "The Pull of the Policy Audience." *Law & Policy* 10(2–3) (1988): 97–166.

Schriro, Dora. *Immigration Detention Overview and Recommendations*. Washington, DC: United States Department of Homeland Security, 2009.

Sellars, Michael (Reserve Officer). "LAPD—'Diverse, Inclusive, Evolved.'" *Rotator*, December 1, 2020.

Selod, Saher. *Forever Suspect: Racialized Surveillance of Muslim Americans in the War on Terror*. New Brunswick, NJ: Rutgers University Press, 2018.

Shachar, Ayelet. "The Shifting Border of Immigration Regulation." *Stanford Journal of Civil Rights & Civil Liberties* 3 (2007):165–193.

Shaw, Adam. "At Helm of DHS, Chad Wolf Vows to Confront the Gangs Behind Illegal Drugs, Guns and Migrants." Fox News, November 25, 2019. www.foxnews.com/politics/dhs-chief-wolf-gangs-drugs.

Shepherd, Katie, and Mark Berman. "'It Was Like Being Preyed Upon': Portland Protesters Say Federal Officers in Unmarked Vans Are Detaining Them." *Washington Post*, July 17, 2020.

Singh, Balbir K. "Decoding Dress: Countersurveillance Poetics and Practices under Permanent War." *Surveillance & Society* 17(5) (2019):662–680.

Singh, Nikhil Pal. *Race and America's Long War*. Oakland: University of California Press, 2017.

Sklansky, David A. "Crime, Immigration, and Ad Hoc Instrumentalism." *New Criminal Law Review* 15(2) (2012):157–224.

Smith, David. "Trump Announces 'Surge' of Federal Officers into Democratic-Run Cities." *Guardian*, July 22, 2020.

Smith, Dorothy E. *Institutional Ethnography: A Sociology for People*. New York: AltaMira, 2005.

———. *Writing the Social: Critique, Theory, and Investigations*. Toronto: University of Toronto Press, 1999.

Sooknanan, Joanna, Donna M. G. Comissiong, and Balswaroop Bhatt. "Life and Death in a Gang: A Mathematical Model of Gang Membership." *Journal of Mathematics Research* 4(4) (2012):10–27.

Speri, Alice. "Detained, Then Violated." The Intercept, April 11, 2018.

SRA International, Inc. Introduction to ICEGangs PowerPoint presentation. N.d.

———. *RFQ#HSCEMD-13-Q-00013, Department of Homeland Security (DHS), Immigration and Customs Enforcement (ICE), Homeland Security Investigations (HIS), Worksite Enforcement Unit (WSE) and Public Safety Unit, Community Shield Section (PSU/CSS) Intelligence Analyst and Programmer Support.* 2013.

———. *Technical Proposal in Response to RFQ#HSCEMD-10-Q-00035, Department of Homeland Security, US Immigration and Customs Enforcement, Intelligence Analyst Support.* 2010.

———. *White Paper: GangNet Software.* N.d.

SRA International ORION Center for Immigrations [*sic*] and Customs Enforcement. *ICE Investigations and Intelligence Systems Training.* N.d.

Stamm, Sola, Arora, Reena, Redman, Laura, and Evelin Gomez. *Detained and Denied: Healthcare Access in Immigration Detention.* New York: New York Lawyers for the Public Interest, 2017.

Starr, Sonja B. "Evidence-Based Sentencing and the Scientific Rationalization of Discrimination." *Stanford Law Review* 66 (2014):803–872.

Stern, Mark Joseph. "Bad Liars: ICE Claimed a Dreamer Was 'Gang-Affiliated' and Tried to Deport Him: A Federal Judge Ruled That ICE Was Lying." *Slate,* May 18, 2018.

Stop LAPD Spying Coalition. *Fuck the Police, Trust the People: Surveillance Bureaucracy Expands the Stalker State.* Los Angeles: Stop LAPD Spying Coalition, 2020.

Strahilevitz, Lior. "Reputation Nation: Law in an Era of Ubiquitous Personal Information." *Northwestern University Law Review* 102(4) (2008):1667–1738.

Stumpf, Juliet P. "The Crimmigration Crisis: Immigrants, Crime, and Sovereign Power." *American University Law Review* 56 (2006):367–420.

Sullivan, Abby. "On Thin ICE: Cracking Down on the Racial Profiling of Immigrants and Implementing a Compassionate Enforcement Policy." *Hastings Race & Poverty Law Journal* 6 (2008):101–146.

Taylor, Margaret H., and T. Alexander Aleinikoff. "Deportation of Criminal Aliens: A Geopolitical Perspective." Working paper, Inter-American Dialog, 1998.

Temple, Jonah M. "The Merry-Go-Round of Youth Gangs: The Failure of the U.S. Immigration Removal Policy and the False Outsourcing of Crime." *Boston College Third World Law Journal* 31(1) (2011):193–215.

Tieu, Hong H. "Picturing the Asian Gang Member among Us." *Asian Pacific American Law Journal* 11 (2006):41–74.

Timmermans, Stefan, and Ido Tavory. "Theory Construction in Qualitative Research: From Grounded Theory to Abductive Analysis." *Sociological Theory* 30(3) (2012):167–186.

Topak, Özgün E. "Humanitarian and Human Rights Surveillance: The Challenge to Border Surveillance and Invisibility?" *Surveillance & Society* 17(3/4) (2019):382–404.

Torpey, John C. "Coming and Going: On the State Monopolization of the Legitimate 'Means of Movement.'" *Sociological Theory* 16(3) (1998):239–259.

Trevizo, Perla. "A Privately Funded Border Wall Was Already at Risk of Collapsing If Not Fixed: Hurricane Hanna Made It Worse." ProPublica, July 29, 2020. www.propublica.org/article/a-privately-funded-border-wall-was-already-at-risk-of-collapsing-if-not-fixed-hurricane-hanna-made-it-worse.

Trevizo, Perla. "Beyond the Wall." *Arizona Daily Star*, July 10, 2016.

Tsuda, Takeyuki. "'I'm American, Not Japanese!': The Struggle for Racial Citizenship Among Later-Generation Japanese Americans." *Ethnic and Racial Studies* 37(3) (2014):405–424.

United States Citizenship and Immigration Services. *Consideration of Deferred Action for Childhood Arrivals.* USCIS Form I-821D. 2019www.uscis.gov/i-821d.

——. *DACA Refresher Training—Evaluating Issues of Criminality, Public Safety, and National Security.* PowerPoint presentation, n.d., accessed by author via FOIA request.

——. *Revised Guidance for the Referral of Cases and Issuance of Notices to Appear (NTAs) in Cases Involving Inadmissible and Removable Aliens.* PM-602-0050. 2011.

United States Congress, House Committee on Foreign Affairs, Subcommittee on the Western Hemisphere. 2018. *Combatting Transnational Criminal Threats in the Western Hemisphere: Hearing before the Subcommittee on the Western Hemisphere of the Committee on Foreign Affairs, House of Representatives,* 115 Cong. 2nd Sess. (May 23, 2018).

——. *Deportees in Latin America and the Caribbean: Hearing and Briefing before the Subcommittee on the Western Hemisphere of the*

Committee on Foreign Affairs, House of Representatives, 110 Cong. 1st
Sess. (July 24, 2007).

——. *Violence in Central America: Briefing and Hearing before the
Subcommittee on the Western Hemisphere of the Committee on Foreign
Affairs, House of Representatives*, 110 Cong. 1st Sess. (June 26, 2007).

United States Congress, House Committee on Oversight and Government
Reform, *Criminal Aliens Released by the Department of Homeland
Security: Hearing Before the Comm. on Oversight and Government
Reform, House of Representatives*, 114 Cong. 9 (2016) (statement of
Sarah Saldaña).

United States Customs and Border Protection. "About CBP." N.d. www
.cbp.gov/about.

——. "Air and Marine Operations Operating Locations." N.d. www.cbp.gov
/BORDER-SECURITY/AIR-SEA/OAM-OPERATING-LOCATIONS.

——. "CBP Attaches [*sic*]." N.d. www.cbp.gov/border-security
/international-initiatives/cbp-attaches.

——. "CBP through the Years." N.d. www.cbp.gov/about/history.

——. *Other Border Wall RFP.* 2017.

——. "Trusted Traveler Programs." N.d. www.cbp.gov/travel/trusted
-traveler-programs.

——. "Western Hemisphere Travel Initiative (WHTI) Frequently Asked
Questions." N.d. www.cbp.gov/travel/us-citizens/western-hemisphere
-travel-initiative/faqs.

United States Department of Homeland Security. "Advance Passenger
Information System (APIS)—Privacy Impact Assessment." 70 Fed.
Reg. 17857–17861 (April 7, 2005).

——. *ENDGAME: Office of Detention and Removal Strategic Plan,
2003–2012.* 2003.

——. *Fact Sheet: ICEGangs.* May 25, 2006.

——. "Immigration and Enforcement Operational Records (ENFORCE)
System of Records." 75 Fed. Reg. 9238–9244 (March 1, 2010).

——. "Immigration and Enforcement Operational Records (ENFORCE)
System of Records." 75 Fed. Reg. 10633–10634 (March 9, 2010).

——. "Immigration and Enforcement Operational Records (ENFORCE)
System of Records." 75 Fed. Reg. 23274–23279. (May 3, 2010).

——. "Immigration and Enforcement Operational Records (ENFORCE)
System of Records." 80 Fed. Reg. 24269–24273 (April 30, 2015).

——. "Office of the Secretary [DHS–2006–0060]." 71 Fed. Reg. 64543–
64546 (November 2, 2006).

———. *Privacy Impact Assessment for CBP License Plate Reader Technology.* DHS/CBP/PIA-049. 2017.

———. *Privacy Impact Assessment for ICE Investigative Case Management.* DHS/ICE/PIA-045, 2016.

———. *Privacy Impact Assessment for the Enforcement Integrated Database (EID).* DHS/ICE/PIA-015, 2010.

———. *Privacy Impact Assessment for the Enforcement Integrated Database (EID) ENFORCE Alien Removal Module (EARM 3.0).* DHS/ICE-PIA-015(b). 2011.

———. *Privacy Impact Assessment for the TECS System: Platform.* DHS/CBP/PIA-021. 2016.

———. 2010. *Privacy Impact Assessment for the TECS System: CBP Primary and Secondary Processing.* 2010.

———. *Privacy Impact Assessment Update for the Alien Criminal Response Information Management System (ACRIMe) & Enforcement Integrated Database (EID).* 2010.

———. *Privacy Impact Assessment Update for the CBP Portal (e3) to EID/IDENT.* DHS/CBP/PIA-012(a). 2017.

———. *Privacy Impact Assessment Update for the Enforcement Integrated Database (EID).* 2010.

———. *Privacy Impact Assessment Update for the Enforcement Integrated Database (EID).* DHS/ICE/PIA-015(f). 2014.

———. *Privacy Impact Assessment Update for the Enforcement Integrated Database (EID) Criminal History Information Sharing (CHIS) Program.* DHS/ICE/PIA-015(h). 2016.

———. *Privacy Impact Assessment Update for the Enforcement Integrated Database (EID)—EAGLE.* DHS/ICE/PIA-015(e). 2012.

———. *Privacy Impact Assessment Update for the Enforcement Integrated Database (EID) Law Enforcement Notification System (LENS).* DHS/ICE/PIA-015(g). 2015.

———. *Privacy Impact Assessment Update for the Enforcement Integrated Database (EID) Prosecutions Module (PM), Electronic Removal Management Portal (eRMP), Operations Management Module (OM²), Law Enforcement Notification System (LENS), and Compliance Assistance Reporting Terminal (CART).* DHS/ICE/PIA-015(i). December 3, 2018.

———. *Privacy Impact Assessment Update for the Enforcement Integrated Database (EID) Risk Classification Assessment (RCA 1.0), ENFORCE*

Alien Removal Module (EARM 5.0), and Crime Entry Screen (CES 2.0). DHS/ICE/PIA-015(d). 2012.

——. "U.S. Customs and Border Protection, Automated Targeting System, System of Records." 72 Fed. Reg. 43650–43656 (August 6, 2007).

——. "U.S. Customs and Border Protection 011 TECS System of Records Notice." 73 Fed. Reg. 77778–77782 (December 19, 2008).

——. *Yearbook of Immigration Statistics, 2003*. Washington, DC: U.S. Government Printing Office, 2004.

——. *Yearbook of Immigration Statistics, 2015*. Washington, DC: Office of Immigration Statistics, 2016.

United States Department of Justice. *Attorney General Sessions Gives Remarks to Federal Law Enforcement in Boston about Transnational Criminal Organizations*, September 21, 2017. www.justice.gov/opa/speech/attorney-general-sessions-gives-remarks-federal-law-enforcement-boston-about.

——. "Deportable Alien Control System (DACS) System of Records." 60 Fed. Reg. 52690–52705 (October 10, 1995). AAG/A Order No. 108-95.

——. "Deportable Alien Control System (DACS) System of Records." 62 Fed. Reg. 59732–59734 (November 4, 1997). AAG/A Order No. 144-97.

United States Department of Justice, Civil Rights Division. *Investigation of the Baltimore City Police Department*. 2016.

United States Department of the Treasury. "Treasury Enforcement Communications System (TECS) System of Records." 66 Fed. Reg. 53029 (January 3, 2001).

United States General Accounting Office. *Information on Criminal Aliens Incarcerated in Federal and State Prisons and Local Jails*. Washington, DC: US GAO, 2005.

United States Immigration and Customs Enforcement. *Fiscal Year 2017 ICE Enforcement and Removal Operations Report*. 2018.

——. *Fiscal Year 2018 ICE Enforcement and Removal Operations Report*. 2019.

——. *ICE Air Operations Fact Sheet*. August 13, 2020. www.ice.gov/factsheets/ice-air-operations.

——. "International Operations." N.d. www.ice.gov/about-ice/homeland-security-investigations/international-operations.

——. *Risk Classification Assessment ICE Leadership Scope Brief*. 2011.

——. *Targeting Operations Subscription Data Service Request*. 2017.

United States Immigration and Customs Enforcement, National Gang Unit. *Operation Community Shield.* PowerPoint presentation, n.d., accessed by author via FOIA request.

University of Washington Center for Human Rights. 2019. *Hidden in Plain Sight: ICE Air and the Machinery of Mass Deportation.* April 23, 2019.

Valdez, Inés. "Immigration Enforcement, Technology, and the Banishment of Politics." In *Latinx Politics Conference: Resistance, Disruption, and Power.* New York University, September 25, 2020.

———. "Reconceiving Immigration Politics: Walter Benjamin, Violence, and Labor." *American Political Science Review* 114(1) (2020):95–108.

Valdez, Inés, Mat Coleman, and Amna Akbar. "Missing in Action: Practice, Paralegality, and the Nature of Immigration Enforcement." *Citizenship Studies* 21(5) (2017):547–569.

Van Cleve, Nicole Gonzalez. *Crook County: Racism and Injustice in America's Largest Criminal Court.* Stanford, CA: Stanford University Press, 2016.

Van Gennip, Yves, Blake Hunter, Raymond Ahn, Peter Elliott, Kyle Luh, Megan Halvorson, Shannon Reid, Matthew Valasik, James Wo, George E. Tita, Andrea L. Bertozzi, and Jeffrey P. Brantingham. "Community Detection Using Spectral Clustering on Sparse Geosocial Data." *SIAM Journal on Applied Mathematics* 73(1) (2013):67–83.

Van Hofwegen, Sara Lynn. "Unjust and Ineffective: A Critical Look at California's Step Act." *Southern California Interdisciplinary Law Journal* 18 (2009):679–702.

Vega, Irene I. "Empathy, Morality, and Criminality: The Legitimation Narratives of U.S. Border Patrol Agents." *Journal of Ethnic and Migration Studies* 44(15) (2017):2544–2561.

Volpp, Leti. "The Indigenous as Alien." *UC Irvine Law Review* 5 (2015):289–326.

Walia, Harsha. *Border & Rule: Global Migration, Capitalism, and the Rise of Racist Nationalism.* Chicago: Haymarket Books, 2021.

Ward, Geoff. "Living Histories of White Supremacist Policing: Towards Transformative Justice." *Du Bois Review* 15(1) (2018):167–184.

Warner, Judith Ann. "The Social Construction of the Criminal Alien in Immigration Law, Enforcement Practice and Statistical Enumeration: Consequences for Immigrant Stereotyping." *Journal of Social and Ecological Boundaries* 1(2) (2005):56–80.

Washington-Baltimore High Intensity Drug Trafficking Areas. "Who We Are." N.d. www.hidta.org/about-hidta/.

Werth, Robert. "Theorizing the Performative Effects of Penal Risk Technologies: (Re)producing the Subject Who Must Be Dangerous." *Social & Legal Studies* 28(3) (2018):327–348.

Winston, Ali. "Prosecutors Are Using Gang Laws to Criminalize Protest." The Appeal, September 1, 2020. https://theappeal.org/gang-laws -criminalize-protest/.

Winston, Ali. "You May Be in California's Gang Database and Not Even Know It." Reveal News, March 23, 2016. https://revealnews.org/article /you-may-be-in-californias-gang-database-and-not-even-know-it/.

Wonders, Nancy A. "Flows, Semi-Permeable Borders and New Channels of Inequality." In *Borders, Mobility and Technologies of Control*, edited by S. Pickering and L. Weber, 63–86. Dordrecht, Netherlands: Springer Press, 2006.

———. "Globalization, Border Reconstruction Projects, and Transnational Crime." *Social Justice* 34(2) (2007):33–46.

Wonders, Nancy A., and Lynn C. Jones. 2019. "Doing and Undoing Borders: The Multiplication of Citizenship, Citizenship Performances, and Migration as Social Movement." *Theoretical Criminology* 23(2) (2019):136–155.

Woods, Jordan B. "Systemic Racial Bias and RICO's Application to Criminal Street and Prison Gangs." *Michigan Journal of Race & Law* 17 (2012):303–358.

Yoshino, Erin R. "California's Criminal Gang Enhancements: Lessons from Interviews with Practitioners." *Southern California Review of Law and Social Justice* 18(1) (2008):117–152.

Zilberg, Elana. "Fools Banished from the Kingdom: Remapping Geographies of Gang Violence between the Americas (Los Angeles and San Salvador)." *American Quarterly* 56(3) (2004):759–779.

———. "Gangster in Guerilla Face: A Transnational Mirror of Production between the USA and El Salvador." *Anthropological Theory* 7(1) (2007):37–57.

———. *Space of Detention: The Making of a Transnational Gang Crisis between Los Angeles and San Salvador*. Durham, NC: Duke University Press, 2011.

Index

Founded in 1893,
UNIVERSITY OF CALIFORNIA PRESS
publishes bold, progressive books and journals
on topics in the arts, humanities, social sciences,
and natural sciences—with a focus on social
justice issues—that inspire thought and action
among readers worldwide.

The UC PRESS FOUNDATION
raises funds to uphold the press's vital role
as an independent, nonprofit publisher, and
receives philanthropic support from a wide
range of individuals and institutions—and from
committed readers like you. To learn more, visit
ucpress.edu/supportus.